FORD MADOX FORD: THE CRITICAL HERITAGE

THE CRITICAL HERITAGE SERIES

General Editor: B. C. Southam

The Critical Heritage series collects together a large body of criticism on major figures in literature. Each volume presents the contemporary responses to a particular writer, enabling the student to follow the formation of critical attitudes to the writer's work and its place within a literary tradition.

The carefully selected sources range from landmark essays in the history of criticism to fragments of contemporary opinion and little published documentary material, such as letters and diaries.

Significant pieces of criticism from later periods are also included in order to demonstrate fluctuations in reputation following the writer's death.

FORD MADOX FORD

THE CRITICAL HERITAGE

Edited by

FRANK MACSHANE

London and New York

First published in 1972
Reprinted in 1997 by Routledge

2 Park Square, Milton Park,
Abingdon, Oxon, OX14 4RN
&
711 Third Avenue, New York, NY 10017

Routledge is an imprint of the Taylor & Francis Group, an informa business

Transferred to Digital Printing 2007

First issued in paperback 2013

Compilation, introduction, notes and index © 1972 Frank MacShane

All rights reserved. No part of this book may be reprinted or reproduced or utilized in any form or by any electronic, mechanical, or other means, now known or hereafter invented, including photocopying and recording or in any information storage or retrieval system, without permission in writing from the publishers.

British Library Cataloguing in Publication Data

ISBN13: 978-0-415-15921-0 (hbk)
ISBN13: 978-0-415-84770-4 (pbk)

Publisher's Note
The publisher has gone to great lengths to ensure the quality of this reprint but points out that some imperfections in the original may be apparent

General Editor's Preface

The reception given to a writer by his contemporaries and near-contemporaries is evidence of considerable value to the student of literature. On one side we learn a great deal about the state of criticism at large and in particular about the development of critical attitudes towards a single writer; at the same time, through private comments in letters, journals or marginalia, we gain an insight upon the tastes and literary thought of individual readers of the period. Evidence of this kind helps us to understand the writer's historical situation, the nature of his immediate reading-public, and his response to these pressures.

The separate volumes in the *Critical Heritage Series* present a record of this early criticism. Clearly, for many of the highly productive and lengthily reviewed nineteenth- and twentieth-century writers, there exists an enormous body of material; and in these cases the volume editors have made a selection of the most important views, significant for their intrinsic critical worth or for their representative quality—perhaps even registering incomprehension!

For earlier writers, notably pre-eighteenth century, the materials are much scarcer and the historical period has been extended, sometimes far beyond the writer's lifetime, in order to show the inception and growth of critical views which were initially slow to appear.

In each volume the documents are headed by an Introduction, discussing the material assembled and relating the early stages of the author's reception to what we have come to identify as the critical tradition. The volumes will make available much material which would otherwise be difficult of access and it is hoped that the modern reader will be thereby helped towards an informed understanding of the ways in which literature has been read and judged.

B.C.S.

Contents

ACKNOWLEDGMENTS	*page*	xii
INTRODUCTION		1
NOTE ON THE TEXT		17

Early novels and prose writings

1. Unsigned review of *The Shifting of the Fire*, *Athenaeum*, November 1892 — 19
2. JOSEPH CONRAD on *The Inheritors*, letter in *The New York Times Saturday Review*, August 1901 — 20
3. Unsigned article on *Romance*, New York *Bookman*, August 1904 — 23
4. Unsigned review of *The Fifth Queen*, *Athenaeum*, April 1906 — 24
5. C. F. G. MASTERMAN on *An English Girl*, *Daily News*, September 1907 — 25
6. R. A. SCOTT-JAMES on *The Fifth Queen Crowned*, *Daily News*, March 1908 — 28
7. Unsigned review of *The Fifth Queen Crowned*, *Academy*, May 1908 — 31
8. ARNOLD BENNETT on *A Call*, *New Age*, March 1910 — 33
9. PERCY F. BICKNELL on *Memories and Impressions (Ancient Lights)*, *Dial*, May 1911 — 35
10. Unsigned review of *The New Humpty-Dumpty*, *English Review*, September 1912 — 40
11. Unsigned review of *Henry James: A Critical Study*, *The Times Literary Supplement*, January 1914 — 42
12. REBECCA WEST on *The Good Soldier*, *Daily News*, April 1915 — 44
13. THEODORE DREISER on *The Good Soldier*, *New Republic*, June 1915 — 47
14. REBECCA WEST on *Between St. Dennis and St. George*, *Daily News*, November 1915 — 51

CONTENTS

Collected Poems (1913)

15 EZRA POUND, review in *New Freewoman*, December 1913 page 55
16 E. BUXTON SHANKS, review in *Poetry and Drama*, December 1913 59
17 Unsigned review, *English Review*, January 1914 62
18 EZRA POUND, review in *Poetry*, June 1914 63

On Heaven and Poems written on Active Service

19 CONRAD AIKEN, review in *Dial*, November 1918 70
20 HARRIET MONROE, review in *Poetry*, January 1919 75

Collected Poems (1936)

21 WILLIAM ROSE BENÉT's introduction to *Collected Poems, 1936* 79
22 JOHN PEALE BISHOP, review in *Poetry*, September 1937 83

The Tietjens novels

23 Unsigned review of *Some Do Not*, *The Times Literary Supplement*, April 1924 87
24 Unsigned review of *Some Do Not*, *Nation & Athenaeum*, May 1924 89
25 JOSEPH WOOD KRUTCH on *Some Do Not*, *Saturday Review of Literature*, October 1924 90
26 LOUIS BROMFIELD on *Some Do Not*, *New York Bookman*, February 1925 93
27 MARY COLUM on *No More Parades*, *Saturday Review of Literature*, January 1926 94
28 BURTON RASCOE on *No More Parades*, *Arts and Decoration*, February 1926 98
29 Unsigned review of *A Man Could Stand Up*, *The Times Literary Supplement*, October 1926 101
30 ISABEL PATERSON on *Some Do Not*, *No More Parades* and *A Man Could Stand Up*, *New York Herald Tribune Books*, October 1926 103
31 L. P. HARTLEY on *A Man Could Stand Up*, *Saturday Review*, November 1926 108

CONTENTS

32 WILLIAM MCFEE on *Last Post, New York Herald Tribune Books*, January 1928   page 110
33 L. P. HARTLEY on *Last Post, Saturday Review*, February 1928   113
34 H. C. HARWOOD on *Last Post, Quarterly Review*, April 1929   115

Miscellaneous controversies

35 W. M. ROSSETTI, letter on *Ancient Lights, Outlook*, April 1911   117
36 J. K. PROTHERO on *Zeppelin Nights, New Witness*, January 1916   122
37 Correspondence following PROTHERO's review of *Zeppelin Nights*, 1916   125
38 H. G. WELLS and ETHEL COLBURN MAYNE, letters on *Thus to Revisit, English Review*, August 1920   128

Joseph Conrad: A Personal Remembrance

39 MRS JOSEPH CONRAD, letter in *The Times Literary Supplement*, December 1924   131
40 EDWARD GARNETT, review in *Nation & Athenaeum*, December 1924   133
41 CHRISTOPHER MORLEY, review in *Saturday Review of Literature*, December 1924   137
42 EDWARD GARNETT, review in *Weekly Westminster*, February 1925   140
43 H. L. MENCKEN, review in *American Mercury*, April 1925   142
44 WILLIAM MCFEE, letter in *New York Bookman*, June 1925   145

Later fiction, reminiscences and criticism

45 JOHN MIDDLETON MURRY on *Thus to Revisit, Nation & Athenaeum*, May 1921   148
46 L. P. HARTLEY on *A Little Less Than Gods, Saturday Review*, November 1928   152
47 MORTON DAUWEN ZABEL on *Return to Yesterday*, New York *Nation*, April 1932   154
48 V. S. PRITCHETT on *It Was the Nightingale, Fortnightly Review*, July 1934   157
49 GRAHAM GREENE on *Great Trade Route, London Mercury*, February 1937   159

CONTENTS

50 GRAHAM GREENE on *Vive Le Roy*, London Mercury, August 1937   page 162
51 V. S. PRITCHETT on *Mightier than the Sword*, London Mercury, March 1938   164
52 CHARLES WILLIAMS on *Mightier than the Sword*, Time and Tide, March 1938   166
53 JOHN PEALE BISHOP on *The March of Literature*, New Republic, October 1938   169
54 GRAHAM GREENE on *Provence*, London Mercury, December 1938   172
55 EDWARD SACKVILLE-WEST on *The March of Literature*, New Statesman and Nation, November 1939   175
56 GRAHAM GREENE on *The March of Literature*, Spectator, November 1939   177
57 Unsigned review of *The March of Literature*, The Times Literary Supplement, December 1939   180

General articles on Ford

58 HERBERT GORMAN in New York *Bookman*, March 1928   186
59 GRANVILLE HICKS in New York *Bookman*, December 1930   194
60 DOUGLAS GOLDRING in *English Review*, December 1931   205
61 GRAHAM GREENE in *Spectator*, July 1939   212
62 EZRA POUND in *Nineteenth Century and After*, August 1939   215
63 SHERWOOD ANDERSON in *Coronet*, August 1940, and *New Directions Number 7*, 1942   219
64 JOHN GOULD FLETCHER in *New Directions Number 7*, 1942   222
65 KATHERINE ANNE PORTER in *New Directions Number 7*, 1942   225
66 ALLEN TATE in *New Directions Number 7*, 1942 and *Minnesota Review*, 1960   227

Later evaluations

67 EDWARD CRANKSHAW on *The Last Pre-Raphaelite*, National Review, August 1948   231
68 R. A. SCOTT-JAMES, preface to the Tietjens novels, 1948   240
69 MORTON DAUWEN ZABEL on *Trained for Genius (The Last Pre-Raphaelite)*, Nation, July 1949   246
70 WILLIAM CARLOS WILLIAMS on *Parade's End*, Sewanee Review, January–March 1951   250

CONTENTS

71 CAROLINE GORDON, *A Good Soldier*, 1963   page 258
72 ROBERT LOWELL, foreword to *Buckshee*, 1966   264
    BIBLIOGRAPHY   268
    INDEX   269

Acknowledgments

For arrangements made with authors, their representatives and publishing houses to reprint copyrighted material, and for the courtesy extended by them, the following acknowledgments are gratefully made. All possible care has been taken to trace ownership of the selections included and to make full acknowledgment for their use.

Mrs Dorothy Cheston Bennett for a review by Arnold Bennett, written under the pseudonym of Jacob Tonson, of *A Call* in *New Age*, 17 March 1910; Brandt and Brandt for 'The Function of Rhythm' by Conrad Aiken. Copyright © 1919 by Conrad Aiken; David Garnett for two reviews by Edward Garnett of *Joseph Conrad: A Personal Remembrance*; Caroline Gordon for selection from *A Good Soldier*. Copyright 1963 by Caroline Gordon; L. P. Hartley for reviews of *A Man Could Stand Up*, *Last Post* and *A Little Less than Gods*; Granville Hicks for 'Ford Madox Ford—A Neglected Contemporary' 1930; Robert Lowell for the 'foreword' to *Buckshee* by Ford Madox Ford, Pym-Randall Press, 1966; William McFee's review, 'Tietjens Once More'. Copyright 1928, New York Herald Tribune Inc. Reprinted by permission of W. C. C. Publishing Co., Inc.; 'The Conrad Wake' by H. L. Mencken. Copyright 1925 by H. L. Mencken. Appeared in *American Mercury*, reprinted by permission of Alfred A. Knopf Inc.; the *Nation* for 'Trained for Genius' by Morton Dauwen Zabel, 1949; the *New Statesman* for review by J. Middleton Murry of *Thus to Revisit*, 1921 and review by E. Sackville-West of *The March of Literature*, 1939; Harold Ober Associates and New Directions Publishing Corporation for statement by Sherwood Anderson. Copyright 1942 by *New Directions*; Harold Ober Associates for selection from Sherwood Anderson's *Memoirs*. Copyright 1942, 1969 by Eleanor Anderson; Penguin Books Ltd for the preface by R. A. Scott-James, printed in their edition of *Some Do Not*, *No More Parades*, *A Man Could Stand Up* and *Last Post*, 1948; A. D. Peters and Co. for review by Edward Crankshaw of *The Last Pre-Raphaelite*, 1948. Reprinted by permission of A. D. Peters & Co.; *Poetry* for 'Great Poetry' by Harriet Monroe, 1919, and for 'Poems of Ford Madox Ford' by John Peale Bishop, 1937; Laurence Pollinger Ltd for reviews by Graham Greene of *Provence*,

ACKNOWLEDGMENTS

Great Trade Route, Vive Le Roy and *The March of Literature*, and for article 'Ford Madox Ford' (*London Mercury*, 1937, 1938; *Spectator*, 1939); Katherine Anne Porter for untitled statement on Ford Madox Ford. Copyright © 1942 by Katherine Anne Porter; Ezra Pound for 'Homage to Ford Madox Ford' from *New Directions in Prose and Poetry, No. 7*. Copyright 1942 by New Directions Publishing Corporation. Reprinted by permission of Mrs Dorothy Pound, Committee for Ezra Pound; Ezra Pound for 'The Prose Tradition in Verse'. Ezra Pound: *Literary Essays*. All Rights Reserved. Reprinted by permission of New Directions Publishing Corporation; Ezra Pound for 'The Prose Tradition in Verse'. Reprinted by permission of Faber and Faber Ltd from *Literary Essays*; *Princeton University Library Chronicle* for 'Ford Madox Ford: The Personal Side' by Herbert Gorman, 1948; V. S. Pritchett for review of *Mightier than the Sword*. Copyright 1938, 1965 by V. S. Pritchett. Reprinted by permission of Harold Matson Co., Inc.; V. S. Pritchett for review of *It Was the Nightingale*. Copyright 1934, 1961 by V. S. Pritchett. Reprinted by permission of Harold Matson Co., Inc.; the *Saturday Review* for 'Joseph Conrad and His Circle' by Christopher Morley, 1924, for review by Joseph Wood Krutch of *Some Do Not*, 1924, and review by Mary Colum of *No More Parades*, 1926; Allen Tate for untitled statement in *New Directions No. 7*, 1942, and for selection from 'Random Thoughts on the 1920's', *Minnesota Review*, 1960; *The Times Literary Supplement* for reviews of *Henry James*, 1914, *Some Do Not*, 1924, *A Man Could Stand Up*, 1926 and *The March of Literature*, 1939. Reproduced from *The Times Literary Supplement* by permission; *Time and Tide* for review of *Mightier than the Sword*, by Charles Williams, 1938; the Estate of H. G. Wells for a letter written by H. G. Wells to the editor of the *English Review* in 1920, and a letter written by H. G. Wells in defence of Ford Madox Ford, published in Maisie Ward's *Gilbert Keith Chesterton*; Dame Rebecca West for reviews of *The New Humpty-Dumpty*, the *English Review*, 1912, *Between St. Dennis and St. George* and *The Good Soldier*, *Daily News*, 1915; William Carlos Williams, 'Parade's End' from William Carlos Williams, *Selected Essays*. Copyright 1951 by William Carlos Williams. Reprinted by permission of New Directions Publishing Corporation.

Introduction

Ford Madox Ford (*né* Hueffer) began to write at a time when political, social and artistic standards were starting to change in a radical way, without yet taking on definite new characteristics. The long Victorian era, with its dominating, even domineering, figures like Dickens and Thackeray, Arnold and Tennyson, Browning, Carlyle and the Rossettis, was drawing to a close, leaving in its trail what appeared to be a school of minor figures, many demoralized by the prospect of trying to equal the work and attain the status of their predecessors. With its gradual dissemination of literature to the masses, the nineteenth century had created a much larger audience than had previously been known, and a great number of books of all kinds were published every year. Although the expansion of the reading public was generally beneficial, it was accomplished mainly by an increase in what Ford was to call 'nuvvle writers'—men and women for whom the novel was entertainment only, who wrote romances of the sort that today appear on television. In this new flood of fiction, serious artists tended to lose their identity. The difficulties they encountered in gaining recognition were increased by the tendency of journals and newspapers to devote little space to the reviewing of fiction. The long quarterly articles of the early nineteenth century were replaced by omnibus reviews in which half-a-dozen or more novels were dealt with in a few hundred words. Critics and reviewers gave most of their attention to histories, biographies and topical works of sociology and politics.

The neglect of serious imaginative literature indicates a lack of critical thinking during much of the period that led up to the First World War. The extraordinary affluence and material prosperity of English life encouraged this blandness. The large middle class was self-satisfied, happy with the combination of industrialism and imperialism that brought millions of pounds into British banks every year. This new class had obtained considerable political and social power, replacing the older aristocracy and landed gentry, and had no intention of giving it up. The Press, which it controlled, supported the *status quo* and was hostile to any questioning of commercial standards. The national genius for compromise encouraged moderation, and the new commercial forces gained power without much disorder. Ideas and influences that could not be reconciled with them were ignored; if that did not work, they were suppressed, as the Boer War and the suffragette movement testify.

From the literary point of view, the irresponsibility of this society is revealed by the absence of serious literary people on the staffs of the literary journals. Many of the more important of these, starting with the *Quarterly Review* and the *Edinburgh Review* and continuing on down through *Blackwood's*, the *Athenaeum*, the *Academy* and the *Saturday Review*, had been founded in the early years of the century by poets and novelists and by others who had mature literary standards and a sense of purpose. But by the 1890s most of them had become intellectually moribund though still influential. Most of the contributors to these papers were not literary: neither novelists nor poets, they rarely wrote books of any kind. Their lack of experience in literary creation made them self-indulgent and may well account for the querulousness that was so widespread in journalistic criticism during the decades that led up to 1914. It certainly explains the academic viewpoint of many of the articles—their remoteness both from life and from an understanding of the intention of artistic creation.

The widespread indifference and hostility expressed by the English journals towards imaginative literature led to a gradual withdrawal of writers from the official world of letters. In the 1850s the Pre-Raphaelite Brotherhood had tried to influence public opinion by working within the system: they hoped to convince by sound argument rather than by confrontation. But their efforts failed, and they were either ignored or laughed at. The successors to the Pre-Raphaelites were therefore forced into extreme positions. Angered by the rigidity of established codes of morality, the aesthetes of the 1890s flung their challenges directly into the faces of the middle classes. They were outrageous because they thought the middle classes were outrageous. The spirit of Oscar Wilde and of the decadence would never have become so widespread had not the literate public not become so unnaturally protectionist, allowing its own feelings of humanity to dry up.

The Wilde scandal released the latent hostilities of the middle classes towards the arts. Many writers were fearful that this case would be permanently damaging to English letters, discrediting them for good. In a period of growing conformity, this was a disquieting possibility. For this reason a group of writers, among them W. E. Henley and R. L. Stevenson, emphasized the need for experience, for living a life

INTRODUCTION

of adventure and action. Despite its fresh air of manliness, the implication of this movement was that experience was more important than literature. This attitude, which reached its apogee in the work of Kipling, was in its way as damaging to serious literary activity as was the behaviour of the decadents.

More than most young writers, Ford was aware of the nuances of these events and the consequent politics of English artistic criticism. His father, Francis Hueffer, was music critic for *The Times* and, through conversations with his uncle by marriage William Michael Rossetti and with Christina Rossetti, Ford knew a good deal about the making and breaking of literary and artistic reputations. After the death of his father, he was brought up by his grandfather, Ford Madox Brown, who had been a mentor to a number of the original Pre-Raphaelite Brotherhood. Through his acquaintance with the work of these painters, Ford learned how a man could become corrupted, how, for example, Millais with his extraordinary talent, could cheapen his art with sentimental paintings and even advertisements. Millais was elected President of the Royal Academy and made over £100,000 in a year, whereas his contemporary, Ford's grandfather, stubbornly maintaining his standards, remained poor, little exhibited and less known.

Brought up in this atmosphere, Ford learned at an early age how influential personal friendships and enmities could be; how criticism was so much a matter of private opinion, often a combination of mixed and suspect motives. These experiences discouraged him so much that he was tempted to do anything rather than be an artist. Later, when he realized that he had to write, he began as an author of children's books. After early work in a minor key, he developed his own standards, basing them on precepts learned from his father and his grandfather. Madox Brown devoted himself entirely to his work, refusing to alter his art for any purpose, either to teach a moral lesson or to flatter a prospective buyer. He was capable of spending twelve years on a single painting, as he did for *Work* and he did not die a rich man. Moreover, he gave Ford a 'rule of life' which Ford himself always tried to follow:

Fordie, never refuse a lame dog over a stile. Never lend money; always give it. When you give money to a man that is down, tell him that it is to help him to get up; tell him that when he is up he should pass on the money you have given him to any other devil that is down. Beggar yourself rather than refuse assistance to any one whose genius you think shows promise of being greater than your own.[1]

From his father, Ford learned the need for internationalism in the arts. Dr Hueffer was a German by birth, and he introduced Ford to European culture, especially French literature and German music. This experience made him realize how ignorant and parochial most English critics and writers were, and he therefore devoted a tremendous amount of energy to encouraging what he later called an international republic of letters. During the period of his collaboration with Joseph Conrad, Ford became one of a small group of men who took a Continental attitude towards writing and who addressed their English audience with the seriousness that neither the decadents of the 1890s nor the hearties of the 'Henley Gang' had attempted. Realizing that these writers, including Henry James, were not properly appreciated and that there was no journal in England giving them the understanding they deserved, Ford in 1908 founded the *English Review* in which he published the work of Hardy, Hudson, Wells, Conrad, James, Galsworthy, Cunninghame Graham, Yeats, Belloc, Pound and introduced Wyndham Lewis, D. H. Lawrence and Norman Douglas. At the same time Ford wrote editorials which he later collected under the title *The Critical Attitude* (1911) and in which he attempted to establish a set of criteria for judging literature.

Ford's intentions were partly influenced by his Pre-Raphaelite background and by his experience as an art critic. His books on Holbein, Rossetti and Madox Brown show his attraction to the methods of art criticism. A critic of painting or sculpture does not dwell on the subject of the work but discusses the way in which it is executed. Ford wanted literary criticism to place a similar emphasis on technique. Even before founding the *English Review*, he had written to Edward Garnett, who had edited a series of art books, suggesting that Garnett's publishing house bring out a similar series 'conceived on the broad general idea of making manifest, to the most unintelligent, how great writers *get their effects*. As distinct from the general line of tub-thumping about moral purposes, the number of feet in a verse, or the amiable and noble ideas entertained by said Great Writers, of Elevating and making the world a better place.'[2]

This last sentence reveals Ford's own experiences as a subject for reviewers. The critics of the 1890s wanted optimism; they wanted the world in which they played an influential role to be praised. They wished current standards to prevail or to be slightly improved on a moral scale; they preferred the formal rhetoric that acceded to these standards to the colloquial and informal which questioned them. On

INTRODUCTION

the whole, despite their bookishness, the critics of Ford's early work are extraordinarily vacuous in their comments (No. 1). The reviewer in the *Academy* (12 November 1892) writes of Ford's fairy story, *The Feather*: 'The story begins well and goes on pretty well and ends in absurdity.' In a later number of the same magazine, another children's book is criticized in this way: 'The story is well, but not too well, written. . . .' These emptinesses are balanced elsewhere by a general distaste for Ford's openness and freedom in using the vernacular. Thus the *Athenaeum* (5 November 1892): 'Mr. Hueffer's latest excursion into the domain of fairyland is marred by two conspicuous defects—the infelicitous choice of names and the still more infelicitous intrusion into the dialogue of the "scores", the "chaff" and the puns of the modern humorist.' Or the *Saturday Review* (5 November 1892) on his first novel: '. . . if the object be to present people and events at once odious and tiresome, unnatural and commonplace, flippant and dull, no better method can be devised. . . . It would not be easy to write a worse book in a worse way . . . [The characters] are in perfect accord with the author as to bad grammar and wrong spelling.'

Discouraged by such reviews, Ford was also upset when a book was ignored. In 1904 he wrote to H. G. Wells that three months after the publication of his book of poems, *The Face of the Night*, he had received only five reviews, three of them in provincial papers, and that as a consequence only four copies of the book had been sold. The variety of Ford's literary undertakings may have brought about this neglect, since critics, who like categories, did not know whether to call him poet, novelist, biographer, topographer, art historian or fairy-story writer. Even the collaboration with Joseph Conrad, which was designed to bring fame and riches to both men, proved useless, for although there were more reviews than usual and a certain amount of interest in the collaboration itself, the various books were ill received. On the whole, the first ten years of Ford's writing career were disastrous. The apprenticeship was to prove beneficial later on, but the period itself was depressing. Then, in 1905, with the publication of the first of a trilogy dedicated to the English countryside, his fortunes changed. Edward Garnett told Galsworthy what had happened:

By the way you will be interested to hear that Hueffer has at last been boomed, boomed furiously! And has come into his own. I am so very, very glad. I think that this success may go a long way to putting him definitely on his feet.

A young enterprising firm took up his London book and brought it out with the title: *The Soul of London*. The manager happened to strike on Harmsworth accidentally—and H. read the book for 10 minutes, and said 'We'll give it a column.' The manager, most astutely, went to the *Chronicle* and *Daily News* etc., and said 'H. is going to give this a col., what'll *you* give?' *They* said a col. and a half! etc. etc. So the boom came off all on one day, and the glorious Press was filled with trumpetings of *The Soul of London*.

It *is* very good, you know; the best thing he's done. And I hope and trust it will definitely pick him up, for if ever a man wanted recognition, poor Ford does.[3]

Unfortunately, this 'boom' was short lived, and Ford's critical reception gradually declined to its usual level. As editor of the *English Review* from 1908 to 1909 his position did nothing to improve his status; on the contrary, as Edgar Jepson was later to explain, it was positively damaging:

Ford demanded a quality of writing in that review such as no review had demanded before, or has since, and it was by that demand that he so hindered the recognition and advancement of his novels. As editor he rejected the work of so many critics. For the life of me I do not see what else he could have done; there was his standard of writing, and they could not reach it. I felt sorry for them, for they tried so hard to write. But after all it is hardly fair to expect a man, who makes it his business to teach other people to write, to be able to write himself.[4]

The reviews of Ford's books published during the decade that preceded the First World War, reflect the same indifference to his work that typified the earlier period. In 1909 his agent, J. B. Pinker, noted that Ford's sales averaged only 2,000 copies per novel. Pinker was generally able to secure decent advances, but the books rarely sold enough to cover them, with the result that there was little advertising. Moreover, since his books did not sell widely, Ford was forced to move from one publisher to another. *The Good Soldier* was Ford's forty-sixth book, and up to 1915 he had had to deal in England alone with twenty-two different publishers. He appeared on the lists of many publishers, but he was never really important to any one of them. Ford was aware of this situation and expressed his dismay in a 1914 letter to Pinker:

I have worked damned hard for many years to establish my name as a good will and that's all there is to it—conceit or no conceit. I don't need money and, unless I can get a good price, I won't sell my immortal soul to any of your blooming devils.

I want also stability; I can't think it to be either good or gracious to go jumping about from publisher to publisher as I have done in the past.[5]

INTRODUCTION

In a literary sense there was some justification for Ford's poor critical reception, for as Ezra Pound observed, much of his 'best prose was probably lost, as isolated chapters in unachieved and too-quickly issued novels'. Most critics emphasized Ford's failures, rarely recognizing what he was trying to do. Only his fellow professionals, or at least those who understood what writing is, wrote intelligently about him. For this reason, most reviews of Ford's work published during this period are uninteresting today; only the few essays written by Rebecca West (Nos 12 and 14) or Arnold Bennett (No. 8), R. A. Scott-James (No. 6) or C. F. G. Masterman (No. 5), Ford's friend and a member of Asquith's government, have enduring qualities. The importance of *The Good Soldier* was recognized by a few of these writers, including Dreiser in America (No. 13), but coming during the war, it failed to solidify Ford's reputation as a novelist.

Indeed, for the first two decades of his literary career, Ford was mainly respected as a poet. His books of verse were only a small portion of his total work, but they were given critical attention. In part this was due to the greater popularity of some of Ford's fellow novelists, especially Galsworthy, Wells and Conrad, among whom Ford was generally considered a minor and junior practitioner. Among the poets, however, he seemed a pioneer, and in the early period of the *English Review*, he was taken up by a number of younger poets, especially by Ezra Pound, who found him a natural ally and in some respects a mentor. In 1913 Pound wrote of Ford that 'He and Yeats are the two men in London. And Yeats is already a sort of great dim figure with its associations set in the past.'[6] Ford's reputation as a poet was also enhanced by his association with the literary movement known as Imagism, which in the immediate pre-war years brought attention to several of its members, especially Richard Aldington, F. S. Flint, John Gould Fletcher, Hilda Doolittle and above all, Ezra Pound. These poets created a ferment by writing about one another's work, and Ford as an elder statesman, as Madox Brown had been to the Pre-Raphaelites, benefited from their attention (Nos 15–20). A frequent visitor to salons and a noted host himself, Ford was always invigorated by discussions of literary theory. With Conrad and Henry James he had formerly engaged in long conversations which led to theories of fictional impressionism, and these ideas he now applied to the looser forms of verse in which he and his younger contemporaries were writing. Ford's own essays on poetry, especially the article 'On Impressionism' which was later used as a preface to his *Collected Poems*

(1913), were important literary documents, and at least one of the articles written about Ford by other poets, Pound's 'Mr. Hueffer and the Prose Tradition in Verse' (No. 18), has become a landmark in the criticism of modern poetry.

These are the enduring aspects of Ford's literary activities, but at the same time he was involved in a number of affairs and episodes that adversely affected his personal reputation and standing as a literary figure. The most important of these were the legal proceedings that led to his separation from his wife and his establishment in London with Violet Hunt. At a time when divorce and disgrace were synonymous, these events proved to be damaging. Less important but in many ways representative of the pettiness of contemporary literary life in London were the extraordinary personal attacks made on Ford by Ada Elizabeth Jones, later the wife of Cecil Chesterton, using the pseudonym of J. K. Prothero (Nos 36, 37). In a review of a book written in collaboration with Violet Hunt, she attacked Ford as a Jew and a coward. In *Goodbye to All That* Robert Graves has described the hysterical xenophobia which the pressures of the war created among non-combatants, and in *Kangaroo* D. H. Lawrence has recounted the same leaden malice with which he and his wife, Frieda, were treated while living along the south coast in wartime. But the attack on Ford, who was then serving in the Welch Regiment, and the correspondence that followed it seem even more sordid and personal.

A later episode which was also damaging occurred after Conrad's death, with the publication in 1924 of Ford's testimonial volume, *Joseph Conrad: A Personal Remembrance*. Ford said that he had written this book 'at fever heat and in an extraordinarily short time for I had, as it were, to get it out of my system.'[7] Nevertheless, to hostile eyes, it looked as though Ford was cashing in on Conrad's reputation and the attention he was receiving in the months immediately following his death. Mrs Conrad stirred up trouble by publicly refuting some of the statements in the book (No. 39), and that led to a public discussion of the collaboration and of standards of literary accuracy (Nos 41, 43, 44). Ford had written *Joseph Conrad*, as he stated explicitly in his preface, in the form of a novel, because he believed that form most appropriate to his memorial, but to clear his name he documented the facts in an article called 'Working with Conrad'. Today the controversy seems petty, but the reviews of Ford's book, including those written by Edward Garnett (Nos 40, 42), the man who introduced Ford to Conrad, have historical interest as texts in literary attitudes and values.

INTRODUCTION

They relate closely to the question of what truth really is, whether it is an objective reality, perceivable by all in the same way, or whether it is open to personal interpretation and subject to unconscious predilections.

Ford firmly believed in the relativity of truth, and his whole literary stance is based on it. 'Modern life', he wrote, 'is so extraordinary, so hazy, so tenuous, with still such definite and concrete spots in it, that I am forever on the look-out for some poet who shall render it with all its values.'[8] This is what impressionism is: the totality of all the little truths. The little perceptions and observations that affect one another are combined to create an awareness of the complexity of life itself, at a level deeper than that of a simple causal or linear progression. Ford used this method in his fiction, and he also used it in his reminiscences, with predictable results. In his first book of memoirs, *Ancient Lights* (1911), he explained his method:

> This book, in short, is full of inaccuracies as to facts, but its accuracy as to impressions is absolute ... My business in life, in short, is to attempt to discover, and to try to let you see, where we stand. I don't really deal in facts, I have for facts a most profound contempt. I try to give you what I see to be the spirit of an age, of a town, of a movement. This cannot be done with facts.[9]

Despite this assertion, and others like it, which made it clear where he stood, Ford was constantly criticized for the inaccuracies of his reminiscences. Impressionism was acceptable in fiction, but not otherwise and, starting with the reviews of *Ancient Lights*, there were always outraged individuals ready to attack Ford for his alleged untruths. Even his own uncle, W. M. Rossetti, wrote a letter to the editor of *Outlook*, listing the errors, page by page, he found in *Ancient Lights* (No. 35). Ford's attitude towards facts always got him in trouble, and the correspondence columns of the magazines where the reminiscences appeared are full of corrective letters, fortunately not always so solemn as Uncle William's (No. 38). If the Conrad controversy harmed Ford more than any other, the greatest public furore arose from a statement in *Return to Yesterday* in which Ford asserted that King George V had threatened to abdicate in 1914 in order to force the government to agree to his request for a conference at Buckingham Palace to resolve the Ulster question of that year. This statement was reprinted in the papers at the height of the 1931 crisis and caused a considerable uproar. The *Daily Herald* published its story under the front-page headline MONSTROUS STORY ABOUT THE KING and various ex-ministers and palace officials denounced Ford's statement. His publisher, Victor Gollancz, loyally defended it for revealing 'a magnificent example for genuine kingship'.

While this episode has no literary importance, the doubts that were repeatedly linked with Ford's reminiscences damaged his reputation as a literary figure. In fact, Ford belonged to three different literary generations, not counting his Pre-Raphaelite background. The first of these involved his friendship with men like Conrad, James, Galsworthy and Wells; the second, placed in France, brought him into association with many of the leading figures of Paris during the 1920s—Joyce, Gertrude Stein, Hemingway, Pound. The final group was mainly American and included Allen Tate and Caroline Gordon, Katherine Anne Porter, William Carlos Williams and Robert Lowell, then a student. There were many reasons for this progression through literary generations, but one may be traced to the reminiscences and the reviews that accompanied them. By writing so extensively and openly about his associates, Ford eventually alienated them. He was not indiscreet but open, and not all writers, especially those with a developed sense of their own importance, enjoy anecdotes about their early days.

Ford was nearly fifty when, in the early 1920s, he left England for good. As author of *The Good Soldier* and editor of the *English Review* he had achieved much, but had little to show for it. The works he wrote immediately after the war revealed a kind of mental shell-shock: despite several attempts, he was too close to his own war experiences to write well about them; while the books that dealt with pre-war life, such as *Thus to Revisit* (1927), a volume of criticism and memoirs combined, and the satirical *Mr. Bosphorus and the Muses* (1923) seemed self-consciously literary. The move to France, first to Provence and later to Paris, helped his perspective and also gave him a tremendous new impetus. The physical change was invigorating, but Paris in the 1920s was also the literary centre of the world. Ford soon found himself with many old friends and many new, a member of a vigorous post-war literary generation that was eager to throw over the gentilities of earlier literary styles and to confront actuality as it had been revealed in the war and its immediate aftermath. With the encouragement of Ezra Pound in 1924 he founded a new literary magazine, the *Transatlantic Review*, in which he published the work of many writers living in Paris, including fiction and verse by Pound, Joyce, Gertrude Stein and, among younger writers, Cummings, Glenway Wescott and Ernest Hemingway. Although not so controlled and polished as its

INTRODUCTION

predecessor, the *English Review*, the *Transatlantic* was nevertheless a vigorous monthly, experimental, open and, in so far as it took risks, somewhat uneven.

These activities were valuable in their own right, but they also helped bring Ford out of the literary doldrums he had experienced in Sussex immediately after the war. The Anglo-French literary *ambiance* of post-war Paris seemed a natural outgrowth of the wartime alliance; and during this period Ford wrote the four novels that make up the *Parade's End* tetralogy: *Some Do Not* (1924), *No More Parades* (1925), *A Man Could Stand Up* (1926) and *Last Post* (1928). While the publication of these novels was overshadowed by the more immediately resounding successes of Joyce's *Ulysses* and Hemingway's *The Sun Also Rises*, it was evident that Ford was producing major work. For the first time in his life, he found himself a best-seller, and his success with these novels brought him a position and a respect that stayed with him for the rest of his life.

Parade's End did not seem as impressive as *Ulysses* when it came out because it appeared to be comparatively old fashioned, emerging from the impressionist tradition rather than breaking with it. In time, the originality of Ford's achievement was to be recognized, but despite the respectful praise given these novels, most English readers thought him less than Galsworthy and Mottram (whom they understood better), while most Americans considered him less than Joyce. Early reviewers agreed that the novels as they came out were 'remarkable' or 'brilliant' (Nos 23-6), but it was not until the series was completed that critics began to grasp the achievement of the whole work (No. 30). The most perceptive reviewers tended to be fellow-novelists such as L. P. Hartley and William McFee (Nos 31-2), but even these were few in number. As editor and critic, Ford had written extensively on the work of his contemporaries, and of writers much younger than he; he had also printed their work in his magazines and encouraged book publishers to bring out their poems and novels. Yet with rare exceptions, those he helped ignored him. As Katherine Anne Porter noted in 1932:

> I have myself noticed for some time that Ford has a special genius for nourishing vipers in his bosom, and I have never seen an essay or article about him signed by any of these discoveries of his. I can make nothing of this, except that I have learned that most human beings—and I suppose that artists are that, after all—suffer some blow to their self-esteem in being helped, and develop the canker of ingratitude. As if, somehow, they can, by denying their debt, or ignoring it,

wipe it out altogether. . . . If I could really understand this warp in most human minds, or hearts, I would be God, I suppose. . . .¹⁰

In similar fashion, Ford, the most international of English authors, enjoyed no reputation at all on the Continent. In the *Transatlantic Review* he published the work of many European writers, but except for a volume of propaganda published in Paris during the First World War, his own books remained untranslated and unknown. Writing in the tradition of the French novel, while dealing with intensely English subjects, he undoubtedly disappointed the expectations of readers accustomed to H. G. Wells and Arthur Conan Doyle.

Nevertheless, the reputation Ford made with the publication of *Parade's End* (a title not used until the omnibus collection put out by Knopf in 1950) brought about the first articles that dealt with his work as a whole. These all appeared in America, where the Tietjens series earned its greatest success, and they were written by some of the more important journalist-critics of the day. Herbert Gorman and Granville Hicks both wrote extensively about him in the *Bookman* (Nos 58, 59), while Burton Rascoe and M. D. Zabel wrote at length about his life and work in the *Nation* and *Arts and Decoration* (Nos 28, 47). Most of these essays emphasized the fact that Ford was an unjustly neglected writer.

Ford's success as the author of the tetralogy was followed by a low period in the early 1930s. Part of this decline was brought about by financial difficulties. Ford was justified in supposing that he might earn a steady income from his past work, especially after the success of the tetralogy, but he chose an unstable publisher for his most successful work. *Some Do Not* was brought out in New York by a new firm called Seltzer, and the book sold 40,000 copies. Soon afterwards, this publisher failed and Ford never received anything beyond his advance. The Tietjens series was then taken over by the A. C. Boni Company with an agreement to publish both his future work and a selection of his past work to be known as the 'Avignon' edition. Boni did indeed republish *The Good Soldier* in 1927, but refused to bring out other novels in the collected edition, only publishing Ford's new novels in the Tietjens series. Their failure to publish his older work undoubtedly cost Ford a great deal of money since at the time his reputation was at its height and the books would probably have sold well.

Ford's financial difficulties were to be aggravated by the depression; and his powers as a novelist seemed to flag after the exertions required

INTRODUCTION

by *Parade's End*. Most of Ford's best work in the last decade of his life was devoted to reminiscence, literary criticism and topographical writing. These books contributed further to Ford's creation of his own literary legend. The usual charge of inaccuracy continued to be made, but books like *Provence* (1935) and *Great Trade Route* (1937) made it evident that Ford was on to something much more than literary conversation pieces. In these books he was indirectly but deliberately preparing a set of values and a code of decency that despite the war have validity today (No. 49). There was also a testamentary quality in his last work, especially in the long *March of Literature* (1938), his survey of the world's literature from Confucius to the present day. From humdrum reviewers, these books received predictable notices. People like Middleton Murry and Edward Sackville-West, who stood on the fringes of literary life, could not understand Ford's purpose and attacked him for his commissions and omissions (Nos 45, 55), but in fact these attacks were rare. In his last years, Ford created little interest among critics. His works were noticed, generally politely, but with scant enthusiasm.

An inevitable consequence of this neglect was an increasingly desperate financial condition. Towards the end of his life, Ford found it almost impossible to find publishers for his work. He had hoped to write a three-volume *History of Our Own Times*, but no publisher would take it. He was therefore forced to return to the writing of novels, which he did not want to do, and in 1936 even wrote a detective story, *Vive Le Roy* (No. 50). His last five books were brought out by four different New York publishers. In England, where some of his later books were not published at all, he was finally taken up by Sir Stanley Unwin who undertook to publish all his last works and even made him a loan of £250 a few months before his death.

Despite the penury of his last days and the critical neglect he had to endure, Ford was widely respected by fellow novelists. He wrote two experimental novels in his last years, *The Rash Act* (1933) and *Henry for Hugh* (1934), and among Ford enthusiasts these were appreciated. But the young novelists who were most impressed by Ford's work, and wrote most extensively about it, considered his late work all of a piece, as one gigantic literary production in which fact and fiction merged and flowed in and out of each other, and which in sum constituted a marvel of human literature. V. S. Pritchett and Graham Greene, who reviewed nearly all of Ford's last books, admired the tremendous skill and ease with which he handled his material (Nos 48–

51, 54, 56). For Greene especially, who was then at an early stage in his career, Ford was a master whose works were to be read in a professional fashion.

If Greene and Pritchett were almost alone in publicly celebrating Ford's achievement, there was a silent underground appreciation. During the last few years of his life, Ford spent prolonged periods of time in New York and also taught at a small Michigan college called Olivet, where other writers occasionally held classes in writing and literature. These activities involved him with a number of American writers whom he saw frequently and sometimes visited. E. E. Cummings, William Carlos Williams, Katherine Anne Porter, Allen Tate and Caroline Gordon, Ford had known for fifteen years or more; Sherwood Anderson and Theodore Dreiser were his immediate contemporaries, and anxious to welcome him as a colleague. There were yet younger writers, including Robert Lowell and Jean Stafford, for whom he was a mentor and example. Ford's strong sense of literary movements and of co-operative activity among artists led him to found a society which he called 'Friends of William Carlos Williams'. Its purpose was to call attention to Williams and also to Cummings and Edward Dahlberg whose work then lacked recognition. The society would meet for dinner at the Downtown Gallery in Greenwich Village at which there would be readings and discussion of the work of the writer selected for honour on the particular evening. It was a short-lived group, partly because of Ford's own ill-health.

Ford died in June 1939, at a time when the world was preoccupied with the growing European conflict. Except for notices written by Pound and Greene (Nos 61, 62), his obituaries were scant and inaccurate, dismissing him as a man of unfulfilled promise. To counter this neglect, James Laughlin printed a collection of essays and statements honouring Ford in the *New Directions Annual* for 1942. Testamentary in quality, these essays nevertheless reflect the widespread respect Ford's achievement had earned him among other writers (Nos 63–6).

During the war, Ford's name virtually dropped out of sight. The subject-matter of his fiction dated and he faded into the generally obscure shadows of Edwardian literature. Then in 1948, with the publication of Douglas Goldring's biography, he again came to public notice (Nos 67, 69). Goldring had served as Ford's sub-editor on the *English Review*, and his book emphasized the personal side of Ford's life, especially the confusions of his love life. For this reason, it re-

INTRODUCTION

awakened the ghosts of Violet Hunt and Stella Bowen who in their own day had written extensively of their liaisons with Ford.

Despite its emphasis on the private rather than the literary career, Goldring's book created an interest in Ford among a generation that had never read him during his own lifetime. There followed the republication of the four Tietjens novels and *The Good Soldier* by Penguin Books (No. 68) and the publication of a one-volume *Parade's End*, as well as *The Good Soldier*, by Knopf in 1950 and 1951. These books were widely reviewed and praised, and a number of Ford's friends and acquaintances, including Williams and Auden and Caroline Gordon, wrote long appreciative critiques (No. 70). Despite this attention in the Press, the Ford 'boom' never quite came off. One reason was the tendency of reviewers and publishers to emphasize the notion that Ford was a forgotten man who was being rescued from total obscurity. This was overstating the case, and aroused suspicions.

In 1950 it was probably too early for a Ford revival. The post-war years marked the rapid replacement of England by America as a world power, and were therefore temperamentally unpropitious for novels which dealt with the decline and corruption of an earlier order of society. By the 1960s, however, so fast do our reactions follow our actions, *Parade's End* and *The Good Soldier* seemed entirely relevant to a western world undergoing moral and psychological turmoil and collapse. The publication of a number of critical works, as well as a new biography, again revived interest in Ford, but this time with greater understanding and appreciation for his achievement. These studies have in turn encouraged the re-publication of a number of other books by Ford, so that a respectable number of titles are now available.

For the moment, Ford's reputation seems secure. In the relatively short time since his death, his work has suffered neglect and has also received elegant critical appraisal (Nos 71, 72). He has now safely risen from the low status of earlier periods, when he was known mainly as Conrad's collaborator and as editor of the *English Review*, judgments echoed in the brief essay in the *Dictionary of National Biography*. There was a time when Ford was thought of mainly as a mere 'war novelist' while Galsworthy, Bennett, Wells and, of the somewhat younger generation, Maugham and Forster, received all the attention. In the last two decades, however, the emphasis has gradually changed, and these writers, who never experienced the neglect Ford knew, and whose reputations were enshrined in histories of literature, have become less and less interesting to contemporary readers. The fall in their popularity has been almost imperceptible, but it has taken place. Bennett and Wells mainly generate a socio-historical interest, whereas Ford has finally emerged, along with Conrad and Lawrence and Joyce, about whom there has never been much doubt, as one of the few important English writers of the present century.

NOTES

1 Quoted in *Ancient Lights*, 1911, 197–8.
2 Letter to Edward Garnett; quoted in MacShane, *The Life and Work of Ford Madox Ford*, 1965, 64.
3 Letter, 8 May 1905; *Letters from John Galsworthy 1900–1932*, 1934, ed. Edward Garnett, 59.
4 Edgar Jepson, *Memories of an Edwardian*, 1937, 149.
5 Letter to J. B. Pinker, 1914; *The Life and Work of Ford Madox Ford*, 69.
6 Letter to Harriet Monroe, 13 August 1913; *The Letters of Ezra Pound 1907–1941*, 1950, ed, D. D. Paige, 21.
7 Inscription, quoted in E. Naumburg, 'A Catalogue of a Ford Madox Ford Collection', *Princeton University Library Chronicle*, ix, April 1948, 154.
8 *Critical Writings of Ford Madox Ford*, 1964, 142.
9 Pp. xv–xvi.
10 Letter, 6 May 1932.

Note on the Text
Preface

The orderly presentation of the material in this collection presents certain problems. The difficulty has been to try to reconcile chronology with subject-matter, and the result is a compromise. The first section is a chronological consideration of Ford's prose, mainly but not exclusively his fiction, from the beginning to the publication of *The Good Soldier* in 1915. The next three sections cover the critical reception of Ford's poetry during his own lifetime. The fifth section contains contemporary reviews of the four parts of *Parade's End*, which is thought of as Ford's most considerable work. The sixth section is a collection of material that could not satisfactorily appear under any of the earlier headings, including early reviews of Ford's reminiscences and documents concerning the various journalistic controversies that followed their publication; the next section deals with Ford's book on Joseph Conrad. The eighth section is devoted primarily to reviews of Ford's books in the 1930s. There are few interesting reviews of his late fiction, and therefore most of the material here is centred on the last books of topography and reminiscence, *Great Trade Route* and *Provence*, as well as on *The March of Literature*. Graham Greene's and V. S. Pritchett's reviews appear here. The ninth section begins with the literary portraits that were first written after the publication of the Tietjens novels, and contains articles that were written about Ford towards the end of his life, and immediately after his death. Included is some obituary material as well as a number of the testaments published in the *New Directions Annual* for 1942. The final section marks the beginning of the first serious reconsideration of Ford's work a decade or more after his death. The articles republished here are limited to those written by his contemporaries, generally by other writers who knew him.

 Except for the correction of obvious typographical errors and the introduction of uniform punctuation, the texts are reproduced here as they were originally printed.

EARLY NOVELS AND PROSE WRITINGS

1. Unsigned review of *The Shifting of the Fire*, *Athenaeum*

No. 3395, 19 November 1892, 700

This review of Ford's first novel is typical of the many short, and usually anonymous, notices his early work received.

Mr. Hueffer, a very young author already known as a writer of fairy stories, makes a first appearance as a novelist in the first of the 'Independent Novel Series' recently published by Mr. Fisher Unwin. The title of the series to a certain extent prepares us for the contents of *The Shifting of the Fire*. Mr. Hueffer has chosen for his motive a singularly repellent situation—the marriage of a beautiful girl to an entirely loathsome satyr of nearly fourscore—and he has certainly spared no pains to elaborate its hideous incongruity. Pity is inspired in the reader; but it is never unaccompanied with disgust, amounting in several passages to positive nausea. Mr. Hueffer's pages bristle with infelicitous audacity and cynicism, which he will regret when he is older. For example, after describing the scene at the burial of the hero's aunt and the grief of his cousin Kate, he adds, 'Never before did men think themselves, ay, and swear at themselves some five minutes later, for being such blasted sentimental fools as those who happened to see her then.' The dialogue is cast in a similarly realistic form; but Mr. Hueffer has yet to learn that strong language does not make a strong book. And he has also to learn the sovereign lesson of self-effacement, instead of obtruding his own dogmatic generalizations at every turn. Such blunders as 'lusi naturæ' are venial trifles in comparison with the errors in taste and temper which colour the whole story. Mr. Hueffer has talent and imagination; but his method is headstrong and gratuitously aggressive. Happily he is young enough to learn better manners and more legitimate means of attracting readers.

2. Joseph Conrad on *The Inheritors*

Letter to the editor, *The New York Times Saturday Review*,
24 August 1901, 603

The anonymous reviewer of *The Inheritors* (*The New York Times Saturday Review* 13 July 1901, 499) failed to mention that this book was a collaboration and entirely omitted reference to Ford. Moreover, the review was generally unfavourable, reading in part: 'Whoever takes up *The Inheritors* under the impression that he is in store for one of those masterly studies of the sea and sailors which delighted us in *The Nigger of the Narcissus* will lay it down half, or, more probably, a fourth, read, and with the sense of being cheated...' The remainder of the review is mainly a summary, concluding with: 'Mr. Conrad sees the significant facts of life and character. If he sometimes flashes before us what we have fondly hoped was a private view, he does it without malice or coarseness. The book lacks the emotional power of *Lord Jim*, but it is clean, vigorous, and not machine made.' Conrad believed this review did an injustice both to the book and to his collaborator, and therefore wrote the following letter to the editor.

Referring to *The New York Times Saturday Review* of July 13, it is impossible not to recognise in the review of one 'extravagant story' the high impartiality exercised in estimating a work which, I fear, remains not wholly sympathetic to the critic.

A feeling of regret mingles with gratitude on that account. It is a great good fortune for a writer to be understood; and greater still to feel that he has made his aim perfectly clear. It might have been wished, too, that the fact of collaboration had been made more evident on the face of the notice. The book is emphatically an experiment in collaboration; but only the first paragraph of the review mentions 'the authors' in the plural—afterward it seems as if Mr. Conrad alone were credited with the qualities of style and conception detected by the friendly glance of the critic.

The elder of the authors is well aware how much of these generously estimated qualities the book owes to the younger collaborator. Without disclaiming his own share of the praise or evading the blame, the older man is conscious that his scruples in the matter of treatment, however sincere in themselves, may have stood in the way of a very individual talent deferring to him more out of friendship, perhaps, than from conviction; that they may have robbed the book of much freshness and of many flashes of that 'private vision' (as our critic calls them) which would have made the story more actual and more convincing.

It is this feeling that gives him the courage to speak about the book—already written, printed, delivered and cast to the four winds of publicity. Doubtless a novel that wants explaining is a bad novel; but this is only an extravagant story—and it is an experiment. An experiment may bear a certain amount of explanation without confessing itself a failure. Therefore it may perhaps be permissible to point out that the story is not directed against 'some of the most cherished traditions and achievements of Englishmen.' It is rather directed at the self-seeking, at the falsehood that had been (to quote the book) 'hiding under the words that for ages had spurred men to noble deeds, to self-sacrifice, and to heroism.' And, apart from this view, to direct one's little satire at the tradition and achievements of a race would have been an imbecile futility—something like making a face at the great pyramid. Judge them as we may, the spirit of tradition and the body of achievement are the very spirit and the very body not only of any single race, but of the entire mankind, which, without the vast breadth and colossal form of the past would be resolved into a handful of the dying, struggling feebly in the darkness under an overwhelming multitude of the dead. Thus our Etchingham Granger, when in the solitude that falls upon his soul, he sees the form of the approaching Nemesis, is made to understand that no man is permitted 'to throw away with impunity the treasure of his past—the past of his kind—whence springs the promise of his future.'

This is the note struck—we hoped with sufficient emphasis—among the other emotions of the hero. And, besides, we may appeal to the general tone of the book. It is not directed against tradition; still less does it attack personalities. The extravagance of its form is meant to point out forcibly the materialistic exaggeration of individualism, whose unscrupulous efficiency it is the temper of the time to worship.

It points out simply—and no more; because the business of a work striving to be art is not to teach or to prophesy, (as we have been charged, on this side, with attempting,) nor yet to pronounce a definite conclusion.

Thus, the teaching, the conclusions, even to the prophesying, may be safely left to science, which, whatever authority it may claim, is not concerned with truth at all, but with the exact order of such phenomena as fall under the perception of the senses. Its conclusions are quite true enough if they can be made useful to the furtherance of our little schemes to make our earth a little more habitable. The laws it discovers remain certain and immovable for the time of several generations. But in the sphere of an art dealing with a subject-matter whose origin and end are alike unknown there is no possible conclusion. The only indisputable truth of life is our ignorance. Besides this there is nothing evident, nothing absolute, nothing uncontradicted; there is no principle, no instinct, no impulse that can stand alone at the beginning of things and look confidently to the end. Egoism, which is the moving force of the world, and altruism, which is its morality, these two contradictory instincts of which one is so plain and the other so mysterious cannot serve us unless in the incomprehensible alliance of their irreconcilable antagonism. Each alone would be fatal to our ambition. For, in the hour of undivided triumph one would make our inheritance too arid to be worth having and the other too sorrowful to own.

Fiction, at the point of development at which it has arrived, demands from the writer a spirit of scrupulous abnegation. The only legitimate basis of creative work lies in the courageous recognition of all the irreconcilable antagonisms that make our life so enigmatic, so burdensome, so fascinating, so dangerous—so full of hope. They exist! And this is the only fundamental truth of fiction. Its recognition must be critical in its nature, inasmuch that in its character it may be joyous, it may be said; it may be angry with revolt, or submissive in resignation. The mood does not matter. It is only the writer's self-forgetful fidelity to his sensations that matter. But, whatever light he flashes on it, the fundamental truth remains, and it is only in its name that the barren struggle of contradictions assumes the dignity of moral strife going on ceaselessly to a mysterious end—with our consciousness powerless but concerned sitting enthroned like a melancholy parody of eternal wisdom above the dust of the contest.

Joseph Conrad

3. Unsigned article on *Romance*, New York *Bookman*

xix, August 1904, 544

In contrast to the reception given *The Inheritors*, reviewers of *Romance* emphasized that it was a collaboration. Most of the comments were unfavourable. Sometimes Conrad received the blame, as in *The Times Literary Supplement*: 'If Mr. Hueffer, the writer of those delicate little 'Poems for Pictures', is a poet and something of an idealist, Mr. Conrad will seem to many the very antithesis of anything of the kind.' But generally Ford was blamed for the book's failure, as in this comment on Conrad that was printed in the *Academy*: 'This writer has too strong an individuality to be able to do himself justice when writing with anyone.'

The *Bookman* was the first periodical to consider the collaboration in general terms.

Ford Madox Hueffer and Joseph Conrad are jointly responsible for *Romance*. From such a collaboration it is likely that Mr. Conrad will get whatever there is of honour and Mr. Hueffer whatever there is of blame, or be swamped altogether. The fact is, however, that Mr. Hueffer is quite as interesting a person in his way as Mr. Conrad. He is a nephew of the Rossettis, and has a number of successful books to his credit; his first, *The Brown Owl*, has run into ten editions. The history of the collaboration between Mr. Conrad and Mr. Hueffer is interesting from the fact that it was Mr. Conrad who asked to be allowed to work with Mr. Heuffer. The plot of the story almost as it now stands had been flashed into Mr. Hueffer's brain by some incidents in the famous Admiralty trial of Cuban pirates. On having it recounted to him, Mr. Conrad's enthusiasm took flame and he begged to be allowed to collaborate. Forthwith the two began the book. That was some half a dozen years ago, in the beginning of their friendship. Between the starting and finishing of *Romance* the two friends produced another collaboration, *The Inheritors*. Mr. Hueffer is Mr. Conrad's literary adviser, and a good deal of Mr. Conrad's work is done at his house, especially the last chapters of stories, which Mr. Conrad finds most difficult to write. Mr. Hueffer, though a descendant of the Rosettis, makes a good deal of sport of the mysticism and symbolism of the pre-Raphaelites. To an inquisitive person who enquired recently how he wrote, he replied with perfect gravity that he could not write anything unless he was 'standing with a tame duckling fast asleep between his feet'— a story which was quoted seriously and with mild surprise by one of our newspapers.

4. Unsigned review of *The Fifth Queen*, *Athenaeum*

No. 4093, 7 April 1906, 417

This review indicates the tone with which Ford's work was generally received.

Mr. Hueffer makes occasional mistakes; his generalizations are weak and faulty at times; but his writing is not slipshod, though he is prolific. His latest book is perhaps his best, and in the historical novel of England's spacious days he may have discovered his *métier*. The 'Fifth Queen' of the title is Catherine Howard, and the story furnishes noteworthy portraits of the eighth Henry, Privy Seal Cromwell, Bishop Gardiner, and the ill-fated fifth queen herself. The story is good, as such, and some distinction is lent to it by two facts: the author has saturated himself in the atmosphere and colour of the period he deals with, and he has followed history not slavishly, but as one who reads his own conceptions into the records of the age. Here and there we are irritated by the author's regrettable practice of continually reverting to any phrase or word which has pleased him. As his taste in phrases favours the curious and bizarre, this weakness is made the more prominent. Some will find the language used too full-flavoured, but it is not discordant.

5. 'A Romance of Two Worlds': C. F. G. Masterman on *An English Girl*

Daily News, 28 September 1907, 3

This is one of the first extended reviews Ford's fiction was to receive. The author was a Liberal politician and a junior Minister in Asquith's cabinet. Early in the war, he was placed in charge of the British Ministry of Information and asked Ford to write for him. The result was two books, *When Blood is Their Argument* and *Between St. Dennis and St. George*, which Ford wrote under great pressure. Masterman died young before fulfilling his considerable promise.

Mr. Hueffer in this romance has 'arrived.' It is a bigger piece of work than his studies in the historical novel: certainly bigger than those essays in which he has attempted the summary of impressions of the country and the town. *An English Girl* is reminiscent of the work of that great novelist, Mr. Harold Frederic. There is the same clarity of style, the same conviction of reality, the same power of opening through the simplicities of quiet narration and converse large and limitless vistas. Mr. Hueffer traffics in great issues and digs deep into elemental things. Yet he makes no attempt at preaching: the detachment is almost chilling in its indifference. He is one who looks on: seeing it all: accepting it all: not blindly scornful, if not entirely forgiving.

There is practically no action in the story. A millionaire manipulator of a hundred trusts dies suddenly. His son finds himself the richest man on earth. An artist, sensitive, revolting from everything which his father delighted in, he regards his fortune as a burden 'too heavy for a man that hopes for heaven'. He is engaged to an English girl, the child of ancient lineage, bearing easily and almost unconsciously the security given by such an inheritance. They journey from Canterbury to New York across the Atlantic, with high hopes of righting all the wrongs which this wealth is creating. They find they can right nothing at all: that they are absolutely helpless, the play and sport of blind forces. He revolts in disgust from the whole affair: New York: Coney Island: the newest America. She finds excuses for it, and decides even to like it. At length he determines to throw it all up: to let it go its own way, to salvation or abyss; to return to England, and live the life of a country gentleman and artist in modest comfort. He comes back, and they set about furnishing and planning for the future. Suddenly America tugs at his heart. He cannot leave it. He announces his intention of going back again to do what he can with the power which has been entrusted to him, the power of great possessions. She refuses to follow him. They part—and for ever.

The interest of the book lies in the study of action and reaction between these two characters. Both the parents of Don Kelleg had been British: both had emigrated to America. He himself had been educated in an English school and University, yet he remained American. As his stepbrother Canzano writes to Eleanor Greville in a letter at the end—a kind of interpretation of it all, 'Americanism isn't the product of a race; it's a product of a frame of mind. The English who succeed in America are the very English who are stifled at home—who can't stand your atmosphere of accepted ideas. They may have been born in Hampshire, but they are born Americans. What fellowship has such with one who falls back always on the accepted traditions and ideas? "The Englishman's eyes" (in the country family portrait gallery) "are always tranquil: he has formed his ideas: he has never had them formed for him: he *knows*: he is never going to learn any more." "Look in at the glass," he breaks out, "at your own fine, brown, and beautiful eyes. You will see that look—and the same thing is expressed in every one of your slow, powerful features. It is the strong, placid, powerful gaze of the bull that looks away over the pastures and reflects".'

Don Kelleg's philanthropy, in face of that roaring turmoil of life, without standard, traditions, or ideals, proves an utterly vain and futile thing. With his hundred millions, and his vast control, he appears as impotent as a little child. No one wants him to break and destroy his Trusts. All that each desire is an opportunity to come in 'at bedrock prices' into some of his ventures. His father had started his great wealth by swindling Kratzenstein, a barber of the West, out of a copper mine. The son desires to make reparation. They hunt up the fat, contented man, plying his trade in New York. In a scene of real humour they propound their proposals. He flares into fury at any suggestion of gift or charity. All he is prepared to accept is the inflation of his thousand shares in a worthless gold company to four hundred dollars apiece.

And as with this man, so all. 'What the population wanted was not the abolition of Trusts. It was just the chance to turn worthless stocks into half a million dollars.' Kelleg became 'simply appalled at New York—at its squalid back streets, at its hard voices, at its hideous language, at its physical recklessness, and at the fact that he hadn't discovered, anywhere, a trace of desire for anything morally better. They only wanted, all these people, plush instead of cotton, six-course dinners instead of one meal of canned meat, a chance of a million dollars instead of a daily wage of one dollar twenty-five cents.'

Mr. Greville, an extraordinarily wise and not unpleasant observer, had prophesied it all on the outward journey. 'He'll found institutions, and find that they breed beastlier chaps than ever. He'll raise cooperative factories, and find the hands will dissipate all the profits on shove-halfpenny. I wouldn't mind wagering that he'll try to purify the municipal politics of some wretched town, and he'll find that his money is being used by his reforming lieutenants to bribe into existence the worst Tammany that's ever been known.'

Mr. Hueffer does not love America. Into many of his descriptions he infuses an element of bitterness. His picture of the American woman, especially, the American woman will find it difficult to forgive. Yet his own opinion would appear to be most clearly expressed in the more tranquil philosophy of Canzano. 'Consider them as children.' Leave all the standards behind. 'The moment that one begins to judge, one condemns. But as long as one forces oneself to accept one has the best time in the world.' 'It's not a question of class and class. It's a question of another race: of a different planet: of a different species even.' 'Don't judge; observe. Just have a good time.'

And as for ideals and philanthropies 'Poor Don,' is the genial conclusion, 'will soon get tired of trying to put the sky where the sea is, and trying to make cette dame wear colours that won't set our teeth on edge. He'll have eventually the sense to see that his compatriots too are having in their own way the best kind of time, and only want to be let alone.'

6. R. A. Scott-James on *The Fifth Queen Crowned*, *Daily News*

26 March 1908, 4

This is one of the first reviews of Ford's work written by a fellow-practitioner, and the difference between this notice and the one immediately following it in this collection will be evident. Scott-James (1878–1959) was literary editor of the periodical in which this article appeared and he followed a literary and journalistic career that eventually led to the editorship of the *London Mercury*. Scott-James also wrote the introduction to the Penguin edition of the Tietjens novels (see No. 68).

In this volume Mr. Hueffer brings to an end his trilogy, the three volumes which present three stages in the tragedy of Katharine Howard, fifth Queen of Henry VIII. In the first we had the coming to Court of the young lady, under the clumsy escort of her cousin, Thomas Culpepper; in the second the career and downfall of Thomas Cromwell, Lord Privy Seal, and the unsought triumph of Katharine; and in the third, the book now before us, we find Katharine crowned, admired, fondled, and petted by the King, surrounded by enemies, and at last the victim of their plots.

It is a bold task that Mr. Hueffer has essayed. For let it be said at once that his aim has nothing in common with that of the too well-known writers of roystering, gushful romance, who take a few historical facts and set them in a ridiculous halo of knight-errantry and heroic love and villainous intrigue. Nor, to put it on a higher plane, is his aim the same as that of a Walter Scott, who aims at showing the panorama and romantic movement of history. His object is nothing less than to combine the qualities of historical romance with those of the modern schools of realists and psychological novelists.

The writer who described Macaulay's History of England as 'my favourite work of fiction' was the first critic who described a way of approaching history which has been justified in modern literature.

Macaulay presented a 'view' or 'reading' of the English Revolution; George Meredith presents a reading of an historical fact in *The Tragic Comedians*; Mr. Maurice Hewlett in more books than one; and Mr. Ford Madox Hueffer in his three novels of the fifth Queen. The novelist has this added advantage in presenting his view, that he is allowed to add such facts as he cares to invent, provided they do not contradict history or the known characters of individuals so far as history has fixed them.

Mr. Hueffer has kept closely to the historical version; and with this object in view he must have studied in no cursory manner the archives and the monuments of the time. For he has not been content to present incidents alone; he describes to us the exact furniture of a room, the characteristic garments which this or that person was wearing, all those small, nice details which, implying as they do not little research, make the scenes real and alive for us. He is skilled too in hinting at delicate personal facts, which we are afraid to associate with historical personages lest we should make them too much like ourselves. Thus, for instance, Mary Tudor, hard, shrewd, unflinching, embittered as she is, is not presented as a rigid, statuesque type. Here is one moment of unbending—and there are others which follow:

Thus, around the Lady Mary, whilst she wrote, the people of the land breathed more peace. And even she could not but be conscious of a new softness, if it was only in the warmth that came from having her window-leads properly mended. She had hardly ever before known what it was to have warm hands when she wrote, and in most days of the year she had worn fur next her skin, indoors as well as out. But now the sun beat on her new windows, and in that warmth she could wear fine lawn, so that, in spite of herself, she took pleasure and was softened, though, since she spoke to no man save the Magister Udal, and to him only about the works of Plautus or the game of cards that they played together, few knew of any change in her.

Of the three novels now completed the last is probably the most successful. The story itself is more decisive, ending naturally, in the restrained pathos of Katharine's last speech to the King, and the simple official announcement, without any gruesome preliminaries:

> Katharine Howard was executed on
> Tower Hill, the 13th of February,
> in the 33rd year
> Of the reign of King Henry VIII.
> MDXLI-II.

The Katharine whom Mr. Hueffer has drawn is an idealised Katharine, a martyred Katharine, who might have been put among the saintly heroines of history, whose devotion to her religion, whose almost quixotic disdain of the intriguing methods of courts made her the victim of her enemies. Yet for all that she is a pathetically human Katharine, girlish, impetuous, gay, proud, optimistic, supremely confident, convinced that through the King's return to religion and her own sincere purpose she can bring back peace to the Court, and happiness to the country. With the Court and the country she does not prevail; but it is in a delicate series of character pictures that Mr. Hueffer shows how she prevails over the adamantine heart of the Lady Mary. She meets with some hard snubbings when she seeks to reconcile Mary with the King; but she persists and persists in her efforts, kneeling to her daughter-in-law, vowing that she will come to her again and again till she has succeeded. Then suddenly there comes a moment when she has refused to soil her hands by listening to a spy who would have warned her. The Lady Mary rises, and this time it is she who kneels to the Queen.

'I acknowledge thee to be my mother,' she said, 'that have married the King, my father. I pray you that you do take me by the hand and set me in that seat that you did raise for me. I pray you that you do style me a princess, royal again in this land. And I pray you to lesson me and teach me that which you would have me do as well as that which it befits me to do. Take me by the hand.'

'Nay, it is my lord that should do this,' the Queen whispered. Before that she had started to her feet; her face had a flush of joy; her eyes shone with her transparent faith. She brushed back a strand of hair from her brow; she folded her hands on her breasts, and raised her glance upwards to seek the dwelling-place of Almighty God and the saints in their glorious array.

'It is my lord should do this!' she said again.

'Speak no more words,' the Lady Mary said. 'I have heard enow of thy pleadings. You have heard me say that.'

This change in Mary is not melodrama. When Katharine, too simple to understand her soured daughter-in-law, ejaculates 'This is the gladdest day of my life,' Mary cries out: 'Pray you get you gone from my sight and hearing for I endure ill the appearance and sound of joy.'

That Mr. Hueffer completely vindicates his heroine from all shadow of guilt follows from what has been said. Thomas Culpepper is the same loutish braggart that he was in *The Fifth Queen*—even Henry himself could entertain no suspicion against the drunken, senseless creature whom Katharine's enemies thrust into her rooms. The King, violent, bull-like, strong in muscle and in appetite, unrestrained in every jovial or tyrannical impulse, is in turn the devoted slave of his meek wife, the clever wielder of retorts in an emergency, and again the slave of those about him, who make him put away and kill the woman he still loves.

Mr. Hueffer uses an artificial historical language which he has intentionally adopted in order, presumably, to keep up the atmosphere of the period into which he introduces us. It is doubtful if this conventionalised language is necessary; but beyond question the author uses it well and to good effect. For all his obvious elaboration, there is often a ruggedness in the description which very admirably expresses the northward process of the King, the tripping up of that sturdy fellow Thomas Culpepper, and other passages where there is movement and action. But elsewhere he is soft and delicately refined in his style, which well adapts itself to the subject in hand. On the whole, this is a very singular combination of historical romance and the intimate study of character.

7. Unsigned review of *The Fifth Queen Crowned*, *Academy*

lxxiv, 9 May 1908, 766

Unlike Scott-James's essay, this review typifies the academic critic's reaction to Ford's early work, especially his fiction. The reviewer's ignorance and venom are not unusual.

This is, apparently, the third of a series of novels dealing with the life of Henry VIII.'s fifth Queen, Katharine Howard. Not that there is anything in the book itself, except its general air of incompleteness, to show the reader that it is a sequel; but from the advertisements at the beginning and end we learn that the two previous volumes were very good. After perusal of the volume in front of us we find it difficult to believe in the excellence of the forerunners, *The Fifth Queen Crowned* having both in matter and style very little to recommend it. There are at least two ways of writing an historical novel, the discreet and the indiscreet. *Esmond* and *John Inglesant* belong to the former method, where the principal characters of the book are unknown, or unimportant historically, and the great personages of history are only there incidentally and as a setting. In this case the principal characters are Henry VIII., Archbishop Cranmer, the Duke of Norfolk, and Katharine Howard, and their most intimate thoughts and intentions are given at length until the mixture of fact and fiction becomes a folly. Even this defect might have been overlooked to some extent if there had been beauties of style and workmanship in compensation; but the whole book—the narrative part as well as the conversations—is written in a style which has now become commonly known as 'Wardour Street English,' from that well-known Soho thoroughfare where antiques and, more especially, sham antiques were to be found in such abundance. Mr. Hueffer, indeed, gives us the impression that he has had at his elbow the catalogue of some second-hand emporium. We have no doubt that much of this antiquarian lore will pass muster, but we should very much like to know whether the little chapel of Edward IV.'s reign was really round-arched.

There is another impression, too, to be gained from this sham archaistic writing, and that is that it has been chosen in order to conceal the author's incapacity for writing plain English. It is always dangerous to point out errors where such a method has been adopted, but we think it will be difficult for any one to justify the following examples that have been culled here and there from the many instances which gave us pause:

As if with furtive eyes and feathery grace of a blonde fox Cranmer's spy came round the great boards.—It was not *till very lately since* this canon of wedding by a holy friar *hath* been derided and contemned in this realm.—May the God to whom *you* have prayed, *that* softened the heart of Paul, soften *thine* in this hour.—Near the doorway it was all shadow, and soundlessly she faded away among *them*.

The italics are all ours. Errors and inelegances peep at us from every page, and we have found it quite impossible to count how often the different characters speak or look 'sardonically,' or 'swallow in their throats', or find their 'eyes suffused with blood;' this last unpleasant trait is, we hope, a strictly Tudor one, and is perhaps the result of Mr. Hueffer's antiquarian researches. But we did take the trouble to count, and we found that he has used the word 'heavy' in a figurative sense seven times in the first two short pages, and has even had to help it out with 'weighty,' which occurs twice. No, not even the *Outlook*, the *Daily Telegraph*, the *Daily News*, and others, aided by the *Revue des Deux Mondes*, whose commendations figure so aggressively on the fly-leaves of this book, shall deter us from saying that *The Fifth Queen Crowned* is a sham, and a 'heavy' sham at that.

8. Arnold Bennett on *A Call*, New Age

vi, 17 March 1910, 471

Writing under the pseudonym of 'Jacob Tonson' (English publisher, 1656–1736, who printed the works of his friends, Addison, Dryden, Pope and others), Arnold Bennett was the most influential literary critic in London before the First World War. Like Ford, Bennett was influenced by French novelists of the nineteenth century, but in his journal he dismissed *A Call*, reviewed below, as 'Slick work, but not, I fear, really interesting. He doesn't get down to the real stuff.'

A novel by the founder of the *English Review* must have at least the interest of its authorship. I believe that Mr. Ford Madox Hueffer's modesty objects to the naming of names in connection with that review. Such an objection is quite futile. Whoever mentions Mr. Hueffer will mention the *English Review*, and if Mr. Hueffer wished to avoid publicity he should have avoided founding the most genuinely 'literary' monthly that, perhaps, ever existed in England. Another instance of Mr. Hueffer's excessive modesty is to be seen in the paltry list of nine works 'by the same author' given opposite the title-page of his new novel, *A Call*. The British Museum catalogue, with its usual generous candour, discloses Mr. Hueffer as the author of some thirty-five separate books.

A Call is a very pretty thing. You can see in it throughout a preoccupation with questions of form, of technique—in short, a preoccupation with the art of literature. A rare quality, and one which must give pleasure to anybody whose reading in fiction has been wide enough, and his judgment sound enough, to enable him to perceive that, for want of that preoccupation, English fiction as a whole is badly second-rate, even the best of it. The style is as a rule distinguished; but in some places it is not, and here and there, in the weak spots, one catches Mr. Hueffer at the craftsman's trick of sticking a word in an unusual situation in a sentence in the hope (vain) of producing distinction by artificial means. In the mere writing, Mr. Hueffer owes something to Mr. Henry James, and perhaps also he has learnt from Mr. James some of the charming grace which is displayed in the construction of the book. It is a mild novel. It deals with tragic matters, but deals with them mildly. It does not engross, and probably is not meant to engross. It induces reverie and reflection. I have seen it upbraided for 'coldness.' It is not cold. But then, fortunately, it is not sentimental; and most reviewers are unable to differentiate between sentimentality and warmth.

I may say that I consider *A Call* to be profoundly and hopelessly untrue to life. It treats of the lazy rich. The characters, with one exception, never do anything except give orders to excellent servants and discuss the states of their bodies and their souls. So far as the novel shows, they have no real interest in any of the arts. They are heroically egotistic. They contribute nothing to the welfare of the Society from which they draw everything. They are, first and last, utterly and in every way idle. The sole thing that can be said in their favour is that they have carried daily manners to a high point of perfection. They are extremely 'class-conscious'; constantly talking to each other of 'our class.' Mr. Hueffer endows these persons with a comprehensive fineness of perception, and a skill in verbal expression, which it is absolutely impossible that they, living the life they do live, could possess. I have never met these persons in their homes, but I have observed them for months at a time on their travels, and I am prepared to defend the proposition that their mental existence resembles much more closely that of the beasts of the field than that credited to them by the amiable idealism of Mr. Hueffer.

Such qualities as Mr. Hueffer illustrates are the fruit only of long and often painful activity in the domains of intellect and of artistic emotion. In this fundamental matter *A Call* is inferior to Mrs. Wharton's enormously over-praised, slabby, and mediocre novel, *The House of Mirth*. But regard *A Call* as an original kind of fairy-tale, and it is about perfect.

9. Percy F. Bicknell on *Memories and Impressions (Ancient Lights)*, *Dial*

1, 1 May 1911, 345–6

From the beginning Ford wrote what used to be called *belles-lettres*—criticism, biography, memoirs—which he treated for the most part as an off-shoot of fiction. Except for poetry, writing was all of a piece for Ford. He was often called a stylist and had as his own definition that the only function of style was to make work interesting. His habit of using novelistic techniques when writing criticism or memoirs had predictable results. Those who enjoyed the use of the imagination were delighted with what he did; others, accustomed to a surface evaluation of facts or used to academic methods, were outraged. The reviews that follow illustrate these varied reactions.

The delightful and surprising thing about Mr. Ford Madox Hueffer's *Memories and Impressions*, a few chapters of which have already whetted the appetite of *Harper's Magazine* readers, is that, although still in his thirties (having been born in 1873), Mr. Hueffer can bring us so many personal reminiscences of such Victorian celebrities as Carlyle, Ruskin, Burne-Jones, Holman Hunt, the Rossettis, Swinburne, Whistler, Ford Madox Brown, William Morris, Millais, and Meredith. Even if some of his memories are of the derivative nature of Edward Everett Hale's, whereby that venerable author was able to produce a book covering a round century of recollections, his narrative is none the worse for that reason.

Being the grandson of Ford Madox Brown, whose artistic genius seems to have been insufficiently recognized in his lifetime, and the son of Francis Hueffer (or, more properly, Franz Hüffer), a Westphalian of encyclopædic learning and an extraordinary command of languages, the author came into the world with such endowments, of varied sorts, as to generate high hopes in his elders that he would develop into a genius of the first rank. Against the parentally prescribed career of a genius, however, he himself early offered vehement objections, and took his fortunes into his own hands, with some noteworthy results that afford interesting matter for certain portions of his book.

As it is the abundance of new and amusing anecdotes, rather than the philosophical reflections prompted by the incidents related, that constitutes the main attraction of Mr. Hueffer's chapters, and as these anecdotes bring the Pre-Raphaelites before us in the veritable warmth and glow of flesh-and-blood reality, we can do the reader no better service than to reproduce a few of the more characteristic manifestations of genial idiosyncrasy, as noted by the observant author. First, of the Pre-Raphaelite poets as a body, he says what many a reader of their verses must have said to himself at times, and at least half in earnest:

They took themselves with such extreme seriousness—these Pre-Raphaelite poets—and nevertheless I have always fancied that they are responsible for the death of English poetry. My father once wrote of Rossetti that he put down the thoughts of Dante in the language of Shakespeare; and the words seem to me to be extremely true and extremely damning. For what is wanted of a poet is that he should express his own thoughts in the language of his own time. This, with perhaps the solitary exception of Christina Rossetti, the Pre-Raphaelite poets never thought of.

But an assertion far too sweeping follows soon after, to the effect that ever since Rossetti's day 'the idea has been inherent in the mind of the English writer that writing was a matter of digging for obsolete words with which to express ideas forever dead and gone.'

Of Christina Rossetti, Mr. Hueffer's favorite among the nineteenth-century poets (despite her connection with the Pre-Raphaelites), he presents a pathetically beautiful picture. The marriage connection that united the two families gave him abundant opportunity to cultivate

Christina's acquaintance. Most engaging is her modest shrinking from any open recognition of her merit.

Ruskin pooh-poohed her because she was not important. And I fancy he disliked her intuitively because importance was the last thing in this world that she would have desired. I remember informing her shortly after the death of Lord Tennyson that there was a strong movement, or at any rate a very strong feeling abroad, that the Laureateship should be conferred upon her. She shuddered. And I think that she gave evidence then to as strong an emotion as I ever knew in her. The idea of such a position of eminence filled her with real horror. She wanted to be obscure, and to be an obscure handmaiden of the Lord, as fervently as she desired to be exactly correct in her language. Exaggerations really pained her. I remember that when I told her that I met hundreds of people who thought the appointment would be most appropriate, she pinned me down until she had extracted from me the confession that not more than nine persons had spoken to me on the subject.

The author's father, a brilliant and versatile man of letters, and a music critic of authority, is the subject of an amusing anecdote illustrating his unusual powers of memory and his extraordinary audacity. The story refers to the arrival of a certain Prussian prince at Berlin, where young Hüffer was about to take his degree.

One evening my father was sitting upon his balcony, while next door the worthy rector [of the University] read the address that he was afterward to deliver to the prince. Apparently the younger members of the institution addressed the prince before the dons. At any rate, my father having heard it only once, delivered word for word the rector's speech to his Royal Highness. The result was that the poor man, who spoke only with difficulty, had not a single word to say, and my father was forthwith expelled without his degree. Being, though freakish, a person of spirit, that same day he took the express to Göttingen and, as a result, in the evening he telegraphed his mother: 'Have passed for doctor with honors at Göttingen,' to the consternation of his parents, who had not yet heard of his expulsion from Berlin.

Certain glaring improbabilities, especially the incredible celerity with which the journey to Göttingen and the securing of a degree were accomplished, in the same day with a necessarily tedious public function at the Berlin university, make it impossible to accept the story in its present form; but one is ready to believe extraordinary things of a man who, while his native tongue was German, acted for many years as music critic to the London *Times*, London correspondent to the *Frankfurter Zeitung*, London music correspondent to *Le Menestrel* of Paris and to the Rome *Tribuna*, and was at the same time an authority on the Troubadours and the Romance languages, and the author of poems in the Provençal dialect.

A homely detail, delightfully characteristic, is brought out in connection with Ford Madox Brown's patronage of Whistler, whose etchings the older artist especially admired. Going on a certain occasion to a tea party at the Whistlers' in Chelsea, Mr. Brown 'was met in the hall by Mrs. Whistler, who begged him to go to the poulterer's and purchase a pound of butter. The bread was cut, but there was nothing to put upon it. There was no money in the house, the poulterer had cut off his credit, and, Mrs. Whistler said, she dare not send her husband, for he would certainly punch the tradesman's head.' It was a troubled and more or less quarrelsome (genially and good-naturedly quarrelsome) existence led by the artists and the authors with whom Mr. Hueffer was brought in daily contact during his boyhood, which appears to have been largely spent in his grandfather's large old house at No. 120 Fitzroy Square,—the very house once occupied by Colonel Newcome, if we are to credit the combined testimony of Thackeray and Mr. Hueffer. The admirable part, however, of the turbulent conduct of all these irritable bards and fractious painters was that, however hotly they abused one another to one another, they loyally championed the common cause and defended their comrades against assaults from without.

In the latter part of his book the author gives expression to some unexpectedly pessimistic opinions concerning modern ideals, modern literature and art, and modern literary methods. He professes to find the commercial instinct predominant in writers, and the beautiful enthusiasms all dead and buried. Surely Mr. Hueffer is not yet old enough to be entitled to the privileges of a *laudator temporis acti*. It must be the buoyancy of youth that makes him indulge in this luxury of lamentation, an indulgence common to all of us before we thoroughly learn how many hard knocks and how many cruel disillusionments we can receive without appreciably diminishing the zest of life. However, let us quote from one of his despondent pages, if only for variety's sake:

And along with all this there has gone the tremendous increase in the cost of living and the enormous increase of the public indifference to anything in the nature of the arts. This last—and possibly both of these factors—began with the firing of the first shot in the Boer War. That was the end of everything—of the Pre-Raphaelites, of the Henley gang, of the New Humor, of the Victorian Great Figure, and of the last traces of the mediæval stiuperstion that man might save his soul by the reading of good books.

If it were not that so many others, in all ages, had solemnly assured their contemporaries that the bottom had dropped out of everything, we should be alarmed by the foregoing and other passages in the same key. As it is, we shall continue to take hopeful pleasure in life and in literature, including in the latter Mr. Hueffer's excellent book. A single regret tempers our satisfaction, and that is that Mr. Hueffer has not more of his aunt Christina's passionate desire to be 'exactly correct' in the use of language,—a little more of the Pre-Raphaelites' fondness for digging into the old authors for lessons in style. Not all those who lived before the blessed seventies and eighties are dead yet.

10. Unsigned review of *The New Humpty-Dumpty* by 'Daniel Chaucer', *English Review*

xii, September 1912, 332

Two of Ford's novels, *The Simple Life Limited* and *The New Humpty-Dumpty*, were written under the pseudonym of 'Daniel Chaucer' so that the earnings he made from them might not have to go towards the payments he was required to make his first wife as a consequence of a legal separation between them. Rebecca West (b. 1892) wrote the review printed below and when she identified Ford as the author of the novel, she was invited to meet Ford and his new wife, Violet Hunt, who explained the use of the pseudonym. It was the beginning of a long friendship. In later years Rebecca West established herself as one of the most distinguished writers of her generation, a novelist (*The Thinking Reed* and others) and an author of political journalism, in such books as *Black Lamb and Grey Falcon* and *The Meaning of Treason*.

'Miss di Pradella explained how you were taught to do the splits. You stood upon two chairs and they were gradually drawn apart. . . .' There is only one serious novelist whose mind is stored with such weighty secrets of the music-hall as this. This phrase, a respectful reference to the Empire Ballet, a savage contempt for tradespeople, and familiar conversation concerning the forms of the Roman Catholic and the Greek Churches, betray the identity of Daniel Chaucer. *The New Humpty-Dumpty*, in its fine detail and lucid statement of complex adventure, is another stage in the development of a genius that is struggling from a youth spent in the subtlest impressionism to the most literal realism of treatment; from *The Fifth Queen* to *The Panel*, in fact. Yet again, it is an echo from the past, when Joseph Conrad collaborated with another to write *Romance*. There was in that the same manly combat with Fortune, the same adoration for the noble highwayman. But this is touched with the virtues of experience. There is a fine mastery over events in the story of the splendid Count Sergius Mihailovitch Macdonald, who, for his ideal of benevolent despotism, moves a counter-revolution in the Republic of Galizia, and sets on the throne the boy-king who would like to be a chauffeur, and who, having served his ideal, is shot down on the night of victory because he once refused to admire the poetry of the elder Dumas. There is a new power in the gnome-life figure of the wretched little Mr. Pett, the Socialist turned Nietzschean Tory, and a wilder humour about the merry and disreputable Miss di Pradella, with her passion for embroidered pillow-slips. Of course, Daniel Chaucer is always very childlike; and one of the habits of childhood is to chuckle over jokes that it cannot explain. So the savage satire with which he cudgels Countess Macdonald, a horrible picture of what a wicked Fabian would be like, is sometimes incomprehensible. The same combination of wit and obscurity, that made one feel the force of the satire one was not permitted to understand, was observable in *High Germany*. But the book as a whole is a complete reaction against Daniel Chaucer's earlier manner. One can remember the time when Daniel Chaucer committed the sin of Henry James in every supersubtle sentence. But that influence has gone. The last pages, which contain Mrs. Pett's description of the death of Sergius Mihailovitch, belong to the manner of Joseph Conrad. The weathercock veers to many winds, but it is always the same weathercock. And the individuality of Daniel Chaucer is always precious, whatever wind it follows.

11. 'The Quest of the Golden Bowl', unsigned review of *Henry James: A Critical Study*

The Times Literary Supplement, 22 January 1914, 38

Mr. Hueffer tells us that he considers Mr. Henry James the greatest of living writers, and in consequence, for him, the greatest of living men. He does not, in the course of his 'critical study,' offer any evidence that he is acquainted with the greater number of Mr. James's books. He appears to be familiar with but two or three of them. The rest are passed over without remark; most of them are not even named. He finds the manner of the later novels bewildering. He only touches *The Wings of the Dove* in an allusion to two of the characters under wrong names; *The Golden Bowl* is barely mentioned; *The Awkward Age*, *The Ambassadors*, and most of the later short stories are entirely overlooked. He reads *The American Scene* 'with a sense of deep, of complete, and finally of utter, non-comprehension.' He thinks that all the English novelists, from Defoe to Meredith, 'remained psychologically upon the level of Sir John Mandeville'; he could not find 'much more than three sentences to say of the methods of any one of them.' He takes, as he lengthily tells us, hardly any interest in Balzac. He has a knowing and jaunty style of humour, very freely indulged, which suggests the essay of the schoolboy who discovers, as he approaches his subject, that he has nothing to say. These are a few of Mr. Hueffer's qualifications for writing a study of Mr. Henry James.

Of a book so raw and so uninformed no criticism is possible. Mr. Hueffer makes no attempt to measure the development of the most deliberate artist of our time, and as a tribute to 'The greatest of living men' his farrago of irrelevances is a piece of trifling which cannot be seriously considered. But that at this time of day such an effusion can be offered as a 'study' of Mr. James's work is a singular illustration of the depth of that work's originality. For some forty years the English language has possessed a writer who has never rested in his patient and daring investigation of the power, the beauty, the character of the art of fiction. As he has elaborated his criticism, so every step has been marked, every discovery embodied, in the series of his published works. He has tested and exemplified every method of representation; he has devised and worked out ever more intricate problems, he has thrown open to both novelist and critic a field of research that is practically virgin soil. His books may be as deeply admired by some as by others they are heartily feared: in either case they form a body of work which can be matched in no other language for its significance as a conscious inquiry into the aims and the methods of the art of the novel. It is an inquiry that is not likely to attract an inconvenient crowd, and nobody can pretend that Mr. James has been greatly concerned to make it easy. On the other hand, in the introductory essays prefixed to the collected edition of his works, he has explicitly shown the way. In these essays he has not merely examined his work in the making, he has defined and illustrated, for the art which he practises, a theory of criticism of which little enough has before been heard. The result is, no doubt, extremely difficult reading. But to refuse the task of mastering his conclusions, to dismiss them with a few words of puzzled astonishment, is to resign all claim to regard Mr. James as either the greatest of living writers or the most misguided. His latest critic, while lavishly quoting from the prefaces, does so with the explanation that Mr. James has anticipated what he had intended to say himself. The comment would be more convincing if it were accompanied by any attempt to expose the general progression, the line of argument, by following which the author of *Roderick Hudson* has become the author of *The Golden Bowl*. It is open to anyone to hold that the last novel represents a certain method carried to an inconvenient extreme, so long as, in maintaining such an opinion, the critic shows us that he understands the principle of growth on which the book is developed. But the task of tracing the how and the why of Mr. James's steady advance from the simplicities of narrative to the complex adjustments of 'drama' and 'picture' (to use his own nomenclature) in his latest novel, is one, interesting and rewarding as it would be, which still remains to be accomplished. Meanwhile all talk of the 'difficulty' of those novels is beside the mark, for the very shape of Mr. James's phrase has been governed by the general law of the form in which he has worked. The large and leisurely consistency with which Mr. James's art has widened and deepened has expounded its own history, as we said, line upon line, in the long series of his books. There is a better work to be done by the critic than to call these books amazing and exquisite. Mr. Hueffer calls them so and evidently feels them to be so, and once or twice we recognize that he seems to be starting on a further flight. But the flight is not taken, and we realize more than ever that it is time to pay Mr. James's work the compliment, not of holding up our hands in wonder, but of beginning to understand and to analyse its meaning.

12. Rebecca West on *The Good Soldier*, *Daily News*

2 April 1915, 6

Although now acknowledged as one of Ford's finest novels, *The Good Soldier* was not so recognized when it was first published. The anonymous critic in the *Observer* found it remarkable, commenting on the story that 'there are not three people in England who could have told it, or two who could have told it just that way'. But the *Saturday Review* characteristically found it 'no more than a chronicle of sordid treachery and vice . . .' while for the reviewer of the *Athenaeum*, the novel was simply 'unpleasant—about that there cannot be two opinions'. In the circumstances, it is pleasant to note that one fellow novelist in England recognized *The Good Soldier* for what it was.

Mr. Ford Madox Hueffer is the Scholar Gipsy of English letters: he is the author who is recognised only as he disappears round the corner. It is impossible for anybody with any kind of sense about writing to miss some sort of distant apprehension of the magnificence of his work: but unfortunately this apprehension usually takes the form of enthusiastic but belated discoveries of work that he left on the doorstep ten years ago.

The Good Soldier will put an end to any such sequestration of Mr. Hueffer's wealth. For it is as impossible to miss the light of its extreme beauty and wisdom as it would be to miss the full moon on a clear night. Its first claim on the attention is the obvious loveliness of the colour and cadence of its language: and it is also clever as the novels of Mr. Henry James are clever, with all sorts of acute discoveries about human nature, and at times it is radiantly witty. And behind these things there is the delight of a noble and ambitious design, and behind that, again, there is the thing we call inspiration—a force of passion which so sustains the story in its flight that never once does it appear as the work of a man's invention. It is because of that union of inspiration and the finest technique that this story, this close and relentless recital of how the good soldier struggled from the mere clean innocence which was the most his class could expect of him to the knowledge of love, can bear up under the vastness of its subject. For the subject is, one realises when one has come to the end of this saddest story, much vaster than one had imagined that any story about well-bred people, who live in sunny houses, with deer in the park, and play polo, and go to Nauheim for the cure, could possibly contain.

It is the record of the spiritual life of Edward Ashburnham, who was a large, fair person of the governing class, with an entirely deceptive appearance of being just the kind of person he looked. It was his misfortune that he had brought to the business of landowning a fatal touch of imagination which made him believe it his duty to be 'an overlord doing his best by his dependents, the dependents meanwhile doing their best by the overlord'; to make life splendid and noble and easier for everybody by his government. And since this ideal meant that he became in his way a creative artist, he began to feel the desire to go to some woman for 'moral support, the encouragement, the relief from the sense of loneliness, the assurance of his own worth.' And although Leonora, his wife, was fine and proud, a Northern light among women, she simply could not understand that marriage meant anything but an appearance of loyalty before the world and the efficient management of one's husband's estate. She 'had a vague sort of idea that, to a man, all women are the same after three weeks of close intercourse. She thought that the kindness should no longer appeal, the soft and mournful voice no longer thrill, the tall darkness no longer give a man the illusion that he was going into the depths of an unexplored wood.' And so poor Edward walked the world starved.

His starvation leads him into any number of gentle, innocent, sentimental passions: it delivers him over as the prey of a terrible and wholly credible American, a cold and controlled egoist who reads like the real truth about an Anne Douglas Sedgwick or Edith Wharton heroine. And meanwhile his wife becomes so embittered by what she considers as an insane, and possibly rather nasty, obsession, that she loses her pride and her nobility and becomes, in that last hour when Edward has found a real passion, so darkly, subtly treacherous that he and the quite innocent young girl whom he loves are precipitated down into the blackest tragedy. All three are lost: and perhaps Leonora, robbed of her fineness, is most lost of all.

And when one has come to the end of this beautiful and moving story it is worth while reading the book over again simply to observe the wonders of its technique. Mr. Hueffer has used the device, invented and used successfully by Mr. Henry James, and used not nearly so credibly by Mr. Conrad, of presenting the story not as it appeared to a divine and omnipresent intelligence, but as it was observed by some intervener not too intimately concerned in the plot. It is a device that always breaks down at the great moment, when the revelatory detail must be given; but it has the great advantage of setting the tone of the prose from the beginning to the end. And out of the leisured colloquialism of the gentle American who tells the story Mr. Hueffer has made a prose that falls on the page like sunlight. It has the supreme triumph of art, that effect of effortlessness and inevitableness, which Mengs described when he said that one of Velasquez's pictures seemed to be painted not by the hand but by pure thought. Indeed, this is a much, much better book than any of us deserve.

13. 'The Saddest Story': Theodore Dreiser on *The Good Soldier*

New Republic, iii, 12 June 1915, 155–6

In the late 1920s and 1930s, when Ford spent much of his time in the United States, he saw a good deal of Theodore Dreiser (1871–1945), who was an almost exact contemporary of his, and he also devoted a chapter to him in *Mightier than the Sword*. Although Ford always thought of Dreiser as a careful and self-conscious stylist, the two men would appear to have had quite different artistic temperaments. Their similarities and differences are revealed in Dreiser's review of *The Good Soldier*, which is an essay on how, as author of *Sister Carrie* and *Jenny Gerhardt*, he would have written the book.

Captain Edward Ashburnham, heir of a wealthy British family, is wedded for reasons of family courtesy to Leonora Powys, the daughter of a financially embarrassed Irish landlord. The Captain is a sentimentalist, his wife a practical-minded moralist. Uninterested and unhappy in his wedded state he approaches or takes up with (1) La Delciquita, a Spanish coquette, (2) Mrs. Basil, wife of a British Major in India, (3) Maisie Maidan, wife of another British officer, (4) Florence Dowell wife of an American globe-trotter who is the friend of the Ashburnhams, who tells the story, and (5) Nancy Rufford, a ward. Both her religious training and her social code compel Mrs. Ashburnham to keep up all those appearances which she deems that these and her dignity and social rights demand. She devotes her life to the task of standing by, saving, and reforming her husband. This results in her supervision of both his finances and his love affairs, to the end that her own soul is tortured while she tortures his. The minor characters suffer also, and in the end the Captain kills himself, his last love goes mad, and Leonora accomplishes her ideal, a happy marriage. Previous to this, one flame has died, another committed suicide, and the wise

Spaniard has milked the Captain to the tune of twenty thousand pounds.

I have, I am aware, told this story in a very rambling way, so that it may be difficult for any one to find their path through what may be a sort of maze. I cannot help it. I have stuck to my idea of being in a country cottage with a silent listener, hearing between the gust of the wind and amidst the noises of the distant sea, the story as it comes. And, when one discusses an affair—a long, sad affair—one goes back, one goes forward. One remembers points that one has forgotten, and one explains them all the more minutely since one recognizes that one has forgotten to mention them in their proper places, and that one may have given, by omitting them, a false impression. I console myself with thinking that this is a real story, and that, after all, real stories are best told in the way that a person telling a story would tell them. They will then seem most real.

Thus Mr. Hueffer in explanation of his style; a good explanation of a bad method.

In this story, as has been said, the author makes Dowell, Florence's husband, the narrator, and it is he who dubs it the 'saddest one.' This is rather a large order when one thinks of all the sad stories that have been told of this mad old world. Nevertheless it is a sad story, and a splendid one from a psychological point of view; but Mr. Hueffer, in spite of the care he has bestowed upon it, has not made it splendid in the telling. In the main he has only suggested its splendor, quite as the paragraph above suggests, and for the reasons it suggests. One half suspects that since Mr. Hueffer shared with Mr. Conrad in the writing of *Romance*, the intricate weavings to and fro of that literary colorist have, to a certain extent, influenced him in the spoiling of this story. For it is spoiled to the extent that you are compelled to say, 'Well, this is too bad. This is quite a wonderful thing, but it is not well done.' Personally I would have suggested to Mr. Hueffer, if I might have, that he begin at the beginning, which is where Colonel Powys wishes to marry off his daughters—not at the beginning as some tertiary or quadrutiary character in the book sees it, since it really concerns Ashburnham and his wife. This is neither here nor there, however, a mere suggestion. A story may begin in many ways.

Of far more importance is it that, once begun, it should go forward in a more or less direct line, or at least that it should retain one's uninterrupted interest. This is not the case in this book. The interlacings, the cross references, the re-re-references to all sorts of things which subsequently are told somewhere in full, irritate one to the point of one's laying down the book. As a matter of fact, except for the perception that will come to any man, that here is a real statement of fact picked up from somewhere and related by the author as best he could, I doubt whether even the lover of naturalism—entirely free of conventional prejudice—would go on.

As for those dreary minds who find life morally ordered and the universe murmurous of divine law—they would run from it as from the plague. For, with all its faults of telling, it is an honest story, and there is no blinking of the commonplaces of our existence which so many find immoral and make such a valiant effort to conceal. One of the most irritating difficulties of the tale is that Dowell, the American husband who tells the story, is described as, first, that amazingly tame thing, an Englishman's conception of an American husband; second, as a profound psychologist able to follow out to the last detail the morbid minutiae of this tragedy, and to philosophize on them as only a deeply thinking and observing man could; and lastly as one who is as blind as a bat, as dull as a mallet, and as weak as any sentimentalist ever. The combination proves a little trying before one is done with it.

This story has been called immoral. One can predict such a charge to-day in the case of any book, play, or picture which refuses to concern itself with the high-school ideal of what life should be. It is immoral apparently to do anything except dress well and talk platitudes. But it is interesting to find this English author (German by extraction, I believe) and presumably, from all accounts, in revolt against these sickening strictures, dotting his book with apologies for this, that, and another condition not in line with this high-school standard (albeit it is the wretched American who speaks) and actually smacking his lips over the stated order that damns his book. And worse yet, Dowell is no American. He is that literary packhorse or scapegoat on whom the native Englishman loads all his contempt for Americans. And Captain and Mrs. Ashburnham, whom he so soulfully lauds for their love of English pretence and order, are two who would have promptly pitched his book out of doors, I can tell him. Yet he babbles of the fineness of their point of view. As a matter of fact their point of view is that same accursed thing which has been handed on to America as 'good form,' and which we are now asked to sustain by force of arms as representing civilization.

After all, I have no real quarrel with the English as such. It is against smug conventionalism wherever found, too dull to perceive the import of anything except money and social precedence, that I uncap my fountain pen. It is this condition which makes difficult—one might almost fear impossible at times—the production of any great work of art, be it picture, play, philosophy, or novel. It is the Leonoras, the Dowells, and the Nancys that make life safe, stale, and impossible. They represent that thickness of wit which prospers impossible religions, and moral codes, and causes the mob to look askance at those finer flowers of fancy which are all the world has to show for its power to think in the drift of circumstance. All the rest is formalism and parade, and 'go thou and do likewise.' We all, to such a horrible extent, go and do likewise.

But you may well suspect that there is a good story here and that it is well worth your reading. Both suppositions are true. In the hands of a better writer this jointure of events might well have articulated into one of the finest pictures in any language. Its facts are true, in the main. Its theme beautiful. It is tragic in the best sense that the Greeks knew tragedy, that tragedy for which there is no solution. But to achieve a high result in any book its component characters must of necessity stand forth unmistakeable in their moods and characteristics. In this one they do not. Every scene of any importance has been blinked or passed over with a few words or cross references. I am not now referring to any moral fact. Every conversation which should have appeared, every storm which should have contained revealing flashes, making clear the minds, the hearts, and the agonies of those concerned, has been avoided. There are no paragraphs or pages of which you can say 'This is a truly moving description,' or 'This is a brilliant vital interpretation.' You are never really stirred. You are never hurt. You are merely told and referred. It is all cold narrative, never truly poignant.

This is a pity. This book had the making of a fine story. I half suspect that its failure is due to the author's formal British leanings, whatever his birth—that leaning which Mr. Dowell seems to think so important, which will not let him loosen up and sing. The whole book is indeed fairly representative of that encrusting formalism which, barnacle-wise, is apparently overtaking and destroying all that is best in English life. The arts will surely die unless formalism is destroyed. And when you find a great theme marred by a sniffy reverence for conventionalism and the glories of a fixed condition it is a thing for tears. I would almost commend Mr. Hueffer to the futurists, or to anyone that has the strength to scorn the moldy past, in the hope that he might develop a method entirely different from that which is here employed, if I did not know that at bottom the great artist is never to be commended. Rather from his brain, as Athena from that of Zeus, spring flawless and shining all those art forms which the world adores and preserves.

14. 'The Novelist in Controversy': Rebecca West on *Between St. Dennis and St. George*

Daily News, 11 November 1915, 4

Ford's two propaganda books, requested by his friend C. F. G. Masterman, who had been appointed to the directorship of the then secret Ministry of Information, were intended to encourage close feelings with England's traditional enemy, France, and antagonism towards Germany, with whom England had racial ties and even the same royal family. For such works, Ford's usual impressionistic techniques would not serve and he therefore produced two closely argued and fully documented books. Much of the documentation was provided by Ford's assistants, who included Richard Aldington and Alec Randall, later knighted and a distinguished diplomat. Written during a time of high feeling, these were among Ford's most controversial books, as Rebecca West's review suggests.

It is really not quite fair that a man who spends his whole existence in the consideration of beauty, the values of life, and the niceties of language, should be able to stroll out of his garden, look on for a minute at the fight of the controversialists in the highway, and say the right, the illuminating, the decisive thing that settles the whole affair, and leaves them sitting, hot and silly, in the dust. But here, in *Between St. Dennis and St. George: a Sketch of Three Civilisations*, we have Mr. Ford Madox Hueffer, who was notable before the war for his conviction that a writer reading a newspaper was as shameful a spectacle as a judge eating his lunch out of a paper bag, who practised to perfection that humped indifference to all human organisations which Mr. Henry James and Mr. Conrad advocate as the proper attitude for the artist: and we see him, with no abandonment of his languor, and his preoccupation with style, picking up that good creature, Mr. George Bernard Shaw, by the scruff of the neck, and shaking him to rights. It seems unfair that he should be so casually right where Mr. Shaw has been so conscientiously wrong. And it seems unfairer still that it is just because of Mr. Hueffer's immoral abstention from political interests and luxurious indulgence in literature, that he can deal with this devoted servant of the commonweal who has sat on committees as ardently as Mr. Hueffer has read Flaubert. He does not, in the appendix to this book which dissects 'Common Sense About the War,' raise the bellow of a goaded patriotism; but treats it properly as an artistic and not a moral tragedy. It mattered hardly at all that Mr. Shaw tried to put the nation wrong about the war, since the crimes of Germany were constantly putting us right about it: but it mattered a lot to Mr. Shaw. For it meant that the tide of mental slovenliness of which the rising had been observable in the revised edition of *The Quintessence of Ibsenism* had risen very high above that great intellect.

It is with that essential tragedy of the situation that Mr. Hueffer concerns himself in his discussion of that undocumented attempt to prove the psychology of Germany identical with that of England. 'Is it the method of good art,' he asks in effect, 'to call Sir Edward Grey and Mr. Winston Churchill Junkers when you do not know what a Junker is?' And he holds Mr. Shaw's head in Chancery while he administers a good drubbing-in of the principles of the Junkers and the Junkerpartei. 'They desire,' he explains, 'the strictest possible protection for agricultural products, the limitation of the vote of the industrial populations, the abolition of death duties on real estate, and the maintenance of the present system of binding contracts for agricultural labourers, so that the existing system of State serfdom in the Ostelbische territories may not be weakened,' and he begs to be told when Sir Edward Grey advocated the like of these. And when Mr. Shaw tries to persuade us that we can give Germany points and a beating in the matter of militarist writers, Mr. Hueffer produces a hundred examples of Satanist sentiments expressed in the German militarist propaganda which is 'promoted, subsidised, enjoined, and enforced by the Prussian State.' 'May God,' prays one professor, 'deliver us from the inertia of other European peoples, and give us a good war, fresh and joyous, traversing Europe with fury, passing the nation through a sieve and disembarrassing us of the scrofulous canaille who fill up space and make it too narrow for other people.' It hurts Mr. Hueffer that an artist can let his critical faculty rust to the extent of taking this sort of thing as the fair Teutonic response to the mild opinion held by Lord Roberts that, on the whole, it would be as well to have trained men to resist an invasion.

He addresses to Mr. Shaw an inquiry which is not, as might have been expected, 'Is this British?' but 'Is this workmanlike?' And that, when one comes to think of it, is an appeal on much higher grounds. It is a condemnation of our slipshod Press that this analysis, superior in matter and manner to the pamphlet to which it replied, should not itself have been issued as a pamphlet and given as wide publicity. For though Mr. Shaw has wiped out this unlucky adventure by a dozen helpful and intelligent statements on the war, his first errors live persistently in that vast new public the existence of which should make every writer or speaker on the side of progress shiver with a sense of his responsibility. This public consists of starved people who have sufficient character to be infuriated with the intolerable state of things caused by our present social and political systems, and will follow with all the passion of their minds any assault on them. It is not in the least to their discredit, since they have no tradition of culture and no education in the use of the critical faculty, that in the wildness of their discontent they listen to and believe in any attack on established things or the doings of established persons. But it should make the writer scrupulous as a priest.

One is surprised when one reads this masterly appendix that an artist can make so fine a controversialist; but as one reads the book of which that is only the sting in the tail one wonders how any but an artist can ever be a controversialist. It is not only that Mr. Hueffer enormously increases one's pride in the alliance with France by reminding one how innocent of all aggressiveness she was, how till August of last year her military glory seemed but a grave by which she wept. 'The rustling of those immortelles as I first saw them, when a boy in the icy December wind, in that most windswept of all open spaces—the rustling of those immortelles round the base of that crowned, enthroned stone figure seemed to commemorate a death as absolute and irrevocable as that commemorated by the immortelles rustling over the grave of a dead and forgotten ploughman.' Or by looking across the little Provençal hills of grey, bare stone, tufted with rosemary, to the white ruin of the Château d'Amour, and reflecting that 'all chivalry, then, all learning, all the divine things of life came from that triangle of the world which holds the Château d'Amour, midway between Les Baux, Arles and Avignon. From there they spread up the Rhine across the Ile de France; across the Pas de Calais, to the Port of London, to Oxford, to Edinburgh, to Dublin, and a little way—but alas, such a little way!—across the Rhine.' But also it observes complicated political processes with the patience of the disciplined artist and describes them with the lucid beauty by which an artist makes his observations immortal in his reader's brain.

COLLECTED POEMS (1913)

15. Ezra Pound, review in *New Freewoman*

i, 15 December 1913, 251

Despite the tepid response Ford's early individual books of verse received from critics, his *Collected Poems* elicited a great deal of interest. The volume, published by his former sub-editor at the *English Review*, Douglas Goldring, appeared just when a younger group of poets, most of them included in the series of Imagist anthologies that had been started by Ezra Pound, began really for the first time to create modern English poetry in this century. Many of these poets found Ford's work interesting in this context. Like theirs, his work differed markedly from the poetry of the nineteenth century against which the rebellion was directed, and he was therefore considered with respect for what he had accomplished earlier, and alone.

Of his contemporaries and near-contemporaries, Pound championed Ford's work more than anyone else. An extraordinarily active and energetic publicist of good letters, he wrote long articles for numerous periodicals, especially the *Little Review* and *Poetry*, in an effort to call attention to the work of those in whom he believed. What initially attracted him to Ford was the naturalness of Ford's language and his ability to write verse in a colloquial fashion free of the inversions of phrase and rhetorical habits of much Victorian writing.

Mr. Ford Madox Hueffer is presented to us as the father or at least the shepherd of English Impressionist writers—not that Mr. Hueffer is an institution. Mr. Hueffer is younger by a decade than most of the English Institutions. Mr. Hueffer has preached 'Prose' in this Island ever since I can remember. He has cried with a high and solitary voice and with all the fervors of a new convert. 'Prose' is his own importation. There is no one else with whom one can discuss it. One is thankful for Mr. Hueffer in land full of indigenous institutions like Gosse, and Saintsbury, and the *Daily Mail* professor at Cambridge for the reluctance of Abraham to take these three upholders of obsolete British taste to his once commodious bosom is a recurring irritation to nearly every young artist.

Mr. Hueffer having set himself against them and their numerous spiritual progeny, it is but natural that he is 'not taken seriously' in Institutional quarters.

Mr. Hueffer has written some forty books, very good, quite bad, and indifferent. He can and, sometimes, does write prose. I mean Prose with a very big capital letter. Prose that really delights one by its limpidity.

And now they have collected his Poems. And he has written a charmingly intelligent and more or less inconsequent preface. He has written a preface that one can take seriously as criticism because he declines to lie. He frankly says what he likes—a paradigm for all would-be critics. And for the most part the things he likes are good and the things he dislikes abominable.

It is true that he invents a class of German lyricists, and endows them with qualities more easy to find among the French writers. He supposes a whole tribe of Heines, but no matter. The thing that he praises is good; it is direct speech and vivid impression.

As for the poems themselves one does not need to be a devotee of letters to be amused by 'Süssmund's Address to an Unknown God.' It is a 'conversation' such as one might have heard from the author in any drawing-room at any one of his more exasperated moments this five years. We feel that that author has expressed himself and has mirrored the world of his day. *His* world that is, London, a circle of diners and writers. And his refrain

> God, fill my purse and let me go away.

is its soul cry and its sum of all wisdom.

The acme of intelligence is again reached in 'The Three-Ten.'

> When in the prime of May-Day time dead lovers
>   went a-walking,
> How bright the grass in lads' eyes was, how easy
>   poet's talking.
> Here were green hills, etc.

The stanza is rather obscure, but we learn that he is comparing the past and present, the fields of Bayswater with the present pavement, and implying the difference in custom. He ends,

> But see, but see! The clock marks three above
>   the Kilburn Station,
> Those maids, thank God! are 'neath the sod and
>   all their generation.

It is a light song, but one has only to open the pages of Cowper to return and sing it with fervour.

Of course Mr. Hueffer is obscure, but after knowing his poems for three or four years one finds oneself repeating his phrases with an ever-increasing passion.

When Mr. Hueffer is not reactive; when he is not 'getting things off his chest' and off all our chests altogether, he shows himself capable of simple, quite normally poetic poetry, as in 'Finchley Road.'

> . . . .
> 'You should be a queen or a duchess rather,'

In some very ancient day and place as follows:

> Lost in a great land, sitting alone
> . . . .
> And you'd say to your shipmen: 'Now take your
>   ease,
> To-morrow is time enough for the seas.'
> And you'd set your bondmen a milder rule
> And let the children loose from school.
> No wrongs to right and no sores to fester.
> In your small, great hall 'neath a firelit daïs,
> You'd sit, with me at your feet, your jester,
> Stroking your shoes where the seed pearls glisten,
> And talking my fancies. And you, as your way is,
> Would sometimes heed and at times not listen,
> But sit at your sewing and look at the brands.

Mr. Hueffer has in his poems the two faces that one has long known in his novels—the keen modern satires as in that flail of pomposities 'Mr. Fleight' and the pleasant post-pre-Raphaelite tapestry as we find is in such chapters as that on the young knight of Edgerton in his bath, or in 'The Young Lovell.'

His emotions make war on his will, but his perception of objects is excellent. From a technical point of view the first poems in the book are worthy of serious study. Because of his long prose training Mr. Hueffer has brought into English verse certain qualities which younger writers would do well to consider. I say younger writers for the old ones are mostly past hope.

I do not mean that one should swallow the impressionist manner whole or without due discrimination.

In 'The Starling' the naturalness of the language and the suavity with which the rhyme-sounds lose themselves in the flow of the reading, are worthy of emulation.

Naturalness of speech can of course be learned from Francis Jammes and other French writers, but it is new and refreshing in contemporary English.

As Mr. Hueffer in his opening bow declares himself to be, not a poet but merely a very distinguished amateur stepping into verse from the sister art, one need not carp at his occasional lapses. And there is no doubt whatever that this is the most important book of verse of the season, and that it, moreover, marks a phase in the change which is—or at least which one hopes is coming over English verse. (I refer to the first three sections of the book, the reprints of earlier work need not come into discussion.) Mr. Hueffer has also the gift for making lyrics that will sing, as for example the 'Tandaradei' more or less after Von der Vogelweide, and 'The Three-Ten' which I have mentioned. This is no despicable gift and there is no man now living in England who is possessed of it in more notable degree.

Hang it all, if 'a lyric' means a song calculated to be sung to music such as we know it, we would not be far wrong in calling Mr. Hueffer the best lyricist in England. This métier he certainly knows and he calculates for both composer and vocalist. The 'Tandaradei' is one of the few things in modern English that Brahms might have set without being wholly disgusted.

16. E. Buxton Shanks, review in *Poetry and Drama*

i, December 1913, 492–3

E. Buxton Shanks (1892–1953) was a literary journalist, editor and lecturer. He was author of many books of verse and was the first winner, in 1919, of the Hawthornden Prize.

At the beginning of his introduction Mr Hueffer makes an indirect appeal to critics which is so pathetic and so acute that no honest man, certainly no man who has enjoyed these poems, could bring himself utterly to disregard it.

And as for trusting any friend to make a selection, one cannot bring oneself to do it either. They have—one's friends—too many mental axes to grind. One will admire certain verses about a place, because in that place they were once happy; one will find fault with a certain other paper of verses because it does not seem likely to form a piece of prentice work in a school that he is desirous of founding.

Mr Hueffer has foreseen, with devilish penetration, the use which critics, with their mental axes, will make of him: and, so far as he can, he has provided for the danger. And yet this book is clearly destined to provoke dispute: there are in it some eighty or more queer, refreshing, puzzling poems, and beyond that a critical and autobiographical introduction which is more important than any other pronouncement on poetry made in our time.

The author is essentially a modern critic in that he provokes thought rather than precipitates it, and allows the play of his own irrational prejudices to be freely seen. Were a man to-day to attempt a work of such ridiculous scope and title as Eckermann's *Beiträge zur Poesie*, he could hardly do better than make it a commentary on this essay, for Mr Hueffer has touched inconclusively yet magically upon every question that might agitate a student of æsthetics. He speaks of his ability to judge the form of his novels and of his inability to say anything concerning his poems, and so he passes on, leaving the reader vaguely struggling with a distinction between invention and imagination, a distinction that would deserve an essay to itself. Further on, he inquires why the chasm between literary and colloquial speech is broader in England than in France, and why in Germany it does not exist at all; but he only sighs that it should be so, and hurries on with a disconsolate shrug of the shoulders. In this point, however, I think lies the significance of the whole book—as apart from its positive poetic value—for Mr Hueffer does not as a rule write literary verse. He instances German poetry as an example of unliterary work with a curious sense of longing and deprivation: for, after all, if these verses be not *lieder* there are none in England. In any case, there are probably no others. But, in this connection, he does not seem to care how German poetry came to have so precious an heritage. It was not always so, for the Breslau school in the seventeenth century and the writers of *Dämonund Phyllis-Poesie* in the eighteenth were as literary as Carew and Pope. These writers, however, were not very important, and German literature was practically created by Goethe, who, influenced in his sage youth by folk-song and always pleased rather by the contemplation of things than of ideas, had little temptation to depart from the ordinary ways of speech.

Mr Hueffer, while deploring the impossibility of achieving such sincerity in English, has more than once achieved it; he has had mostly the courage to say what he means without literarifying his language, though he has singularly avoided the modern subjects he pleads for. Even when he writes of Finchley Road, he drifts off quickly, though quite naturally and sincerely, into—

> A tiny town
> Where all the roads wind up and down
> From your little palace—a small, old place. . . .

But what makes his poems lovable is the want of effort in them. He speaks himself of their genesis; first a vague rhythm, then the first line, and afterwards the rest flowing out. They seem to have been composed mentally and sung over for the poet's own pleasure, as, I suppose, 'The trees they do grow high' and 'High Germany' were first sung in the fields by a countryman at his work. It is encouraging to those who believe that literary poetry is bankrupt and that we must go back behind the Elizabethans, and behind Chaucer even, and take up the thread again where Romance influences cut it off. (In saying this,

I do not imply that the folk-song we now know is chronologically anterior to the Romance influences in English; merely that it comes of an older root, and represents a different sort of writing.) I have come perilously near to exhibiting Mr Hueffer as the founder of a new school and for this I ask his forgiveness: I have certainly neglected the letter of his poems for theories based on their general nature.

The songs are the best part of the book, and it is difficult to choose among them. They are certainly songs in the true sense of the word; calling for music. The only fault to be found with them is that nearly all are in the minor key, literally, that is to say a composer would be obliged to set them in the minor. Here is a verse of one that demands such qualification and no other:

> Close the book and say good-bye to everything;
> Pass up from the shore and pass by byre and stall,
> —For the smacks shall sail home on the tail of the tides,
> And the kine shall stand deep in the sweet water-sides,
> And they still shall go burying, still wedding brides;
> But I must be gone in the morning.

Viewed chronologically, the book shows no change in Mr Hueffer, only a progressive individuality and clearness. Two poems in the latest written section, 'The Starling,' and 'In the Little Old Market-place' show more evidence of sustained power than any of the earlier poems except the almost perfect 'Suabian Legend.' Another long poem in this section, 'To all the Dead,' is tedious: it gives me an impression of Mr Hueffer writing and writing because he was too tired to stop. But for yet another, 'Süssmund's Address to an Unknown God,' no praise can be too high and no gratitude extravagant, for in it Mr Hueffer has impartially and eloquently cursed this age and all the earnest and officious persons who would make it unbearable, if they could.

It remains to say that Mr Hueffer has, in spite of his introduction, taken upon himself to select some of his poems for oblivion. This volume does not contain 'Every Man,' which appeared in *Songs from London*, and I cannot say that I regret it; but I do regret the absence of 'Two Making Music,' which was published in *From Inland and other Poems*.

17. Unsigned review, *English Review*

xvi, January 1914, 302

The author of this article was in all likelihood Norman Douglas, who succeeded Goldring when the magazine was taken over by Austin Harrison.

In the present superfoetation of the Muses, the *Collected Poems* of Mr. Hueffer come as a great relief. Here is a real poet. He does not boast of having lived only in slums. He does not proudly proclaim that he refuses to scan or rime. He is a real man and thinks real thoughts, and he expresses them in a rugged yet musical form. There is a good deal of passion, a good deal of shrewd sense, a good deal of human sentiment, which never lacks virility. Some critics have remarked that his style resembles Browning, but Browning has not the charming inconsequence of Mr. Hueffer. Even in Browning's best lyrics the schoolmaster's ferule of intellectualism keeps the fairy class in order.

This writing is excellently simple in thought, and the thought is always pure in the true sense of the word. He sees cleanly. He can write, 'John kissed Jane,' which is a very difficult thing to do when so many people insist on writing 'The wicked John—Heaven bring him to naught!—kissed the good Jane—Mary Mother have mercy upon her!'

So much in this book is excellent that I do not wish to quote, and I sincerely trust that my readers will see to it that they gain rather than lose by my omission.

18. 'Mr. Hueffer and the Prose Tradition in Verse': Ezra Pound, review in *Poetry*

iv, June 1914, 111–20

The most extended statement Pound wrote about Ford in his lifetime appeared as a second review of the *Collected Poems* published in *Poetry*. This article shows further thought by Pound on the subject, with its conclusion that Ford's naturalness as a poet derives from his skill as a prose writer. Prose values were to be very important in Pound's work, and this essay is his first extended treatment of the subject. T. S. Eliot thought it important enough to be included in his edition of Pound's *Literary Essays*.

In a country in love with amateurs, in a country where the incompetent have such beautiful manners, and personalities so fragile and charming, that one can not bear to injure their feelings by the introduction of competent criticism, it is well that one man should have a vision of perfection and that he should be sick to the death and disconsolate because he can not attain it.

Mr. Yeats wrote years ago that the highest poetry is so precious that one should be willing to search many a dull tome to find and gather the fragments. As touching poetry this was, perhaps, no new feeling. Yet where nearly everyone else is still dominated by an eighteenth-century verbalism, Mr. Hueffer has had this instinct for prose. It is he who has insisted, in the face of a still Victorian press, upon the importance of good writing as opposed to the opalescent word, the rhetorical tradition. Stendhal had said, and Flaubert, De Maupassant and Turgenev had proved, that 'prose was the higher art'—at least their prose.

Of course it is impossible to talk about perfection without getting yourself very much disliked. It is even more difficult in a capital where everybody's Aunt Lucy or Uncle George has written something or other, and where the victory of any standard save that of mediocrity would at once banish so many nice people from the temple of immortality. So it comes about that Mr. Hueffer is the best critic in England, one might say the only critic of any importance. What he says today the press, the reviewers, who hate him and who disparage his books, will say in about nine years' time, or possibly sooner. Shelley, Yeats, Swinburne, with their 'unacknowledged legislators,' with 'Nothing affects these people except our conversation,' with 'The rest live under us;' Rémy De Gourmont, when he says that most men think only husks and shells of the thoughts that have been already lived over by others, have shown their very just appreciation of the system of echoes, of the general vacuity of public opinion. America is like England, America is very much what England would be with the two hundred most interesting people removed. One's life is the score of this two hundred with whom one happens to have made friends. I do not see that we need to say the rest live under them, but it is certain that what these people say comes to pass. They live in their mutual credence, and thus they live things over and fashion them before the rest of the world is aware. I dare say it is a Cassandra-like and useless faculty, at least from the world's point of view. Mr. Hueffer has possessed the peculiar faculty of 'foresight,' or of constructive criticism, in a pre-eminent degree. Real power will run any machine. Mr. Hueffer said fifteen years ago that a certain unknown Bonar Law would lead the conservative party. Five years ago he said with equal impartiality that Mr. D. H. Lawrence would write notable prose, that Mr. De la Mare could write verses, and that *Chance* would make Conrad popular.

Of course if you think things ten or fifteen or twenty years before anyone else thinks them you will be considered absurd and ridiculous. Mr. Allen Upward, thinking with great lucidity along very different lines, is still considered absurd. Some professor feels that if certain ideas gain ground he will have to rewrite his lectures, some parson feels that if certain other ideas are accepted he will have to throw up his position. They search for the forecaster's weak points.

Mr. Hueffer is still underestimated for another reason also: namely, that we have not yet learned that prose is as precious and as much to be sought after as verse, even its shreds and patches. So that, if one of the finest chapters in English is hidden in a claptrap novel, we cannot weigh the vision which made it against the weariness or the confusion which dragged down the rest of the work. Yet we would do this readily with a poem. If a novel have a form as distinct as that of a sonnet, and if its workmanship be as fine as that of some Pleiade rondel, we complain of the slightness of the motive. Yet we would not deny praise to the rondel. So it remains for a prose craftsman like Mr. Arnold

Bennett to speak well of Mr. Hueffer's prose, and for a verse-craftsman like myself to speak well of his verses. And the general public will have little or none of him because he does not put on pontifical robes, because he does not take up the megaphone of some known and accepted pose, and because he makes enemies among the stupid by his rather engaging frankness.

We may as well begin reviewing the *Collected Poems* with the knowledge that Mr. Hueffer is a keen critic and a skilled writer of prose, and we may add that he is not wholly unsuccessful as a composer, and that he has given us, in 'On Heaven', the best poem yet written in the 'twentieth-century fashion.'

I drag in these apparently extraneous matters in order to focus attention on certain phases of significance, which might otherwise escape the hurried reader in a volume where the actual achievement is uneven. Coleridge has spoken of 'the miracle that might be wrought simply by one man's feeling a thing more clearly or more poignantly than anyone had felt it before.' The last century showed us a fair example when Swinburne awoke to the fact that poetry was an art, not merely a vehicle for the propagation of doctrine. England and Germany are still showing the effects of his perception. I can not belittle my belief that Mr. Hueffer's realization that poetry should be written at least as well as prose will have as wide a result. He himself will tell you that it is 'all Christina Rossetti,' and that 'it was not Wordsworth, for Wordsworth was so busied about the ordinary word that he never found time to think about *le mot juste*.'

As for Christina, Mr. Hueffer is a better critic than I am, and I would be the last to deny that a certain limpidity and precision are the ultimate qualities of style; yet I can not accept his opinion. Christina had these qualities, it is true—in places, but they are to be found also in Browning and even in Swinburne at rare moments. Christina very often sets my teeth on edge,—and so for that matter does Mr. Hueffer. But it is the function of criticism to find what a given work is, not what it is not. It is also the faculty of a capital or of high civilization to value a man for some rare ability, to make use of him and not hinder him or itself by asking of him faculties which he does not possess.

Mr. Hueffer may have found certain properties of style first, for himself, in Christina, but others have found them elsewhere, notably in Arnaut Daniel and in Guido and in Dante, where Christina herself would have found them. Still there is no denying that there is less of the *ore rotundo* in Christina's work than in that of her contemporaries, and that there is also in Hueffer's writing a clear descent from such passages as:

> I listened to their honest chat:
> Said one: 'Tomorrow we shall be
> Plod plod along the featureless sands
> And coasting miles and miles of sea.'
> Said one: 'Before the turn of tide
> We will achieve the eyrie-seat.'
> Said one: 'To-morrow shall be like
> To-day, but much more sweet.'

We find the qualities of what some people are calling 'the modern cadence' in this strophe, also in 'A Dirge', in 'Up Hill', in—

> Somewhere or other there must surely be
> The face not seen, the voice not heard,

and in—

> Sometimes I said: 'It is an empty name
> I long for; to a name why should I give
> The peace of all the days I have to live?'—
> Yet gave it all the same.

Mr. Hueffer brings to his work a prose training such as Christina never had, and it is absolutely the devil to try to quote snippets from a man whose poems are gracious impressions, leisurely, low-toned. One would quote 'The Starling', but one would have to give the whole three pages of it. And one would like to quote patches out of the curious medley, 'To All the Dead',—save that the picturesque patches aren't the whole or the feel of it; or Süssmund's capricious 'Address', a sort of 'Inferno' to the 'Heaven' which we are printing for the first time in another part of this issue. But that also is too long, so I content myself with the opening of an earlier poem, 'Finchley Road'.

> As we come up at Baker Street
> Where tubes and trains and 'buses meet
> There's a touch of fog and a touch of sleet;
> And we go on up Hampstead way
> Toward the closing in of day....
>
> You should be a queen or a duchess rather,
> Reigning, instead of a warlike father,
> In peaceful times o'er a tiny town,
> Where all the roads wind up and down

> From your little palace—a small, old place
> Where every soul should know your face
> And bless your coming.

I quote again, from a still earlier poem where the quiet of his manner is less marked:

> Being in Rome I wonder will you go
>   Up to the Hill. But I forget the name . . .
> Aventine? Pincio? No: I do not know
>   I was there yesterday and watched. You came.

(*I give the opening only to 'place' the second portion of the poem.*)

> Though you're in Rome you will not go, my You,
> Up to that Hill . . . but I forget the name.
> Aventine? Pincio? No, I never knew . . .
> I was there yesterday. You never came.
>
> I have that Rome; and you, you have a Me,
> You have a Rome, and I, I have my You;
> My Rome is not your Rome; my You, not you.
> . . . . . . For, if man knew woman
> I should have plumbed your heart; if woman, man,
> Your Me should be true I . . . If in your day—
> You who have mingled with my soul in dreams,
> You who have given my life an aim and purpose,
> A heart, an imaged form—if in your dreams
> You have imagined unfamiliar cities
> And me among them, I shall never stand
> Beneath your pillars or your poplar groves, . . .
> Images, simulacra, towns of dreams
> That never march upon each other's borders,
> And bring no comfort to each other's hearts!

I present this passage, not because it is an example of Mr. Hueffer's no longer reminiscent style, but because, like much that appeared four years ago in *Songs from London*, or earlier still in *From Inland*, it hangs in my memory. And so little modern work does hang in one's memory, and these books created so little excitement when they appeared. One took them as a matter of course, and they're not a matter of course, and still less is the later work a matter of course. Oh well, you all remember the preface to the collected poems with its passage about the Shepherd's Bush exhibition, for it appeared first as a pair of essays in

Poetry, so there is no need for me to speak further of Mr. Hueffer's aims or of his prose, or of his power to render an impression.

There is in his work another phase that depends somewhat upon his knowledge of instrumental music. Dante has defined a poem as a composition of words set to music, and the intelligent critic will demand that either the composition of words or the music shall possess a certain interest, or that there be some aptitude in their jointure together. It is true that since Dante's day—and indeed his day and Cassella's saw a re-beginning of it—'music' and 'poetry' have drifted apart, and we have had a third thing which is called 'word music.' I mean we have poems which are read or even, in a fashion, intoned, and are 'musical' in some sort of complete or inclusive sense that makes it impossible or inadvisable to 'set them to music.' I mean obviously such poems as the First Chorus of *Atalanta* or many of Mr. Yeats' lyrics. The words have a music of their own, and a second 'musician's' music is an impertinence or an intrusion.

There still remains the song to sing: to be 'set to music,' and of this sort of poem Mr. Hueffer has given us notable examples in his rendering of Von der Vogelweide's 'Tandaradei' and, in lighter measure, in his own 'The Three-Ten':

> When in the prime and May-day time dead lovers went a-walking,
> How bright the grass in lads' eyes was, how easy poet's talking!
> Here were green hills and daffodils, and copses to contain them:
> Daisies for floors did front their doors agog for maids to chain
>   them.
> So when the ray of rising day did pierce the eastern heaven
> Maids did arise to make the skies seem brighter far by seven.
> Now here's a street where 'bus routes meet, and 'twixt the wheels
>   and paving
> Standeth a lout who doth hold out flowers not worth the
>   having.
> But see, but see! The clock strikes three above the Kilburn
>   Station,
> Those maids, thank God, are 'neath the sod and all their generation.
>
> What she shall wear who'll soon appear, it is not hood nor
>   wimple,
> But by the powers there are no flowers so stately or so simple.
> And paper shops and full 'bus tops confront the sun so brightly,
> That, come three-ten, no lovers then had hearts that beat so lightly

As ours or loved more truly,
Or found green shades or flowered glades to fit their loves more
    duly.
*And see, and see! 'Tis ten past three above the Kilburn Station,
Those maids, thank God! are 'neath the sod and all their generation.*

Oh well, there are very few song writers in England, and it's a simple old-fashioned song with a note of futurism in its very lyric refrain; and I dare say you will pay as little attention to it as I did five years ago. And if you sing it aloud, once over, to yourself, I dare say you'll be just as incapable of getting it out of your head, which is perhaps one test of a lyric.

It is not, however, for Mr. Hueffer's gift of song-writing that I have reviewed him at such length; this gift is rare but not novel. I find him significant and revolutionary because of his insistence upon clarity and precision, upon the prose tradition; in brief, upon efficient writing—even in verse.

Ezra Pound.

Note Mr. Hueffer is not an *imagiste*, but an impressionist. Confusion has arisen because of my inclusion of one of his poems in the *Anthologie des Imagistes*.   E. P.

ON HEAVEN AND POEMS WRITTEN ON ACTIVE SERVICE

19. 'The Function of Rhythm': Conrad Aiken, review in *Dial*

lxv, 16 November 1918, 417-18

If Ford was not taken seriously in England as a war poet, or as a poet of any kind, he was known and respected in America, and in particular by fellow practitioners like Conrad Aiken. The appreciative audience he found in the United States was one of a number of reasons that led him to leave England, where he was generally neglected and ignored, in the early years of the 1920s. Thereafter he spent his time equally in New York and Paris because there he could find people who shared his own interests, especially in the technique of good writing.

Conrad Aiken (b. 1889) is a distinguished poet, novelist and writer of short stories who has won most of the high honours accessible to writers in the United States.

In the Preface to his new book of poems, *On Heaven*, Mr. Ford Madox Hueffer remarks:

The greater part of the book is, I notice on putting it together, in either *vers libre* or rhymed *vers libre*. I am not going to apologize for this or to defend *vers libre* as such. It is because I simply can't help it. *Vers libre* is the only medium in which I can convey any more intimate moods. *Vers libre* is a very jolly medium in which to write and to read, if it be read conversationally and quietly. And anyhow, symmetrical or rhymed verse is for me a cramped and difficult medium—or an easy and uninteresting one.

One recollects, further, that Mr. Hueffer has in the past been also insistent, in theory and in practice, on the point that poetry should be at least as well written as prose—that, in other words, it must be good prose before it can be good poetry. Taken together, these ideas singularly echo a preface written one hundred and twenty odd years ago—Wordsworth's preface to the Lyrical Ballads. In the appendix to that volume Wordsworth, it will be recalled, remarked that in works of imagination the ideas, in proportion as they are valuable, whether in prose or verse, 'require and exact one and the same language.' And throughout he insisted on doing away with all merely decorative language and on using the speech of daily life.

On the matter of meter or rhythm, however, the two poets are not so entirely in agreement as they might appear to be. They are in agreement, it might be said, just in so far as they both seem inclined to regard the question of rhythm as only of minor or incidental importance. 'Metre,' said Wordsworth, 'is only adventitious to composition.' Mr. Hueffer, as is seen above, candidly admits that he avoids the strictest symmetrical forms because to use them well is too difficult. Do both poets perhaps underestimate the value of rhythm? In the light of the widespread vogue of free verse at present, it is a question interesting to speculate upon. And Mr. Hueffer's poems, which are excellent, afford us a pleasant opportunity.

Wordsworth's theory as to the function of rhythm was peculiar. He believed that as poetry consists usually in a finer distillation of the emotions than is found in prose, some check must be used lest the excitation arising therefrom, whether pleasurable or painful, exceed desired bounds. Rhythm is to act as a narcotic. 'The co-expression of something regular, something to which the mind has been accustomed . . . in a less excited state cannot but have great efficacy in tempering . . . the passion by an admixture of ordinary feeling. . .' Only by way of incidental emendation did Wordsworth suggest that in some cases meter might 'contribute to impart passion to the words.' This is perhaps to put the cart before the horse. Mr. Hueffer, on the other hand, while equally regarding or appearing to regard meter as a subsidiary element, raises a different and subtler objection to it. In common with a good many champions of free verse he feels that free verse is better than symmetrical verse for the conveyance of more intimate moods. This is a plausible and intriguing theory. At first glimpse it seems only natural that in a freer and more discursive medium the poet should find himself better able to fix upon the more impalpable nuances of feeling. But a steadier inspection leaves one not quite so sure. If one can convey subtler moods in free verse than in symmetrical verse, might one not logically argue that prose could be subtler still than either? And we should have reached the conclusion that poetry should employ, to reach its maximum efficiency, not only the language but also the rhythms of prose—in other words, that it should *be* prose.

The logic is perhaps not impeccable; but it is sufficiently strong to suggest the presence of some error. If prose could convey subtler emotional moods and impressions than poetry, why write poetry? We suspect however that the reverse is true, and that it is poetry which possesses the greater and subtler power of evocation. But the language is, largely speaking, the same in both. And consequently we must assume that this superior quality of evocativeness or magic which we associate with poetry has something to do with the fact that, more artfully than in prose, the language is *arranged*. And this arrangement is, obviously, in great part a matter of rhythm.

This brings us back, accordingly, to the afterthought in Wordsworth's appendix to the *Lyrical Ballads*—the idea that meter may impart 'passion' to words. The truth of this seems irrefragable. When a poet, therefore, discards rhythm he is discarding perhaps the most powerful single *artifice* of poetry which is at his disposal—the particular artifice, moreover, which more than any other enables the poet to obtain a psychic control over his reader, to exert a sort of hypnosis over him. Rhythm is persuasive; it is the very stuff of life. It is not surprising therefore that things can be said in rhythm which otherwise cannot be said at all; paraphrase a fine passage of poetry into prose and in the dishevelment the ghost will have escaped. A good many champions of free verse would perhaps dispute this. They would fall back on the theory that, at any rate, certain moods more colloquial and less intense than those of the highest type of poetry, and less colloquial and more intense than those of the highest type of prose, could find their aptest expression in this form which lies halfway between. But even here their position will not be altogether secure, at least in theory. Is any contemporary poetry more colloquial or intimate than that of T. S. Eliot, who is predominantly a metrical poet? It is doubtful. Metrical verse, in other words, can accomplish anything that free verse can, and can do it more powerfully. What we inevitably come to is simply the fact that for some poets free verse is an easier medium than metrical verse, and consequently allows them greater efficiency. It is desirable therefore that such poets should employ free verse. They only transgress when they argue from this that free verse is the finer form. This it is not.

The reasons for this would take us beyond the mere question of rhythm. When Wordsworth remarked that one could re-read with greater pleasure a painful or tragic passage of poetry than a similar passage of prose, although he mistakenly ascribed this as altogether due to the presence of meter, he nevertheless touched closely upon the real principle at issue. For compared with the pleasure derived from the reading of prose, the pleasure of reading poetry is two-natured: in addition to the pleasure afforded by the ideas presented, or the material (a pleasure which prose equally affords), there is also the more purely esthetic delight of the art itself, a delight which might be described as the sense of perfection in complexity, or the sense of arrangement. This arrangement is not solely a question of rhythm. It is also concerned with the selection of elements in the language more vividly sensuous and with the more adroit combination of ideas with a view to setting them off to sharper advantage. Given two poems in which the theme is equally delightful and effective on the first reading, that poem of the two which develops the theme with the richer and more perfect complexity of technique will longer afford pleasure in re-reading. It is, in other words, of more permanent value.

Mr. Hueffer confesses in advance that he prefers a less to a more complex form of art. As a matter of fact Mr. Hueffer is too modest. When he speaks of free verse he does not mean, to the extent in which it is usually meant, verse without rhythm. At his freest he is not far from a genuinely rhythmic method; and in many respects his sense of rhythm is both acute and individual. Three poems in his book would alone make it worth printing: 'Antwerp', which is one of the three or four brilliant poems inspired by the war; 'Footsloggers', which though not so good, is none the less very readable; and 'On Heaven', the poem which gives the volume its name. It is true that in all three of these poems Mr. Hueffer very often employs a rhythm which is almost as dispersed as that of prose; but the point to be emphatically remarked is that he does so only by way of variation on the given norm of movement, which is essentially and predominantly rhythmic. Variation of this sort is no more or less than good artistry; and Mr. Hueffer is a very competent artist, in whose hands even the most captious reader feels instinctively and at once secure. Does he at times overdo the dispersal of rhythm? Perhaps. There are moments, in 'Antwerp' and in 'On Heaven', when the relief of the reader on coming to a forcefully rhythmic passage is so marked as to make him suspect that the rhythm of the passage just left was not forceful enough. Mr. Hueffer is of a discursive temperament, viewed from whatever angle, and this leads him inevitably to over-inclusiveness and moments of let-down. One feels that a certain amount of cutting would improve both 'Antwerp' and 'On Heaven'.

Yet one would hesitate to set about it oneself. Both poems are delightful. Mr. Hueffer writes with gusto and imagination, and—what is perhaps rarer among contemporary poets—with tenderness. 'On Heaven' may not be the very highest type of poetry—it is clearly of the more colloquial sort, delightfully expatiative, skilful in its use of the more subdued tones of prose—but it takes hold of one, and that is enough. One accepts it for what it is, not demanding of it what the author never intended to give it—that higher degree of perfection in intricacy, that more intense and all-fusing synthesis, which would have bestowed on it the sort of beauty that more permanently endures.

20. 'Great Poetry': Harriet Monroe, review in *Poetry*

xiii, January 1919, 219–24

The title poem of *On Heaven* was written before the war, but Ford considered it appropriate to a volume of war verse because, as he was later to demonstrate in the Tietjens tetralogy, much of the horror of warfare derives from a soldier's worry about his wife and family at home. Belonging to an older generation, Ford has rarely been considered as one of the famous group of 'war poets' (Rosenberg, Owen, Read, Graves and others), and so Harriet Monroe's comments on this point are interesting. Founder and for many years editor of *Poetry*, Harriet Monroe (d. 1936) was a staunch admirer of Ford's work.

Has England any up-to-date, twentieth-century poet of large calibre? Has she given us any poetry of war true to the motive of *this* war and the spirit of these times, and unlit by the rose-and-purple glint of ancient glamours, of time-exaggerated ideals? Has any of her poets expressed *our* kind of spirituality, the hope and faith and power that carry *us* through *our* days of agony, and bring us *our* flashes of joy?

Yes—this book is the proof of it. A man-size book by a poet who does not shirk the bitterest issues of life and death, and who admits no rose-color of romance between his eyes and the white light of truth; by a poet moreover whose molding of English words into a form fit and shapely and absolutely expressive, has become, after long practice and experiment, as sure as a master potter's molding of clay.

Going through this small volume with a favoring pencil, one finds oneself noting *all* the poems and getting a fresh delight, a fresh illumination, from each. The light shines through them as through prismatic glass, separating into its pure and vivid color-elements, The book has the effect of justifying our modern spirituality—our twentieth-century ideals which have fought and won the greatest of all wars; as against the fragmentary visions, the ecstatic closet-divinations, which fought and won those lesser wars of the past—wars temporal and spiritual that passed the torch along through the centuries. Not that there is any remotest hint of propaganda, any trace of the pulpit or the rostrum: the poet never states, he never directly tells us anything. But through the depth and clarity of his own emotion he makes us feel what he feels; and what he feels, what his illumined mind knows, is simply the whole immense range and beauty of the modern science-illumined search for truth.

One is tempted to compare, or contrast, this soldier-poet—for even 'On Heaven', printed by *Poetry* in June, 1914, reads like a soldier's poem—with that other English soldier-poet, Rupert Brooke. Brooke was moved by all the old romantic glamours: he sang the glory of war, the rapture of death in battle; and, true to type, completed the image by dying in beautiful youth, in inviolate faith. Hueffer is moved by sterner forces; unaided by illusion, he can yet follow his country's flag and the world's hope through four long years of agony, knowing always the criminal absurdity of war, yet always completing the paradox with a deep realization of war's sublimities of devotion and sacrifice. As Brooke's glamorous death was typical, so is it typical that the more modern poet has lived through the four arduous years of battle to face the new struggle for the remaking of the world. And if Brooke's shining muse wore classic draperies, Hueffer makes no apologies for naked beauty in such poems as 'One Day's List', 'Clair de Lune', 'The Old Houses of Flanders', or 'Footsloggers', which begins and ends with this strophe:

> What is love of one's land?
>   Ah, we know very well
> It is something that sleeps for a year, for a day,
> For a month, something that keeps
> Very hidden and quiet and still,
> And then takes
> The quiet heart like a wave,
> The quiet brain like a spell,
> The quiet will
> Like a tornado, and that shakes
> The whole being and soul . . . .
> Aye, the whole of the soul.

Perhaps the whole contrast—the difference between the old and the new—is suggested in 'When the World Crumbled':

> Once there were purple seas—
> Wide, wide....
> And myrtle-groves and cyclamen,
> Above the cliff and the stone pines
> Where a god watched.....
>
> And thou. O Lesbian....
>
> Well, *that's* all done!

The two longer poems, which open and close the book, are 'Antwerp' and 'On Heaven'. Both are written in a rhymed conversational free verse, the rhymes ringing those little bells of surprise which present-day technique aims at rather than the exactly measured chime of the more accepted forms. Mr. Hueffer's *Collected Works* show how expert he has been in the manipulation of the usual measures, but he has graduated into the freer form because—let him tell us:

It is because I simply can't help it. *Vers libre* is the only medium in which I can convey any more intimate moods. *Vers libre* is a very jolly medium in which to write and to read, if it be read conversationally and quietly. And anyhow, symmetrical or rhymed verse is for me a cramped and difficult medium—or an easy and uninteresting one.

In the opinion of at least one reader, Mr. Hueffer's poetry in this medium is as much more beautiful than his earlier work as it is more simple and 'intimate.' The extreme skill which has gone into the making of these poems is most happily concealed under the easy distinction and clarity of an achieved style. The poet complains of 'sloppiness' in 'On Heaven'; indeed for four years he refused to reprint it, leaving to *Poetry* the honor of exclusive publication; and even now the earlier version contains a beautiful passage of thirty lines super-critically omitted from the book. But while the style has not that hardness which the imagists aim at, being more fluent and less patterned than their discreet counsel admits as the latest vogue, it has a silken richness shining and flowing with many colors in the wind, and absolutely responsive in texture and movement to the delicate amenities of the theme.

This theme, 'a materialist's Heaven,' is Mr. Hueffer's present excuse for printing the poem.

I know at least that I would not keep on going if I did not feel that Heaven will be something like Rumpelmayer's tea-shop. . . . For haven't we Infantry all seen that sort of shimmer and shine, and heard the rustling and the music, through all the turmoil and the mire and the horror? . . . . . We must have some such Heaven to make up for the deep mud, and the bitter weather, and the long lasting fears, and the cruel hunger for light, for graciousness and for grace!

It may be questioned whether this Rumpelmayer Heaven is any more material than the mansions of gold and pearl and the harping angels of an earlier revelation. At any rate the poem expresses, in our unpretentious, even a bit humorous, modern way, the same yearning for joy in love and beauty under the divine approval of a super-human but strictly personal God—'a man-and-a-half,' so to speak—which our ancestors, throughout the Christian ages, have persisted in expressing through their more assertive and grandly gesticulatory arts. And moreover it expresses also, in spite of our more difficult modern questionings, their faith that this little earth and its fragile fabric of lives are not the whole story:

> For God is a very clever mechanician;
> And if he made this proud and goodly ship of the world,
> From the maintop to the hull,
> Do you think he could not finish it to the full,
> With a flag and all,
> And make it sail, tall and brave,
> On the waters, beyond the grave?

'Antwerp' is a heroic ode conceived in the modern spirit and fashion —it is a tribute to the bravery of Belgium, to the bravery moreover of the common man:

> With no especial legends of marchings or triumphs or duty—
> Assuredly that is the way of it,
> The way of beauty.

The book, as a whole and in detail, makes us feel that 'that *is* the way of it'; that kings and knights and conquerors and all the pomp and pageantry of human grandeur and bluster have had their day, and that the new 'way of beauty' will follow the footsteps of the common man and penetrate the byways of his homely heroisms.

COLLECTED POEMS (1936)

21. Introduction by William Rose Benét to *Collected Poems* (1936)

Oxford University Press, New York, vii-xi

> Although not published as a review, this introduction gives a good idea of the general critical attitude taken towards Ford's poetry at the end of his life. During the 1930s, William Rose Benét (1886–1950), his brother, Stephen Vincent Benét, and his wife, Elinor Wylie, were important literary influences in New York, and this introduction undoubtedly helped the publication of the volume at a time when Ford's own fortunes were at a low ebb.

Ford Madox Ford (formerly Hueffer) is now advanced in years and has written over fifty books. His post-War novels have especially won fame. His youth knew the world of the pre-Raphaelites. The great Christina Rossetti was his aunt. He was a friend of Henry James, and friend and collaborator with Joseph Conrad.

Mr. Ford professes to be ill-read in English poetry and not to care much about it. This is partly an attitude. He is a born romancer. He has become a citizen of the world. He knows France and Germany, for one thing, as do few younger men. He was born in a literary atmosphere and creative writing is as natural to him as breathing. He has, in his time, been an instinctively fine editor of literary publications. No older writer of whom I know has had greater sympathy with brilliant young talent or done more in the way of its encouragement. Despite any profession of his, it is the poetry in his soul that has endowed him with this perpetual youth, even to its enthusiasms.

Ford—although it may be impertinent of me to say so—is an old sea-lion of the ledges. Still he sings 'Lukannon before the sealers came.' Yet, even while he wheezes old wisdom at you—he will surprise you by a lightning-flash of quite contemporary defiance. He is romantic, sentimental—and at times direly realistic. His poetry—as he wrote it—began traditionally; yet even then the original twist appeared. He thinks his greatest early influence was Christina Rossetti. Browning can be also descried. The period of the Great War found him free of most influences. A poem written at Albert, on active service (he was an officer in the Welch Regiment) impresses me still as it impressed me when I first read it. Possibly it is like something Henley might have written, had Henley known the War. In any case, it is fine description. The last verse runs:

> Dust and corpses in the thistles
> Where the gas-shells burst like snow,
> And the shrapnel screams and whistles
> On the Bécourt road below,
> And the High Wood bursts and bristles
> Where the mine-clouds foul the sky . . .
> But I'm with you up at *Wyndcroft*,
> Over Tintern on the *Wye*.

'Antwerp,' however, is Ford's own favourite among these poems of active service. The management of the following lines is sufficiently remarkable, both in dramatic intensity and true feeling:

> They await the lost who lie in trench and barrier and foss,
> In the dark of the night.
> This is Charing Cross; it is past one of the clock;
> There is very little light.
> There is so much pain.

An accomplished writer of prose, who desires to spurn the poetic 'device,' his natural ear for the subtle rhythm that makes poetry of the most direct statement, his possession of the depth of feeling that decrees to words an inevitable order, illuminate the commonplace. In his best poems the impact of what is not said, through the choice of what *is* said, is of great force:

> I will punt you
> To Paradise for the sugar and onions. . .
> We will drift home in the twilight,
> The trout will be rising. . .

Gas-shells, shrapnel, and mine-clouds . . . sugar and onions . . . are these words for poetry? Yes. Because this is not poeticizing. This is experience. This also:

> I wonder, my dear, can you stick it?
> As we should say: 'Stick it, the Welch!'
> In the dark of the moon,
> Going over. . .

As one grows older it is this record of personal experience, I find, that seems most important in a man's poetry. But the record must be *written*. Not many can write it.

As to phrase, and as to the handling of the flexible rhymed free verse that has become characteristic of Ford, an earlier poem, 'The Starling' contains such lines as

> A multitude, throng upon throng,
> Of starlings,
> Successive orchestras of song,
> Flung, like the babble of surf,
> On the roadside turf—

One can only say 'Admirable!' of that, just as even further back in time, over thirty years ago, this poet could write—in a poem beginning 'Come in the delicate stillness of dawn,'

> You shall fade away and pass
> As—when we breathed upon your mirror's glass—
> Our faces died away.

That is to use words as words should be used, with precision; the conjuring up of the exact sight, or, in the case of the starlings, of the exact sound. That is a large part of the art of writing, and its difficulty cannot be exaggerated.

So much for Mr. Ford's credentials as a poet. Now for a personal, and I hope not too intrusive an opinion. Of his longer poems I cannot disconnect 'On Heaven' from a personal experience of my own. It has for me, as they say, 'sentimental associations,' though the term 'sentimental' does not at all express what the association was, or remains. I knew little about Mr. Ford at the time and did not meet him until years afterward. I still think 'On Heaven' a most remarkable poem, though once, I understand, he wished it suppressed, and I know that he still feels it to be too long. Probably 'A House' is really better. In either, and in both, he is *sui generis*. Those two poems will, I hope, increasingly be read.

Nine years elapsed between the appearance of 'On Heaven' (with the poems written on Active Service) in book-form and the publication in book-form of 'A House.' The same latter volume contains the quite remarkable 'Brantigorn,' which to me is a bit cryptic—but I got no help on that score from putting questions to the author. He smiled somewhat enigmatically and said 'I just wrote it,' or words to that effect.

As to the earliest work, there is a night piece, 'Thanks Whilst Unharnessing,' the interesting dialogue in 'Grey Matter,' the sociological implications of 'From the Soil,' the lyrical spurt of 'The Great View,' the memorable 'Goths' from 'Two Frescoes,' 'The Old Faith to the Converts,' of 1897, and the stoic 'Song of the Women,'

> When ye've 'eered the bailiff's 'and upon the latch,
> And ye've felt the rain a-trickling through the thatch,
> An' y'r man can't git no stones to break ner yit no sheep to
>   watch—

So they come 'a-Christmassing,' with a refrain of despair that is heard today in all the cities of the world.

The technique of the poet has become far more his own since then, but the same feeling can be traced. Compare the cadences of 'The Mother' (A Song Drama) with those of 'A House.'

While 'To all The Dead,' of the section 'High Germany,' is not wholly a good poem, in several passages it is amazing. 'In the Little Market-Place' is distinctly and wholly good.

Ford's poetry is emotional, as the best poetry should be. It is the problem of the artist to present his emotion with the most scrupulous honesty. And whether or not there is such a thing as poetic afflatus, there are certainly moments that must be seized upon, when more precise language than at any other time is ready to hand for the expression of spontaneous feeling. These things Ford knows. He has accepted the dicta of no school. He has followed his instinct. That instinct has frequently been most fortunate.

Finally, I should like to point out that in the early part of a century when verse has been undergoing a great deal of experimentation, this poet has created a type of verse that can now easily be recognized as his own. The vexed definition of style I shall not further confuse. This writer has a style, which is perhaps merely to say that he is saliently an individual. Whatever may be true in the realms of sociology and economics, to sacrifice the individual in the arts is to destroy them. What is valuable in art, as I have noted, is the particular human experience. And for that, this poet has unborrowed language, and sometimes the inevitable word.

22. John Peale Bishop, review in *Poetry*

1, September 1937, 336–41

The publication of Ford's second *Collected Poems* passed almost unnoticed, with two or three scant reviews. Again, as was so often true, the only extended treatment it received was written by a fellow artist, John Peale Bishop (1892–1944). Poet and novelist in his own right, Bishop was also managing editor of *Vanity Fair* in New York and was a close friend of Allen Tate and Edmund Wilson.

Though the *Collected Poems* of Ford Madox Ford now appear for the first time in an American edition, it is not the first volume of that title to be published. *A Preface to Collected Poems*, dated 1911, is here reprinted, with some apology for the frivolity of its tone, none for its opinions. This is as it should be. For if it is hard not to resent the patronizing attitude which Mr. Ford then took toward William Butler Yeats, it must be allowed him that, while his own poetic art shows a sure consistent gain down through the war period, there is, from first to last, no essential change in his point of view. In 1914 there was an English edition of *Collected Poems* which was reissued in 1916. The present volume gathers together all that Mr. Ford has written in verse, from 'The Wind's Quest,' his first poem, printed in 1891, through *Buckshee: Last Poems*, finished in Paris only last year. His famous 'On

Heaven,' which first appeared in *Poetry* in 1914, has here its pride of place, and is followed by the equally unforgettable 'Antwerp.' From these two poems we are led, in the familiar Ford manner, back and forth through time until we have covered a career of forty-five years.

Mr. Ford's position as a poet has been somewhat over-topped by his place as a writer of prose. For it has been his fortune—and it is this that has won him, in so many cities and in more than one country, the esteem and affection of many writers younger than he—to insist upon the professional attitude. He has done it by precept and, more importantly, by example. The novelist might, as he so often told us, practice a *métier du chien*. It was still a *métier*. And nothing less than a complete consciousness of the craft would do. Of course, he was not alone among his contemporaries in holding that the French had a far finer and fuller sense of what it meant to construct a novel than the English; around the turn of the century there were not a few who spoke and wrote his language and like him followed the cult of conscience, ready at any instant to call upon Flaubert as their only saint. But of them none survive who has proved more constant to that faith; none was ever more devout than Ford Madox Ford.

His approach to the novel is in the French manner. But when it comes to poetry, Mr. Ford would have us believe that he is a man of England. It is a country where, as a living French poet has observed, poems grow like grass,—that is to say with apparent ease and an incomparable freshness, secretly sustained by centuries of care. Ford Madox Ford disclaims too profound a concern with poetry, either his own, or others'. If, when he starts a novel, he knows from beginning to the end just how each word is to be placed, he knows—or so he says —practically nothing of how his poems are made. They come to him— a little tune in the head, then words, and then more words, on paper. How should he say if they are good or bad? He has read so little poetry. When he opens the morning paper, it is to turn first to the cricket scores.

This need not really deceive us. Like Congreve, who told Voltaire he did not wish to be visited as a dramatist, Mr. Ford, the poet, prefers to be thought of as among the country gentlemen. Their class, it might be remembered, has made no small contribution to English literature.

Before the War came, Mr. Ford was able to bring to the writing of verse not only the skill and scrupulousness which have distinguished his best novels, but also a good many tricks of his conscious trade. There are, from first to last in his work, poems which have the April spontaneity of grass; but they are not his best poems. At his best, he will be found almost invariably not to have departed too far from his methods in prose. This discourse which is a record of his own emotions and is meant, too, to record the contemporary world; which is so realistic on the surface, so romantic in its depths; which is never so pleased as when adding one discordant passage to another; which slides as smoothly as a *Wagon-Lit* from place to place, and at dead of night from a known country to one that is strange; which is careless with the years and indifferent to the clock as memory is: where have we encountered it before? The verse has a strong insistent, uneven beat; the rhymes arrive unexpectedly. But this cosmopolitan speech, whose English slips so readily into a French or a German phrase, which pauses scarcely an instant and with only a touch of superiority before it turns to slang: where did it come from—if not from the prose of Ford Madox Ford? When he began writing verse, it was under those influences which a young Englishman of independent tastes might have been expected to feel just before the close of the last century. They were soon discarded. Mr. Ford's own manner seems to have been rather easily come by; it has been worn since with comfortable assurance, like an old country-coat of good cut and the best tweed. If at times something in a poem reminds us of one of his contemporaries, that is only because his aim and theirs happen to coincide.

Mr. Ford's contribution to the poetry of his time was to assist in bringing it nearer to the art of prose. It was, when he did it, a necessary thing to do. There were others: Ezra Pound also knew that if poetry was to live and not die in a living and dying world, it must, in his own phrase, catch up with prose; but none of the others knew so much about prose as Ford Madox Ford did.

It is thus that poetry has always been renewed. Jules Romains, in his recent *Preface à l'Homme Blanc*, reminds us that it was so in France, for as late as his own boyhood the charge he constantly heard levelled against Victor Hugo was one of *prosaïsme*, while in the *lycées* Baudelaire was still referred to as a *prosaïeur froid et alambique*. When the Muse's sandal is bound too strictly, there is nothing for her to do but loosen it and for a time go barefoot. When too much that he sees about him in the world is forbidden to the poet there is nothing he can do but lay violent hands on the immense matter of prose and seize whatever he thinks he can appropriate.

So little is now forbidden, that it is not altogether easy for us to conceive how difficult this was for an English poet in the decade before the War. Mr. Ford could conclude a poem on the death of Queen Victoria with these straightforward lines:

> A shock,
> A change in the beat of the clock,
> And the ultimate change that we fear feels
>   a little less far.

But he had to go through no small amount of rather facile poetizing—

> Keep your brooding sorrows for dewy misty hollows,
> Here's blue sky and lark song, drink the air—

before he could come to

> This is Charing Cross:
> It is midnight;
> There is a great crowd
> And no light.

And it is precisely because there were difficulties to be surmounted that there remains so much that is tough and enduring in these poems, despite their constant use of not too particular sentiment.

> They await the lost.
> They await the lost that shall never leave the dock;
> They await the lost that shall never come again
>   by the train
> To the embraces of all these women with dead faces;
> They await the lost who lie dead in trench and
>   barrier and foss,
> In the dark of the night.
> This is Charing Cross; it is past one of the clock;
> There is very little light.
>
> There is so much pain.

This gives, as does no other poem, the feel of a great London in the midst of the war. And more than that, 'Antwerp' remains one of the distinguished poems of our time.

THE TIETJENS NOVELS

23. Unsigned review of *Some Do Not*, *The Times Literary Supplement*

24 April 1924, 252

Although Ford included *The Times Literary Supplement* among the names of academic periodicals unsympathetic to imaginative literature, and believed that this paper 'had a down' on him, he must have been pleased with the reception the Tietjens series received in its columns. The first of these is printed below.

Mr. Ford Madox Ford's new novel, *Some Do Not* . . . is constructed on somewhat the same principles as his last, *The Marsden Case*; and we are not sure that these are quite so suitable to a serious story as to a comedy. The principle is a modification of the purely dramatic; the number of acts and scenes, or 'sets,' is strictly limited, and Mr. Ford manages, with quite extraordinary ingenuity, to dovetail into his admirable dialogue long passages of reflection which reveal the essentials of an extremely complicated tissue of events. It is ingenious, but it is by no means easy for the reader. Nevertheless, Mr. Ford's method justifies itself in this—that it conveys an impression of fullness, of three dimensions, which would make the bulk of modern novels look thin in comparison; and one might say that, seeing all his characters and events and all the relations between them with a Richardson's completeness, his only misfortune was in having to compress into one what Richardson would have taken several volumes of letters to describe.

Within the limits of a review it is impossible to carry compression still further; we should only do a great injustice to the brilliant animation with which the book itself presents, in section, a complete view of English society just before and during the war. From the extraordinary events on the golf links at Rye, where Tietjens prevents the capture of two suffragettes who were harrying a Cabinet Minister, through the still more extraordinary breakfast at Mrs. Duchemin's, where his friend Macmaster falls in love with the wife of a rector afflicted with scatological mania, and the amazing conversation of Sylvia, Tietjens's thoroughly corrupted wife, her mother and Father Consett at Lobscheid, to the confused whirl of the day when Tietjens, finally down and out, returns to the front, the movement is never arrested. And the movement has a plan, which is to contrast 'those who do'—that is, the accommodating consciences, the holders of places, the makers of careers, the arbiters of social prestige, the immoralists and the materialists—with 'those who do not'—namely, the uncomfortable idealists like Tietjens and the girl Valentine, who are too sharp-cornered not to be rejected. Mr. Ford, as we should expect, does not sentimentalize; he presents, coldly but angrily, and with an occasional coarseness of language by which some will be repelled, the social ruin that befell the most brilliant man in England, Christopher Tietjens, son of a Yorkshire country gentleman, a Tory idealist, who sees himself as 'a sort of lonely buffalo, outside the herd.' Sylvia's good name, the 'Whig' Macmaster's success in the Statistics Office, Mrs. Wannop's renewal of prosperity, one might almost say the comfort of the amiable General Campion and the evil-tongued in general, are all promoted by Tietjens's quixotry. His severe morality, even, draws down upon him the direct calumny, and his honesty enables Sylvia to make him out a rogue. He can make no concessions—that is his tragedy and also his pride; and it may be Mr. Ford's tragedy and pride also. His hero is presented as paddling uncouthly, and Valentine as struggling shrilly but dejectedly, in the immoral slime of the 'classes' as represented in modern England. For a while Valentine sees him bedaubed worse than the rest; but that he is cleared in her sight is his only victory. Whether Mr. Ford makes this view of things convincing, whether his whole view of England, as compared with France, is not unbalanced, is a matter for philosophers to discuss; we need only say that here is a novel of unusual power and art.

24. Unsigned review of *Some Do Not*, *Nation & Athenaeum*

xxxv, 24 May 1924, 258

Just as *The Good Soldier* was generally not recognized for what it was when it first appeared, so *Some Do Not* elicited little notice. In many ways this is not surprising for no one knew that it was the first of a projected series, and the quantity of Ford's literary production (six books were published in 1923–4) tended to blunt critical discrimination. Such reviews as there were contained predictable comments. Edwin Pugh in the London *Bookman* declared that 'Mr. Ford's people are uniformly unpleasant and not in the least companionable. . . . Singly they are credible; grouped together they have the aspect of unclean freaks whose likeliness to humanity only makes them the more repulsive.' The reviewer for the *Daily Express* complained that 'It points no noteworthy moral, and is unnecessarily full of crude profanity of the type beloved by pseudo-realists.' These inanities are extreme, if not typical. More intelligent reviewers found the book interesting but bewildering. The notice printed below reflects that opinion.

In the first half of this remarkable novel, Mr. Ford constructs for us an England that Englishmen generally will have some difficulty in recognizing; a strange, erotic land inhabited principally by sexual monomaniacs. This country and people—the time is the year previous to the war and the early days of the war itself—are made astonishingly real to the reader, so that when the preliminaries are over, the strange scenery set, the sex-saturated atmosphere created, and Mr. Ford's wonderfully realistic marionettes get into their stride, the passionate drama that results is continuously enthralling. It is really a triumph of mind over matter. The mind is always there, acutely observing even when most grotesquely misunderstanding; a distinguished mind that moulds everything to its will. If the resulting imbroglio is like nothing that ever was on land or sea, it nevertheless satisfies, for given its premises its argument is almost flawless. Mr. Ford's besetting weaknesses—they are faults of his qualities—are the emphasis he puts upon trifles and a passion for imparting information.

25. 'An Angry Novel': Joseph Wood Krutch on *Some Do Not*

Saturday Review of Literature, i, 18 October 1924, 197

The review printed below is not so much typical as perverse. It is included as an example of the way in which Ford's uncertain literary reputation often interfered with an understanding of his own work.

Born in 1893, Joseph Wood Krutch was for many years an author, naturalist and editor, as well as professor of dramatic literature at Columbia University.

Passion makes a work of art and anger destroys it, yet passion and anger are certainly related states of mind. The latter, of course, is personal and concerned only with self, while the former has detached itself from the ego and embraced a 'cause' or an idea, but it is doubtful if it ever begins except as a sense of personal wrong. That Milton would never have conceived his passion for freedom of speech or for the right of divorce if those passions had not begun as the anger of a strong man thwarted, is a commonplace, but there are other and subtler examples. Because Strindberg was unhappy in his personal relations he came to see the whole world in terms of his own exasperation and many a writer suffering under the smart of even an illusion of persecution has become, because of that, the passionate defender of a race, a creed or, perhaps, of humanity itself. Nor does the nature of the origin detract from the importance of the thing produced—perhaps indeed nothing is more fundamental in artistic creation than this process which transmutes or sublimates, and makes passion out of anger—but the transmutation is the fundamental thing and the distinction between the two is clearly marked. Indeed it would be an interesting though easy task for some critic to discriminate between them as they appear in different pieces of writing and to show how the one produces great work and the other only petulance; how angry writing is confused, violent, and feeble while passionate writing is clear, calm and strong; how the one burns with a bright flame, while the other smokes like an ill-made torch, and blackening the objects around, reveals only uncertain glimpses of their distorted forms.

Mr. Ford Madox Hueffer or, as he now prefers to call himself, Mr. Ford Madox Ford, has hung for years on the edge of literary fame. Back in the forgotten nineties he even contributed to the near sacred *Savoy* and two generations of writers, many of them doubtless unworthy, have passed him on the way to celebrity, leaving him, after a lifetime of literary effort, a name still so vague that his publishers find it advisable to advertise him as 'Joseph Conrad's Famous Collaborator.' Under these circumstances it is not difficult to understand that Mr. Ford should be angry and there is nothing in the nature of the case to explain why he should not transmute this anger into passion and why he should not write a book called *Some Do Not*, which would sear the souls of those unworthy ones who are willing to play the game and rise step by step in the rotten hierarchy which they serve. Unfortunately, however, we are not dealing with a possibility but with a fact, and the actual novel which he has written does nothing of the sort since it rarely rises above the level of angry petulance. It is true that the outward motions of transmutations are gone through. The literary world comes in for only incidental attacks, and the hero, a brilliant mathematician of Tory principles, ruins his career in official not literary circles, yet the anger of a personally disappointed man is more evident than the passion of a great soul. The book, it is only fair to add, is reported to have had a very remarkable reception in England and to have gone through several editions, but one reader at least got as his reward for the close attention necessary to follow its rather obscure method of story telling little except glimpses of a man too angry to be very interesting.

To be specific, the story deals with the life of a very upright man in a very naughty world. Christopher Tietjens, the younger son of an old family, stands for substantial British virtue, sobriety and honor as opposed to the loose living and the sentimentalized immoralities of the modern representatives of his class. As a result his name is smirched with scandal and his world turns him down. It is a simple and dignified theme susceptible of simple and dignified treatment but the author's anger clouds his picture and transforms his hero into a somewhat foul-mouthed scold who obscures his supposed virtues with a torrent of railing. In his thoughts most of the men of his acquaintance appear as 'swine' and the women he calls almost without exception (the diction is his not mine) 'whores.' That is the fact which seems most typical of the book. Perhaps the two epithets are indeed the ones most applicable to the majority of those who constitute upper-class circles in England, but it would require a book less hysterical to convince one of the fact.

26. Louis Bromfield, review of *Some Do Not*, New York *Bookman*

lx, February 1925, 739

The initial response in New York to the first of the Tietjens novels was not very different from that in London, but when, as here, a practising novelist reviewed the book the reaction was generally more sympathetic than usual. Louis Bromfield's comments on *Some Do Not* are part of a longer essay dealing with a number of different subjects.

Novelist, short story writer and playwright, Bromfield was also well known for his writings on farm life. He lived for some time in Lucas, Ohio and died there in 1956.

At least five adventures occurred during the month which made life worth living, five glowing experiences, two of the past and three of present creation. They were encounters with a novel, a play, an actress, a great picture, and a poet.

Some Do Not is the book. It is a revelation of a man who for so many years existed in the public consciousness chiefly as the collaborator of Joseph Conrad. Suddenly, without a word, Ford Madox Ford (né Hueffer) publishes a book which is to our day what *Vanity Fair* was to the early days of Victoria's reign, a book that presents a picture of social life surpassed in poise, penetration, and literary excellence only by Thackeray's great novel. If it were buried now, to be dug up three hundred years hence, the men who dug it up would have an extraordinarily sound picture of the England of the past quarter century. They would know about it virtually all there is to know. And it is no prettier a picture than the *Vanity Fair* which shocked the homebodies of Victoria's neat kingdom. In an autumn remarkable for the wealth of good novels, *Some Do Not* surely stands high above most . . . a book that is built with a sense of form, one that tells a story admirably, one in which the characterization is excellent, and one which has that quality of all great novels—a sublimation of reality, and an inherent glamor that is quite beyond such labels as realism or romanticism.

27. 'New Worlds and Old': Mary Colum on *No More Parades*

Saturday Review of Literature, ii, 30 January 1926, 523

This review by Mary Colum (d. 1957), who was a prominent literary figure in New York and the wife of Padraic Colum, is mainly interesting for what it says about Ford's reputation in America. The Tietjens novels brought Ford financial benefits as well as a critical success that established his name. As to the substance of Mrs Colum's remarks, they helped create the impression that Ford was a 'highbrow' author, with little appeal to the ordinary reader. This view was often repeated, sometimes with philistine hostility, and to a certain extent has endured till the present.

No More Parades . . . deals with a life so new that only those readers abreast with modern ideas can read it with pleasure . . . Mr. Ford's novel is not a thoroughly English book—it is not permeated with English ideals and traditions; it has, in fact, a sort of unconscious anti-English feeling in it as if it were the work of one of those aliens in the British Empire, Celt or Semite, who in their souls resents what England stands for.

No More Parades is probably the most highly praised novel of the year; in fact, one discovers from the more intellectual reviewers that it is a very remarkable book. The *Dial* reviewer gives us to understand that it is a great book; he seems to think that all Mr. Ford's novels are great books—they are written, we are told, 'with integrity, probity, and a single violence of passion that makes them great.' Both the

Tribune and *The Times* reviewer pronounced the book the finest novel of the year. Anyhow, it is perfectly certain that if it had been written one, or two, or three decades ago, or at any time since novels began to be written, few if any would have read it. All our intellectuals are reading it now. Indeed I expect that our young intellectual novelists will be heavily influenced by it or will attempt to imitate a wholecloth imitation of it. At the beginning of a new year it is worth considering why a book like *No More Parades* gets this amount of attention.

It gets attention for exactly the same reason that the work of T.S. Eliot gets attention, and, in a lesser degree, that the work of the new *Dial* prize-winner, E.E. Cummings, who that journal editorially informs us is a great poet. The *Dial* does not explain to us why it considers Mr. Cummings a great poet, nor does its reviewer tell us why he considers Mr. Ford a great novelist. But this is the reason: Mr. Ford, Mr. Cummings, and several other writers of the newer order express, nimbly and accurately, in carefully developed and individual style, certain attitudes of mind, certain sensations, certain emotions and, above all, certain observations of this generation. Mr. Ford is, of course, a much more important writer than Mr. Cummings. They both, however, give expression to a certain rampant and disillusioned intellectualism which is the fashionable literary attitude of the moment.

That a reader should like a writer because he expresses them or something which interests them is understandable enough; this sort of judgment has indeed a certain relation to literary criticism, but it must be considered as relative to other merits. It is the sheerest nonsense to call a writer great because he expresses some facet or some neuroticism of his own generation. For example, I believe that T.S. Eliot expresses a part of me a great deal better than does John Keats or Robert Browning. But I am not for that reason under the delusion that Mr. Eliot is as great as Keats or Browning, or that he is a great poet at all—an excellent poet of sorts he is. An excellent novelist of sorts is Mr. Ford Madox Ford, but neither of them have the stamina, or the passion, or the hard grip on their material of the great writers; they have not added anything to the experience of the race, and, if we are to have any sort of genuine criticism, the indiscriminate calling of such writers great or immortal must be stopped.

An immortal writer is a writer who expresses something immortal; a great writer is a writer who expresses something great—it may be something overwhelmingly great, or it may be simply a strong, fleeting intensity. The expression of fleeting intensities, or even fleeting whimsicalities has often innate in them, if not an immortal flame, at least an immortal spark, and so they, too, live with the greater expressions in the mind of man. Having made my protest against the calling of such books 'great'—and such a protest is, perhaps, the most necessary act of criticism at the present time, let me state that *No More Parades* is an excellent book and worth every intelligent man's or woman's reading once. It has the integrity and the probity which the *Dial* reviewer credits it with; it has not, however, 'the single violence of passion'—it has not, in fact, passion at all; passion is exactly the quality lacking in such books. It has little emotion; it is life portrayed through thin emotions but distinguished intellect—a life where people observe rather than feel things. What intensity it has is nervous and intellectual intensity. It is an outstanding characteristic of such books that they are written out of the nerves and intellect.

The two chief characters, Sylvia and Christopher Tietjens, similarly, are created out of the nerves and intellect, and so have the curious reality and unreality of such creations. The scene of the novel is a basecamp behind the lines in France during the war; naturally we do not get the emotional reactions of people to the war—we get their nervous reactions to minor phases of it. Readers of what are called very modern books will notice that in them great stress is laid on such facets of life as have, up to the present, been omitted altogether in literature or relegated to a minor position. This is due to the influence of the discoveries of psychoanalysis which show that more or less hidden, and sometimes superficial desires, play an unsuspected rôle in the nervous make-up of individuals. When such forces are brought out and made to play the chief rôles the total effect is of patent unreality. In the older English novels such forces had no part to play. For instance, in *Tess of the d'Urbervilles*, Tess is shown acting under powerfully moving influences, in powerfully significant situations, while in a book like *No More Parades* Sylvia Tietjens's character is shown in insignificant circumstances under the sway of neurotic emotions. Her chief desire with regard to her husband is to torture him with infidelities and cruelties. As she sits in a hotel lobby with a man who has been her lover she sees in a mirror her husband enter and hand a card to the hotel servant; she watches his lips moving as he asks for her, sees him see her sitting there. The description of this scene is a triumph of nervous observation. We have all through the book triumphs of nervous observation, but we have no triumphs of emotional revelation; neither Sylvia nor her husband are strongly alive because their creator had not in himself a vital life to give them. He tries to make of Christopher an intellectual, a chivalrous gentleman following public school ethics and the Arnold of Rugby code of honor; what he actually turns out to be is a sort of Sissy without strong emotions, a man who tries to be unfaithful to his wife but cannot succeed. We are told that he won't hit another man before his wife, Sylvia, but he permits his brother to write scurrilous letters about her.

28. 'Contemporary Reminiscences': Burton Rascoe on *No More Parades*

Arts and Decoration, xxiv, February 1926, 57

With the publication of the second part of the Tietjens series, critical opinion began to polarize. There were still those who, like Milton Waldman in the *London Mercury* (November 1925), found Ford's work offensive: 'The nastiness that was immanent in the earlier book breaks through most unpleasantly in this one.' But others, like the reviewer in the *New York Times* (8 November 1925), began to make comparisons with Joyce and Proust. One interesting explanation of the obstacle preventing Ford's recognition appeared in a review of *No More Parades* in the *Observer* (11 October 1925), which said of Ford that he

> has a larger measure of genius than most men now writing, yet he has never reached the place under the public eye where genius should be seated. And it may be because he has a touch of that inhumanity which the public never pardons. He uses us too ill, flagellates and torments us, so that we escape from him quickly and go back to him never ... It may be questioned whether fiction has any right to make one suffer so much.

The review reprinted below is in part an answer to H. L. Mencken's attack on Ford's book, *Joseph Conrad: A Personal Remembrance* (see No. 43) and to that extent again reveals how Ford's private difficulties worked against the favourable reception of his work. Rascoe's defence was salutory, however, since he was one of the more important literary journalists of the day. A critic and literary editor for many magazines, notably the *American Mercury*, Rascoe (1892–1957) also wrote a number of volumes of reminiscences containing entertaining stories of well-known writers.

My revered master, Mr. Mencken, the venerable sage of Baltimore, who sometimes fires at Englishmen without waiting to see the whites of their eyes, about a year ago let go a couple of barrels in the general direction of Ford Madox Ford (*né* Hueffer). He wrote apropos of Ford's *Joseph Conrad: A Personal Recollection*, the biographical importance of which he was quick to see, but he discharged a number of generalities about Ford's abilities as a writer which were obviously not based upon an adequate study of Ford's contributions to literature.

This Ford, (wrote Mr. Mencken) has been a promising young man in England for thirty years. . . . Luck, I fear, is not with him; even his change of name has not got him anywhere. Half German and half English, he is a sort of walking civil war—too much engrossed by the bombs going off in his own ego to make much of an impression upon the rest of the human race. The high, purple spot of his life came when he collaborated with Conrad, and upon that fact, I dare say, his footnote in the literature books will depend.

It is quite true that Ford is more generally known at present through his collaboration with Conrad than through his individual work; but that, surely, is no more basis for judgment than the fact that when Conrad was first heard of he was known only through his association with Ford. Both situations were fortuitous: Ford was at first the better known because he was the brilliant grandson of a Pre-raphaelite painter and now is the lesser known because united critical opinion forced recognition of Conrad. In his book on Conrad, Ford records with a jesting deprecation that Conrad had come to him for literary help on the advice of someone who had told Conrad that Ford was the best stylist writing in English. Conrad enthusiasts have taken great umbrage at this simple statement, with a sort of Well-of-all-the-gall! reaction to what they regard as an impertinence.

Now, not to put too fine a point on it, if Ford is not the best stylist now writing English, he is certainly one of the best. Only one writer, James Joyce, knows as much about the technique of writing English as Ford or is able to write perfectly in as many different manners. Conrad never came within miles of Ford's competence and ease in manipulating the resources of the English language. Fortunately for Conrad, this counted rather to his advantage, for the very uncertainty of his use of the language often contributed to the effect of occult brooding that gives a mystic charm to his work. It slowed up his sentences; and in prose literature as in music the retarding of the tempo makes for an effect of solemnity.

Finally, it is an open question whether Conrad ever wrote a finer novel than Ford's new one, *No More Parades*. There are, of course, very few points at which the two writers meet and so it would be difficult to compare them; but Conrad never created a heroine as real as Sylvia Tietjens, and he never undertook a harder task than Ford undertook in *No More Parades*.

No More Parades is the second book in a projected series, of which *Some Do Not* was the first. What he is doing in this series is recording the revolution that has taken place in the British social structure and the disintegration of a code of conduct—the code of the English Tory gentleman, 'Waterloo was won on the playing field of Eton,' etcetera, etcetera. The revolution, of course, had its economic origin in the break-up of the squirearchy which began before the war. The Tory code was once an effective club wherewith to beat creditors and tradesmen whenever one had no money; but the transvaluation of values which the war brought about and the shake-up of the haves and have-nots put an end to that. The code had other, pleasanter uses, and, in the abstract, it made for nice amenities and a certain dignity of character when adhered to. But abuses of it, and a certain necessary hypocrisy which it involved, together with the progress of the democratic and feministic movement, brought about its ruin.

In *No More Parades* and *Some Do Not*, Ford has presented Christopher Tietjens, a young man who is thoroughly imbued with the Tory ideal by inheritance and environment, and has shown him in conflict with situations wherein the code is a dead letter. What he was trying to do was not so obvious in the first novel. In *No More Parades* it becomes marvelously clear. Because of the critical misunderstanding, the first novel occasioned, Ford has found it necessary to write a preface disclaiming responsibility for the Tory opinions expressed by Tietjens in the story. That critics confounded Tietjens' arguments with Ford's private views is a tribute to the sympathy and insight Ford has brought to the creation of Tietjens. What is perhaps even a greater achievement is that he has accounted for Tietjens' adulterous wife in every particular. You understand why she despised Tietjens in one way and yet came back to him always because in another way she found all other men stupid or insipid in comparison with him.

In *No More Parades*, Ford appears to have studied both Proust and Joyce with profit; but, as always, he is master of a technique with which others have experimented. There is writing in this book to make the judicious weep—with envy. There is every indication that when Ford has completed this series his fame will have grown as did Conrad's and that he, too, will achieve the distinction of seeing a uniform, collected edition of his work. When this occurs, it may surprise Mr. Mencken and some others to discover that Mr. Ford has always written with great distinction, even in *When Blood Is Their Argument*, which he wrote, I believe, as propaganda while attached to the British Intelligence Service. It is the only book with such an aim written in those emotional days that was graced with beauty or with sense, even though Ford would now probably regret its fervor and hyperbole.

29. Unsigned review of *A Man Could Stand Up*, *The Times Literary Supplement*

14 October 1926

This review typifies the English reaction to the Tietjens novels as a whole. The books are admired—in part, but there is little sense of the larger work of which they are a part. This is partly due to the English habit of devoting only limited space to fiction.

This novel, *A Man Could Stand Up*, says Mr. Ford Madox Ford, is the third and penultimate volume of the series that began with *Some Do Not—*. We had rather hoped that the extraordinarily complicated affairs of Christopher Tietjens could have been wound up in three volumes, but it was not to be so. In fact, this particular volume advances them very little, though it actually ends the war. Mr. Ford's epistle dedicatory to his publisher might lead one to suppose that the private affairs of this strange central figure were of small importance to the main intention, which is, it appears, to give so truthful a picture of modern war as to make war seem undesirable; but it is really impossible for the author to support this thesis from his trilogy, taken as a whole.

Indeed, Tietjens, with his loathsome wife and the appallingly complicated difficulties and defamations which he quixotically lets himself in for—chaotically and even exasperatingly as he and they are presented to the reader—is one of the few truly original characters which have appeared in modern English fiction. Without Tietjens, without Sylvia, without General Sir Edward Campion, whose caddish but kindly behaviour to his godson is still an enigma, and without all the background of the Macmasters and Valentine Wannop, this narrative would lose nearly all that makes it a work of art.

Nevertheless, so far as the present volume is concerned, there is some justification for Mr. Ford's assertion that he is dealing chiefly with public affairs. The first and third parts are nothing but a whirligig of Valentine Wannop's mind with intervals of telephone conversations, a meeting with Tietjens and an impromptu celebration in Lincoln's Inn, attended by several officers, all of which occur on Armistice Day. They are not public affairs at all, and those who correctly unravel the private affairs will have good memories and clear brains. But the second part is magnificent. Tietjens, it will be remembered, had been sent to the front as second in command of a battalion after the scandals caused by Sylvia in the base camp. We find him, then, in the trenches, some time in April, 1918. The organized retreat is continuing, strengths are very low, the battalion is in a hot corner, there has been a *strafe* the night before, during which the C.O. has hurled empty bottles at the enemy and refused to obey orders to retreat, the *morale* of the men is just on the point of cracking, a big German attack is due in thirty minutes, and the C.O. will not take the M.O.'s pill. Tietjens, emerging from a low and stifling cellar, has, as usual, to take responsibility for sending the C.O. away, for taking his place, for restoring *morale*, for getting the paperwork of the battalion straight, for organizing communications, and for defying the mad McKechnie and all his foul insinuations.

Between bombardments of various kinds all this is done: he restores the confidence of the men, strained to breaking point by the thrusting of a drunken C.O., he takes over from that C.O., who makes an astonishing confession, defies McKechnie, inspects his trenches, is half buried, saves a young officer under fire, and all to meet an irate General Campion, who curses him for being there at all. The General does not matter, but the picture of a day in the trenches, seen through the mind of an unusually capable and well-educated, but not at all normally reacting man, is a brilliant piece of work, the second and third chapters particularly.

The whole war is compressed into this mental picture, into this wonderfully blended mosaic of incidents, speeches, reflections, retrospects, fears and confidences. What Mr. Ford has seized with such incisive power is that even when fighting and in deadly danger a soldier is not left alone, but is still beset by the worries and complications of an outer world. But this book will be written in vain; nobody who does not know will understand. Yet it would be hard to find a more notable instance of imagination applied to experience.

30. 'Don Quixote in the Trenches': Isabel Paterson on *Some Do Not, No More Parades* and *A Man Could Stand Up*

New York Herald Tribune Books, 17 October 1926, 5

Isabel Paterson was the first reviewer to consider the Tietjens novels as part of a single work, an important step in helping make plain what Ford's general intentions were. As a consequence of this review and of subsequent talks with Miss Paterson, Ford dedicated the final volume of the series to her.

For years Miss Paterson, the author of seven novels, conducted a weekly literary column in the New York *Herald–Tribune*. She died in 1961.

Though these three novels have been published separately, and the first two were reviewed on their publication dates, in 1924 and 1925, they are an organic unit; and the third volume cannot be appreciated at its full value without its predecessors. It resolves the psychological suspense of the situation which was elaborately and compellingly developed in the first two, a solution skillfully postponed by the author, without avoidance of the issue, by the intimation that a man at the front might find the Gordian knot cut for him at any moment.

Indeed, life is always an unfinished story; and even this third installment of the story of Christopher Tietjens makes no factitious pretence in finality. It does, however, come to a definite point, not only with the armistice, but in regard to Christopher's private concerns. It is the end of one phase and, therefore, the beginning of another. There may be a fourth volume, but for the present that is immaterial. These three have a satisfying completeness; they are an astonishing achievement in both form and substance. They rank with Galsworthy's *Forsyte Saga* as a record of the passing of a whole social order and period, the changes being shown by the actions and reactions of two or three significant individuals. Even more cleverly than Galsworthy, Ford avoids the long-winded explanations and sociological footnotes of H. G. Wells; he is dramatically specific. To paraphrase Whistler, he isn't telling you, he's showing you; and seeing is believing.

The result is that Christopher Tietjens emerges as the most vital and fully realized character in post-war fiction. One might go back further still, probably; but there is really no need of comparisons. Christopher is simply himself; and a character can be neither more nor less than that. He is entirely human and quite unlike anybody else; which is the peculiarity of all human beings and the touchstone of character creation.

This is also a genuine novel; that is to say, a manageable portion of life seen through an artist's eyes; and a rule-of-thumb test of that is the fact that knowing the plot in advance will not detract from the intelligent reader's enjoyment of the book. It may, rather, for the non-professional reader, be helpful. Mr. Ford has employed, very brilliantly, the modern structure of the novel, in which the events are linked together, not chronologically, but by their realization or recurrence in the consciousness and memory of the various principal persons involved. The period of elapsed time is unimportant; the intensity and lasting consequences of the events determine their artistic value, and their incidence, their interrelation, whether as cause and effect or as counter-checks, fixes their place in the narrative. This, to readers accustomed only to the chronological march of the old-fashioned novel, is naturally a trifle confusing. Methods of reading are also a matter of habit. But departures from habit are often a source of the keenest pleasure. In this case it is well worth making the effort to follow a new path.

For example, the first volume of the series, *Some Do Not*, ostensibly begins in a railway carriage, en route from London to Rye. Actually, it begins in Christopher Tietjens's mind, which reaches back over an agonized space of time to get to the roots of his marital unhappiness. He remembered that his wife had entrapped him into the marriage. He was not even sure that her child, though born in wedlock, was his own. He knew now that Sylvia had taken him as an escape from another man, by whom she had been seduced. And he knew she had been discreetly unfaithful to him after marriage. Then, on a caprice of hatred, she had run off to Brittany with a man named Perowne. And finally, after three months, learning that Christopher had taken no steps toward divorcing or disgracing her, Sylvia wrote calmly that she was coming back.

He took her back; at least they lived under the same roof again. His conduct was dictated by his code as a gentleman, which he obeyed literally. He held that a gentleman could not divorce his wife, no matter what she did. Women and children came first and must be protected. Consequently, a woman had a right to protect herself, especially if there was a child in question, if she had been 'let down' by another man. Christopher explained that to his wife. The fact that he suffered in this particular instance did not affect the principle.

That was what drove her mad. She was not only 'extravagantly beautiful,' but rich, of high social position and a spoiled darling generally. It was an unbearable situation to find herself shielded and logically justified by the man she had duped. Furthermore, he was the one man who was insensible to her charms. She set herself to make him regret his conscious nobility. She could and did use his child, his mother and father, his friends, to torment him. It need hardly be said she was in love with him, perversely and passionately. She wanted, of course, the one thing she had lost.

Christopher thought he had reckoned the cost of what he was doing. He had not reckoned on two things—both of which happened. He fell in love with a girl of his own kind; and the war broke out. As a gentleman he had to fight, though he regarded the war as a gigantic imbecility. That urged Sylvia to further extremes. The thought of losing Christopher forever, whether she regarded him as husband or victim, sent her after him to France. She had already, while Christopher was home on leave briefly, tried to throw him into the arms of his girl, Valentine Wannop. Partly she was moved by a fleeting impulse of pity, partly by a desire to bring Christopher down to a level with herself by an infidelity. Failing in that, she made a final effort in France to win him back, at least temporarily, make him unfaithful to Valentine. Again she failed. *Some do not.*

But Sylvia's arrival had made such trouble with Christopher's superior officers that he was sent up from the base camp to the front line. He was always in trouble of some sort. Sylvia is not an admirable person; at times she is simply devilish. But her creator makes her comprehensible; and Christopher's indubitable virtues are honestly depicted as exasperating. He made things impossible for other people by living the principles they professed. He showed them up. It was demoralizing; nobody could stand it. He lent money to any man who asked for it, and so got his best friend, Vincent McMaster, hopelessly in debt, which was very bad for McMaster. By condoning Sylvia's misbehaviour he goaded her into devising something that he couldn't condone.

Even in trifles he was a disturbing creature. He injected common sense into situations where no one asked for it; and when common sense would have been to his own advantage he ruined himself with chivalry. He gained a reputation for being 'brilliant, but unsound,' by pointing out the obvious. When his General, Lord Edward Campion, uttered one of the platitudes of 'culture' regarding a Tudor fortification —'We don't build like that nowadays'—Christopher said: 'Look for yourself; it's under your nose. Just rubble behind a facing of cut stone.' But to Campion the theory of 'the good old times' saved thinking; he didn't want to look. In the same way, Christopher uttered inappropriate truths of natural history to a soldier in the trenches who wished to regard skylarks sentimentally.

His attitude toward Valentine was equally correct, and unconsciously cruel. In a moment of desperation he had asked her outright to be his mistress. She said, 'Yes.' Then they both thought better of it and he went back to the trenches; and for almost two years he did not even send her a postcard. They had chosen their course, and he considered that final. At least for the duration of the war.

In *A Man Could Stand Up* he is shown thinking it over, under fire, in the midst of the collective and individual insanity of war. Up to his ears in mud, tripping over the dead and dying, harassed by hysterical fellow officers and dumbly dubious privates, he wasn't quite sure whether he had done right or not. It took a cataclysm to shake his convictions, but they began to give.

Christopher's mind becomes the theatre of war for the reader. The intimacy and immediacy of the effect produced is almost uncanny.

The one glimmering hope they all cherished was that when the war was over perhaps 'a man could stand up on a hill' and look around him. Instead of creeping along, ducking behind parapets to avoid German snipers. That became an obsession. It was their image of peace.

Then the war did end. Christopher went home, and after an attack of pneumonia he thought maybe he was free. Sylvia had informed him she was through with him. He was stripped, discredited, broken in health. But then, if his wife and friends were done with him, he might have his girl. He had discharged his obligation. Valentine came to him.

The final chapter is magnificently ironic. They hardly had time to speak to each other before a group of miscellaneous celebrators of the armistice, men from his regiment, burst in on them, insisted they should join in the general rejoicing. Perhaps they were allowed to escape later to some hilltop, where they could stand up. Perhaps not. One hopes, sentimentally, that they did. For this is one of those rare novels which becomes a part of the reader's personal experience.

31. L. P. Hartley on *A Man Could Stand Up*, *Saturday Review*

cxlii, 15 November 1926, 592

This review indicates the author's awareness of this novel as part of a series, but in common with other contemporary reviewers, he compared it mainly with R. H. Mottram's popular trilogy, *The Spanish Farm*.

L. P. Hartley (b. 1895) is the author of numerous novels including *The Go-Between, A Perfect Woman* and *The Hireling*.

Mr. Ford Madox Ford describes life at the Front as well as any other novelist, perhaps better. His account lacks the sense of proportion which Mr. Mottram's had; it treats the war as a kind of blind catastrophe, repugnant to thought, unrelated to any coherent or tolerable conception of life. Though Mr. Mottram's hero could look beyond his job his mind always turned, without undue distress, to the business in hand and found a refuge there. His robust imagination could eat and digest what was set before it by destiny, however nauseous the fare. Not so Christopher Tietjens. The squire of Groby, landowner and mathematician, lymphatic, resolute, sensitive, quixotic, and most delicately balanced organism, was precisely the man on whose sensibility, on whose sanity even, the war took its heaviest toll. In his married, nominally 'peace-time' life with the odious Sylvia, he had continually presented her, and the world in general, with gestures of generosity which were greeted with incredulity and contempt. And in the war, though he found some heart's ease in the affection of his men, the powers that be, particularly Lord Edward Campion, his wife's lover and David to this poor Uriah, behaved towards him with the maximum of misunderstanding and ingratitude. For saving a man's life under fire, or rather for being dirty and untidy as a result of this heroic act, he was deprived of his command. Stricken in heart and pocket (he was always lending money) he returns to England and to the illicit embraces of Valentine Wannop. Honourable as ever, he feels he must acquaint this lady's mother with his dishonourable intentions:

Her mother, to be in the van of mid-Victorian thought, had had to allow virtue to irregular unions. As long as they were high-minded. But the high-minded do not consummate irregular unions. . . . They would have been ethically at liberty to, but they didn't. They ran with the ethical hare, but hunted with the ecclesiastical hounds. . . Still, of course, she could not go back on her premises just because it was her own daughter!

Unfortunate Tietjens, coming home to find his furniture sold by his wife's orders, and then this delicate disagreeable telephone interview! There was always a fly in his ointment.

Mr. Ford has a romanticism of his own, and in addition he has taken a deep draught of Conrad's. The world loathes and mistrusts the idealist in Tietjens, and Tietjens himself is too humble-minded, too sensitive to his own and other's pain, to find relief in contemplating the nobility of his own character. His motives, like Mr. Ford's method of presenting them, are always complicated, sometimes obscure; he 'reacts' almost equally to the actual needs of the moment and to his proposed standards of conduct. What agonies of adjustment and compromise he goes through! His thoughts, like Mr. Ford's sentences, nearly always lead up to an exclamation mark; the second-rateness of sublimary things and the necessity of taking it into account is a continual surprise to him. Life comes to him not whole but in a shower of fine sparks, bewildering in their multiplicity and their power to sting and burn. The pointillism of Mr. Ford's method emphasizes perhaps unduly the discreteness of human consciousness; there is no real sequence, each moment is like a re-birth, a re-awakening to pain and perplexity. Applied to the war, it imparts the right febrile atmosphere; in ordinary life (so far as Mr. Ford portrays ordinary life) it makes confusion worse confounded. We are sorry to say good-bye to Tietjens, who, besides being a genuine creation, is a most likeable fellow. This third instalment of his history has magnificent moments, but none finer than the passage which gives the book its title.

32. 'Tietjens Once More': William McFee on *Last Post*

New York Herald Tribune Books, 15 January 1928, 3

Owing in part to the success of the earlier volumes in the series, *Last Post* was chosen as a selection for the Literary Guild in New York. It was widely reviewed as a book by itself, as in this article by William McFee.

Born in London in 1881, McFee was for some years a ship's engineer. He later settled in America and was the author of a number of novels with maritime settings. He died in 1966.

Readers will have this opinion and that about these novels by Mr. Ford. They will be enthusiastic, and they will remain mildly indifferent to a very highly-specialized glamour. But they will all fail to agree with the announcement on the jacket-flaps of *The Last Post* that the novels deal with the lives of a small group of representative individuals. That word 'representative' needs some qualification. Those individuals may be described as interesting and convincing and so on, but with the possible exception of Mark Tietjens, they are not representative English people. They are representative of Tory England only in their intense individuality, in their ability to do odd and shocking things without turning a hair.

Mark Tietjens, brother of the unhappy Christopher, holds the center of the stage in *The Last Post*. We find him, on page one, stretched out on a pallet beneath a roof of thatch in a Sussex garden on a hill where he can see four counties falling away below him. That is all he can do now—see, hear and think. Near by Christopher is living with Valentine Wannop, who is going to have a baby. They are in the antique furniture business, Christopher sending his finds to a partner in New York. Mark is being cared for by his wife, Marie Léonie, née Riotor, a big, blonde Norman woman with whom he lived for twenty years before he made her Lady Tietjens after the war.

It turns out, as one suspected while reading *A Man Could Stand Up*, that Mark Tietjens is a much more interesting man than Christopher. He is the real Tory. Christopher has the instincts of his class, but he is too self-conscious to be typical, or even quite credible, until he steps out of his class. Because a self-conscious Tory is almost a contradiction in terms, Christopher runs true to form, but Mark's form is much more true. He is the perfectly inarticulate Englishman, the man whose interests in life are limited to his horses, his women and his job. The trouble with such a character in an ordinary novel is that, as he never speaks in character, he cannot be exploited by the ordinary conventional machinery used in such a novel. He can only be caricatured. Dickens did this in *Dombey and Son* in the case of Mr. Toots to whom everything in the world was 'of no consequence.' Mr. Toots was a genuine Tory of the old school. And so Mr. Ford really loses nothing by bringing on Mark Tietjens bedridden by a stroke that has robbed him of the powers of speech. A Yorkshire Tory never had any powers of speech. What we get in *The Last Post*, through Mr. Ford's fine art, is Mark's thoughts; his thought of Marie Léonie, of Sylvia and young Mark, son of Sylvia and Christopher, who comes from Cambridge full of acquired communistic ideas and ineradicable Tory instincts; of Valentine, and of the American woman, Mrs. Millicent de Bray Pape.

Marie Léonie, indeed, is a person. She is an authentic Frenchwoman. She is convincing in her way as the French girl in *The Spanish Farm* or the other remarkable French girl in one of the best short books Arnold Bennett ever wrote—*The Pretty Lady*. The scene in which Ford describes Mark in his youth accosting Marie Léonie Riotor, of the French Ballet at Covent Garden Opera, 'outside the old Apollo,' in the Edgware Road, and offering her an establishment and two hundred and fifty a year out in St. Johns Wood Park, 'which was the place in those days in which most of his friends had establishments,' is a perfect miniature of Victorian London. It is a thumbnail sketch of the London that flourished between the Crimean War and the Boer War. In Marie Léonie we behold the soul of a real ballet girl, a *coryphée* of Covent Garden. Some of those girls became the wives of peers, so that their sons ruled England.

Throughout this book neither Mark nor Marie Léonie seems aware of the existence of what a more effete generation calls love. In this they are true to their characters. And indeed the dryest of palates will discover no musky sweetness in the story of the Tietjens and their women. Sylvia attends to that. The character of Sylvia percolates through the fiber of the book, embittering the very peasants of the countryside. She is indeed what Mark, with his old Tory's wholesome command of biblical and Elizabethan phrase, mentally calls her. To me, however, Sylvia's character is not crystal-clear at all times, which may perhaps be set down to a childhood and youth spent in the shadow of Whig traditions. Perhaps Sylvia, of all the people in the Tietjens Saga, responds least readily to the 'stream-of-consciousness' method of projecting a character.

But what are we to say of Mrs. de Bray Pape, the American woman who has rented Groby Castle and who, incited by Sylvia, cuts down Groby Great Tree? This extraordinary being believes herself to be the reincarnation of Madame de Maintenon, though her husband has had heavy losses at Miami. Mark, who has scarcely ever spoken to an American in his life, can make nothing of her. We, who have spoken to a great many Americans, can make nothing of her either. She is a grotesque, a caricature put in, one suspects, to make the characters of Mark and Léonie and Valentine seem more solid and tridimensional.

The action—if that is the right word—covers a very brief period. That is the modern way of doing the novel. James Joyce took 400,000 words to deal with 24 hours in one man's life. Mr. Ford requires only 60,000 for an afternoon. But once we are in the stream of consciousness time ceases to have much significance. This is the secret of Mr. Ford's art. He does not give us the almighty lift that came to us while reading *No More Parades*, but it is there. It may be—though this is not laid down as an iron law—that the composition of Sagas, like the reading of them, is a tiresome business. They have to be very good, these later volumes, because they inevitably invite comparison with their forebears, from which they are biologically descended.

Does this last of the Tietjens books, the fourth of the series, come off? The answer is that, so far as technique is concerned, it comes off extraordinarily well. That it is practically flawless. The question immediately arises, however, whether a flawless technique is the whole story. There is a rage among the upper crust of readers for flawless technique, for great reservoirs of memories of past events out of which pour streams of consciousness. But when all is said and done it is only what is in the author's brain that can come out in his book. The chances are that he has to invent his psychology at times just as he had to contrive and shape his plot, if he deigns to have one. And certainly the more flawless his technique the more convincing he can make that psychology. But whether mankind in general will ever cotton to these intricate wordpatterns is doubtful. They are becoming a shade too stenographic. *The Last Post* at times is terribly like a psychopathic ward in some fabulous hospital for world-war wreckage. One is desperately sorry for these people, even though they had a superb time of it in England for a hundred and fifty years. But one is glad at least to get out into the open air again.

33. L. P. Hartley, review of *Last Post*, *Saturday Review*

cxlv, 18 February 1928, 199

The conclusion of the Tietjens series was not marked in England by any real appraisal of the tetralogy as a whole. *Last Post* was either praised or rejected, and rarely was it related to the other three novels. Of the reviews it received, L. P. Hartley's was probably the most perceptive.

Mr. Ford Madox Ford is as mannered a writer as Meredith, and like Meredith he rejoices in his manner. He has mannerisms of thought as well as mannerisms of style: irony dominates the one, fragmentariness characterizes the other. Had he written in the last century he might have been caught up by the comic spirit, for like Meredith's, his attitude towards life is a robust one. Sylvia Tietjens is just such a character as Meredith would have enjoyed drawing; he would have disliked her less than Mr. Ford does, and he would have revelled in her high spirits and in her determination to make everything and everyone bend to her will. Mark Tietjens, through whose troubled mind and before whose dying eyes much of the one day's action of *Last Post* passes, always thought of Sylvia not by her name but by an elegant alias that Meredith also might have employed. To Mark, his brother,

Christopher's wife was simply 'that bitch.' As she rides up on her horse towards the hut where lies the paralysed Squire of Groby, the servant Gunning tries to bar her approach. But 'she exclaimed to Gunning, "By God, if you do not let me pass, I will cut your face in half. . . ."'

Sylvia certainly is sufficiently robust—too robust for Lord Edward Campion, much too robust for her husband. She liked to represent the much-tried Christopher, who appeared 'like a kindly group of sacks,' as 'a triply crossed being, compounded of a Lovelace, Pandarus, and a Satyr.' She had been a thorn in the flesh—

largely because he had seemed to her never to be inclined to take his own part. If you live with a person who suffers from being put upon a good deal, and if that person will not assert his own rights, you are apt to believe that your standards as gentleman and Christian are below his and the feeling is lastingly disagreeable.

Mr. Ford ranges himself on the side of Christopher and Christopher was a quietist who, though not consciously a defeatist, was always worsted in his encounter with life. His creator is an ironist, a child of the present age, who looks askance on the thrusting and the ambitious and the successful, seeing such persons as so many Sylvias. His is therefore not an essential robustness; it expresses itself mainly in the vitality of his writing and in his readiness to fit into his scheme whatever phenomena of existence present themselves to his view; for he is not at all world-weary, nor does his conviction of the hard lot of the righteous take away his appetite for the multifarious experiences of life that, taken together, contribute to making that lot a hard one. On the contrary, all is fish that comes to his net: he greets the seen with a cheer. He is a romantic, of course, and that helps him. His world, that extraordinary world, so unreal when seen in relation to everyday existence, within the high boundary walls of his art and his imagination, has its own validity and moves in harmony with its own laws.

Of all the Tietjens novels *Last Post* is surely the greatest *tour-de-force*; its action takes place in a day, yet seems timeless; the chief actors assemble as though for the brief appearance of a curtain-call, yet each brings the sense of a full lifetime with him. It moves with the *tempi* of life, sometimes tediously slow, sometimes at break-neck speed. It is full of complicated issues, of pure and base motives, of noble endeavours and unhappy outcomes, all bewilderingly mixed—all viewed partially and fleetingly from a hundred angles. It has the richness and the confusion and the profusion of life. Some people may say that although

Mr. Ford's work possesses many of the ingredients and qualities of life the mixture he makes of them is something very different from life; wilful, feverish, self-conscious, inconsequent, and above all artificial. There certainly are moments when he seems exclusively preoccupied with art and with himself as artist. But in the novels of to-day there is so much sterility masquerading as simplicity, so much specialization aping profundity, so much dullness styling itself sincerity, so much coldness calling itself restraint, that we are ready to forgive Mr. Ford all his faults of rhetoric and exaggeration and excess.

34. 'Recent tendencies in English fiction': H. C. Harwood on *Last Post* and other novels of the time

Quarterly Review, cclii, April 1929, 327

Until the 1960s remarkably few surveys of contemporary English fiction contained more than the slightest reference to Ford and his work. This early article, a portion of which is reprinted below, was almost alone in considering the achievement of *Parade's End* as a whole.

To Mr Ford it may come as a shock to be reminded that he is an English novelist, for both his blood and his domiciles may seem to preserve him against so horrid accusations. We have treated him badly. We have failed to see that he was a genius, that his influence upon the English imagination will outlast bronze and marble and the pompous monuments of princes. We have thought of him as just a clever literary gent. Our excuse must be that for so long he was that, and nothing more. The creator of Tietjens came as a surprise. The name of Ford, or as he then was called, of Hueffer, was associated with a dabbling in the decomposition of Stevensonian romance, in particular with that form of decomposition called Conradism, and with brief, acute historical studies too good to be praised. And then, then—neat sparrow turned to albatross or eagle—this competent author suddenly begins to compose works of a passion, an intensity, rarely equalled in our tongue. Novels descriptive of the war are almost weekly acclaimed as immortal. I doubt it. I doubt whether the Great War that last happened will eventually produce more works of genius than the last Great War but One, which, if you happen to remember it at all, you will remember as being badly snubbed by Jane Austen. But Tietjens will live. And Tietjens will live, not because he was a sort of soldier, but because his personality allowed Mr Ford to express an attitude, and excited him to describe a man. The tetralogy is full of errors, in chronology, of character and in taste. Nor should it have been a tetralogy at all. But if it does not outlive bronze and marble and the pompous monuments of princes, the fault will lie in the stern determination of civilised people to commit suicide.

MISCELLANEOUS CONTROVERSIES

35. 'Mr. Madox Hueffer's Inaccuracies': W. M. Rossetti on *Ancient Lights*

Letter to the editor of *Outlook*, xxvii, 22 April 1911, 507–8

Throughout his lifetime, as has already been noted (pp. 9–10) Ford's inaccuracies as a writer of reminiscence angered many of his readers. Sometimes errors in fact were noticed by reviewers; often they were cited in public letters to the editor. One of the more solemn of these was written by Ford's uncle by marriage, W. M. Rossetti (1829–1919), the brother of Dante Gabriel and Christina Rossetti. To this catalogue of mistakes, which naturally had a damaging effect on Ford's reputation for reliability, Ford himself replied in part as follows:

> The whole tenor of my book should have gone to prove that Madox Brown delighted to relate picturesque anecdotes. He did not intend that they should be taken as serious contributions to history. Neither do I . . . I wished, as a filial duty, as an expiation, to make Pre-Raphaelites appear like men . . . I remain, in short, absolutely impenitent, and with as affectionate a regard as ever for my so voluntary and so amiable critic.

Rossetti's amiability was revealed in his own rejoinder in which he pointed out an additional five errors.

Sir,—I lately saw in the *Outlook* for April 8 a review of Mr. Ford M. Hueffer's book, *Ancient Lights and Certain New Reflections*, and I observe that you are sceptical as to an anecdote recited by Mr. Hueffer on the authority (as he states) of Madox Brown. The anecdote purports that, when George Meredith was housed in Cheyne Walk along with Swinburne, my brother Dante Gabriel, and myself, some one of us three, conceiving Meredith to be miserably poor, substituted a new pair of boots for an old and dilapidated one which he had in wear—an act which the novelist justly resented. I hereby affirm that there is not an atom of truth in that anecdote: I did not substitute any such pair of boots, and I feel certain that neither Swinburne nor my brother did so. Meredith in those days, 1862 or 1863, was at least as well-dressed a man as any of the other three. It may be that his income was scanty, but nothing particularly bearing upon that point came under our observation.

With your permission I should like to refer to some other statements in the book of Mr. Hueffer—who is a connection of mine, and against whom I entertain no sort of ill-will. He himself says, in his dedication, that the book 'is full of inaccuracies as to facts,' and I agree with him. He asks the dedicatees, his daughters, to 'go through this book carefully, noting the errors.' This is a task for which the young ladies are perhaps not qualified: but I am as regards some of the instances, and I am willing to replace the Misses Hueffer.

Page 6.—Mr. Hueffer refers to certain statements which were at one time, say 1865, made to the disadvantage of my brother. He says that I took some part in the correspondence, along with Burne-Jones, Swinburne, Marshall (which may mean either John Marshall or Peter Paul Marshall), and C. A. Howell. Now, to the best of my recollection, I knew nothing of that matter at the time. It was Mr. Hueffer himself who, coming into possession of certain letters which had belonged to Brown up to his death in 1893, was so good as to hand them over to my custody.

Page 9.—'Charles Dickens called loudly for the imprisonment of Millais and other Pre-Raphaelites, including my grandfather' (Brown). Dickens never did this. In the early days of Pre-Raphaelitism, 1850, he, or someone contributing to his magazine, wrote in very abusive and absurd terms about some of the Pre-Raphaelite pictures. Mr. Hueffer repeats his statement on p. 214.

Page 24.—Some commercial patrons of art are named: Peter Millar of Liverpool, and Plint of Birmingham. Instead of Peter Miller (not Millar) his father, John Miller, should have been named. Plint belonged to Leeds not Birmingham.

Page 35.—'The Rossettis always circled round Bloomsbury.' Only two Rossettis, my mother and Christina, ever lived in the Bloomsbury district, and they not until 1876. My brother's residences from 1852 to his death were by Blackfriars Bridge and in Chelsea. Christina did not die 'in Woburn Square,' but in Torrington Square. I could give other details disproving the Bloomsbury allegation, but they are not wanted. On p. 64 comes a reference to 'the gloomy and surely glamorous houses that in Bloomsbury the Rossettis successively inhabited.'

Page 50.—'Oliver Madox Brown died in 1875.' No, 1874.

Page 54.—Various inaccuracies as to dates. Rossetti did not print 'his first poem when he was perhaps ten' (on p. 132 it comes to be 'seven or eight'), but when he was fifteen or else fourteen. 'His first published volume of original poetry' did not appear in 'the late seventies,' but in 1870. Christina's *Goblin Market* volume was not 'published in the late sixties,' but in 1862.

Page 66.—It is a mistake to say that Christina, having become engaged to James Collinson when he was a member of the English Church, persisted in the engagement when he became a Roman Catholic. In point of fact, she then withdrew from the engagement. Afterwards she renewed it when he reverted to the English Church; and when he finally recurred to Catholicism she again broke off the engagement.

Page 117.—An account of Madox Brown's death, October 6, 1893, is given as follows:

Just before his death the Town Council of Manchester, with the Lord Mayor at its head, sitting in private, put forward a resolution that his frescoes in the town hall should be whitewashed out, and their places taken by advertisements of the wares of the Aldermen and the Councillors. Thus perished Ford Madox Brown; for this resolution, which was forwarded to him, gave him his fatal attack of apoplexy.

This statement astonishes me: on what foundation is it based? I was living next door but one to Brown, and I saw a great deal of him in the last few days of his life, and never heard anything resembling this account. On the morning of October 3 he seemed to be much in his usual health, which was far from good. On the night of the 3rd, or morning of the 4th, he was struck with apoplexy. He never recovered consciousness, and died in the afternoon of the 6th. I am aware that at one time there had been a collision between Brown and some members of the Manchester Town Council. This was towards 1892 (possibly 1891), when Brown had painted all but one of his pictures (not strictly frescoes). The Council did not like the latest-executed work, and they tried to impose some restriction as to the one which remained to be painted. But Brown persevered, painted his wall-picture, and might, for the brief residue of his life, be regarded as having carried his point maugre the council. The mere idea of whitewashing all his works seems so extravagantly monstrous, that I must be excused if I fail to accept the assertion of Mr. Hueffer. If the town council did pass that resolution in the autumn of 1893, how comes it that they have not acted upon it? The resolution would hardly have been sent to Brown unless it had been actually passed.

Page 132.—Swinburne and Morris 'pushed this great figure [Rossetti] into the exaggerated and loose mediævalism that distinguished his latest period.' His latest period extended up to 1882, and for ten years or more preceding there was hardly any mediævalism in his paintings, to which the context mainly refers. The principal phase of his mediævalism was towards 1855 to 1863; whether Swinburne had much to do with it may be open to question.

Page 135.—'At one period Rossetti's income ran well into five figures'—i.e. it exceeded an annual £10,000. He would have been only too glad to find this true: but in fact he never made so much as £4,000 in a year.

Page 147.—'O'Connell requested Madox Brown, Rossetti, and Holman Hunt to stand for Irish constituencies.' The name O'Connell, when used in this absolute way, can only mean Daniel O'Connell, the Liberator, who died in 1847; but the incident here notified (I will make no suggestion as to its authenticity) appears to be of some such date as 1875.

Page 159.—Cruikshank 'the immortaliser of Pickwick.' He had nothing to do with Pickwick. The physiognomy of that personage was invented by Seymour, and taken up by Hablot Browne.

Page 160.—'Douglas Hannay, a midshipman.' James Hannay is meant; whether James Hannay really had anything to do with Tristram Madox (a cousin of Madox Brown) is not known to me.

Page 178.—Rossetti, when about to publish his poems of 1870, 'was not ashamed to corrupt the Press'—and more to like effect. I regard this as hugely overstated: but it is a fact that my brother took some pains to ensure that editors of reviews should admit critiques of his volume by well-affected reviewers, and I shall therefore say no more on the point.

Page 181.—Madox Brown gave Mr. Hall Caine 'an introduction to Dante Gabriel Rossetti.' He did nothing of the sort. Mr. Caine introduced himself to Rossetti by sending him a printed lecture which he had delivered on the poems of the latter. It was Rossetti who at a later date introduced Caine to Brown.

Page 182.—To call Rossetti 'a man of as many irregularities as one man could reasonably desire in one earthly existence' is really nonsense; I speak with knowledge, but can only leave the readers to judge between Mr. Hueffer's statement and mine. At the close of this paragraph Flaubert's *Madame Bovary* is mentioned: it ought to be *Salammbô*.

Page 206.—'Madox Brown went upstairs to bed, and died in his sleep.' This statement gives a very inaccurate idea of the facts. He had gone to bed on the night of October 3: then, being struck with apoplexy, he lingered on unconscious for two days and a half.

Page 225.—Here comes an anecdote about my having accidentally made a clatter with fire-irons in Brown's studio. He, 'jumping to his feet, would shout, "God damn and blast you, William, can't you be more careful?"' I remember this petty circumstance, and I assert in the most positive terms that Brown did not use any such violent or profane language. He exhibited a momentary irritation, naturally enough, but he said nothing to which any exception could be taken on any ground. I knew Brown with great intimacy from 1848 up to his death, becoming his son-in-law in 1874, and I do not believe that I ever once heard him use any such expression as 'God damn and blast.' He could on occasion indulge in some rather decided expletives: but all in a moderate measure and with comparative temperance—quite different (according to my ample experience) from what Mr. Hueffer has represented in this instance and in some others. Brown's general demeanour was quiet and decorous in an eminent degree, and I should truly regret if anything of a contrary kind, written by Mr. Hueffer in what may be called a picturesque spirit, should produce a different impression on his readers, or on future writings concerning Brown's personality.—I am, Sir, yours, &c.,

WM. M. ROSSETTI

3 St. Edmund's Terrace, N.W.,
    April 19.

36. 'Mr. Hueffer and his Cellar *Garnis*': J. K. Prothero on *Zeppelin Nights*

New Witness, vii, 6 January 1916, 293

The article reprinted below is probably the most vicious personal attack ever made in print against Ford. Its consequences are discussed in No. 37 (pp. 125–7).

Mr. Ford Madox Hueffer has written a series of stories under the title of *Zeppelin Nights*; and Miss Violet Hunt has collaborated with him. There are flashes of Miss Hunt's genius dispersed throughout the volume, and one is sensible that she has made a heroic attempt to leaven the mass of Mr. Hueffer's dull offensiveness. But the fugitive gleams of patriotism supplied by the lady are not sufficient to redeem the ponderous panic of the co-author. It is generally supposed that Mr. Hueffer is not exactly of pure European extraction, and this book certainly tends to confirm such impression. The following lines, descriptive of London cowering in the throes of Zeppelinitis, seem to indicate that the writer's fear of bodily hurt is more acute than one associates with men of our blood:—

> All day in London we moved under a curse, towards evening we grew sick with anticipation of the dusk which must fall in due course, and we trembled, for there was no longer the prelude to the cheerful access of lighting to which we were accustomed . . . Lips were compressed, eyes were turned inwards or anxiously searched other eyes whose owners might perhaps be in receipt of more recent intelligence. To know! To know! To know more! . . Over us in the daytime the spectre, brooding, her proportions shrunken to the sum of a man's waking thoughts, waited for the night to come to closer grips and to accentuate her monstrous spell; but she was there, and men drew every breath as if it were their last free suspiration, anxious, obsessed, paralysed, mentally incapable even of the civil word that turneth away wrath.

After this we are not surprised to gather that Mr. Hueffer sought refuge in a cellar *garnis*—presumably one of the many which he assures his readers during the summer were advertised, and it was apparently while he inhabited this delightful shelter, that he composed—with some assistance from Miss Hunt—a series of sketches dealing with the notable events of the world from the year 490 B.C. down to the coronation of King George V. People of an inferior type of mind less gifted with soaring imagination might pause before reviewing the world's history under the influence of abject terrors in a cellar *garnis*. The author, however, is quite content to wallow in horrors, and reads his own fear into the minds of the nation with whom he resides.

Had Mr. Hueffer confined himself to the description of his own sensations under the influence of 'the German spectre which rode us all those summer months, terrifying some of us beyond mental endurance,' the document would have been an interesting one and have preserved certain valuable psychological truths. When, however, from the safety of his cellar *garnis* he describes London as 'profoundly wretched and uneasy, filled with a wretchedness that was worse than pain,' he is merely writing for German consumption. Had the inhabitant of the cellar *garnis* ventured from his refuge into the London streets at such time as Zeppelins were anticipated, or had indeed arrived, he would have found an amazing absence of terror, an almost bewildering jocularity. Far from hiding in cellars—*garnis* or otherwise—the people of London rushed into the streets at the first hint of the approach of what the author calls 'the German Night Hag.' I have myself heard odds freely offered and taken as to whether the anti-aircraft guns would hit the Zep. within the first six shots, and the men and women who watched the progress of the death-ship through the heavens betrayed none of that paralysis, physical and mental, suggested by the author of *Zeppelin Nights*. Mr. Hueffer apparently is unable at the present time correctly to apprehend any of the human emotions save through a thick mist of blinding fear. This fear leaks out in the episode of the 'House of the Water Clock,' which describes how the news was brought of the victory of Marathon, and is continued through the accounts of the writing of the Gospel of St. Mark and the Martyrdom of Joan of Arc.

The German policy of frightfulness can claim at least one convert to the belief of its cardinal dogma. Mr. Hueffer is helpless before the 'Night Hag', and paints the English people in a condition of such paralysis, such utter spiritual and moral decadence, that they can imagine nothing more frightful than death; he conceives them as grovelling face downwards in their cellars, anxious only to escape the perils of what *he* regards as the apotheosis of terror—what the Cockney describes as 'one of them there gas-bags of the Kaiser.'

It is, I believe, true that in certain parts of London, notably in the foreign quarters of Whitechapel—and by 'foreign' I mean those parts which are inhabited by non-Europeans—the fear of the 'German Night Hag' has created something of a panic; but between these aliens on the one side and the people who seek refuge in cellars *garnis* on the other, are the people of London, who not only refrain from cowering by day and palpitating by night, but with their own particular sense of humour, have turned the terror that walks in darkness as devised by Berlin and ratified by Mr. Hueffer into a joke, and can find something humorous to say even when the 'Night Hag' succeeds in murdering a few women and children.

The end of the book, however, shows us Serapion Hunter, the teller of these tales—devised, according to Mr. Hueffer, to find 'mental rest . . . just as the inhabitants of that old Italian city of Florence found refuge in the dreary institution of the Decameron,' grown tired of living in a cellar *garnis*; and having decided that death is by no means the most terrible thing in life, shaking off his paralysis forthwith enlists—possibly under the influence of Miss Hunt. This is quite obviously the European view of things. The view, which is quite as clearly un-European, insists that the horror of the 'Night Hag' 'slowly upspreads from its nodus on the panting human breast where she squats and crouches . . . until moon and stars and all clarity of thought and vision are blotted out under the loathsome burden. . . . We lay helpless and could only long in our bitter abjection, for the dispelling crow of the cock, for the gay noises of dawn.'

For this condition which Mr. Hueffer aptly describes as 'abjection,' there is only one cure.

37. Correspondence concerning Prothero's review of *Zeppelin Nights*

New Witness, vii, 13 January 1916, 321; vii, 20 January 1916, 352; vii, 27 January 1916, 385; vii, 3 February 1916, 416; vii, 10 February 1916, 449; letter by H. G. Wells printed in Maisie Ward, *Gilbert Keith Chesterton*, London, 1944, 350–2

This extraordinary attack on an author who at the time was serving as a lieutenant in the Welch Regiment brought several rejoinders, the first from the playwright, J. M. Barrie, who wrote in part:

Mr. Hueffer has committed the heinous offence of producing, with the assistance of Miss Violet Hunt . . . one of the stupidest and dreariest pot-boilers ever published in London . . . That is no reason why you should go out of your way to insult Mr. Hueffer by calling him a Jew and a coward. Mr. Hueffer is not a Jew, but a Catholic; and as for being a coward, he has succeeded in obtaining, at the rather asthmatic age of forty-five or so, a commission in the Army . . . The reviewer in question . . . probably does not know the real case against Lieutenant Hueffer, which is that he considers Ezra Pound a good poet.

To this letter, the reviewer replied as follows:

Sir,—Your correspondent J. M. may be interested to know that I was aware of Mr. Ford Madox Hueffer's curious poetical preferences; I was also aware that he had written a novel centering round a particularly brutal type of sensualist which he published under the title of *A Good Soldier*! I cannot, however, lay the claim to the prescience of your correspondent who, although 'not personally acquainted with Mr. Hueffer,' has had it revealed unto him that the gentleman is asthmatic, forty-five, and, in spite of these drawbacks, has succeeded in obtaining a commission in the Army. These facts hardly being of European importance I am content to be labelled 'ignorant' concerning them, as I am of the 'fact' that because a man adopts the Catholic religion he ceases to be a Jew. One might as reasonably say that if a black-a-moor adopts Calvanism he immediately turns white.—Yours, &c.,

This extraordinary statement elicited another letter, this time from Ford's old friend, E. S. P. Haynes:

Sir,—I do not feel it my duty as a personal friend of Mr. Hueffer to intervene in this controversy. He is absent on military service, and no doubt enjoys a controversy which deliciously recalls some of the 'Epistolae Obscurorum Vivorum.' Mr. Hueffer's age can be verified from *Who's Who*. He is not asthmatic.

But as an occasional contributor to the literary columns of the *New Witness* I claim to record my conviction that *The Good Soldier* is one of the ten greatest novels so far published in the twentieth century, and that J. K. Prothero's astonishing remark about it represents an individual opinion which every reader of the novel with whom I am acquainted would regard as at best eccentric.

Unrepentant, J. K. Prothero replied as follows:

Sir,—The statements concerning Mr. Hueffer's age and bodily condition were not made by me, but by your correspondent, J. M. I am ignorant and indifferent as to whether Mr. Hueffer is or is not asthmatical and quite content to remain so. I note Mr. Haynes' conviction that *The Good Soldier* 'is one of the ten greatest novels so far published in the twentieth century;' but in regard to his statement that my 'astonishing remark'—which it may be remembered concerned the moral character of the hero and not the literary merits of the book—represents 'an individual' and 'at best eccentric opinion,' I should like to point out that the opinion is shared by at least one literary critic of considerable distinction. In the *New Witness* of June 3, 1915, Mr. Thomas Seccombe places it on record that 'the usurpation of such a title by Mr. Hueffer's hero is nothing short of profanation.'

This letter was followed by a new attack in the form of a letter from 'M.F.':

Mr. Hueffer, personally, has been wittily dismissed with the sentence that he considers Ezra Pound a good poet. The title of his book [*The Good Soldier*] cannot be so lightly condoned. Charming women, to whose refined minds the exploits of a vigorous stallion have no interest, are buying the book, in the belief . . . that it is a grateful tribute, from the pen of an able and delightful writer, to their men. Men whom they have born and trained to be 'Good Soldiers' in the truest and finest sense of the word. 'The Perfect Stallion' would have been an appropriate title for a book which none of Mr. Hueffer's admirers can have read without wondering what necessity he saw, in this hour when men have so gloriously fought for and entered into their Kingdom, to portray them in such a despicable light.

With this astonishingly perverse comment, the editor closed the correspondence, but in the meantime, H. G. Wells wrote the following letter to G. K. Chesterton:

This business of the Hueffer book in the *New Witness* makes me sick. Some disgusting little greaser named —— [J. K. Prothero] has been allowed to insult old F. M. H. in a series of letters which make me ashamed of my species. Hueffer has many faults no doubt, but first he's poor, secondly he's notoriously unhappy and in a most miserable position, thirdly he's a better writer than any of your little crowd and fourthly, instead of pleading his age and his fat and taking refuge from service in a greasy obesity as your brother has done, he is serving his country. His book [*The Good Soldier*] is a great book —— ['M. F.'] just lies about it—I guess he's a dirty-minded priest or some such unclean thing—when he says it is a story of a stallion and so forth. The whole outbreak is so envious, so base, so cat-in-the-gutter-spitting-at-the-passer-by, that I will never let the *New Witness* into the house again.

Chesterton wrote a conciliatory letter to Wells and peace was made between them. J. K. Prothero turned out to be Ada Elizabeth Jones who later married Cecil Chesterton, the actual editor of the *New Witness*.

38. 'A Footnote to Hueffer' and 'Another Criticism': H. G. Wells and Ethel Colburn Mayne on *Thus to Revisit*

Letters to the editor of the *English Review*, xxxi, August 1920, 178–9

Thus to Revisit, a book combining criticism with reminiscence, was published serially in the United States and England and elicited these letters from two of the subjects mentioned. Both writers knew Ford well, especially during the time of the founding of the *English Review*. Wells (1866–1946) had originally planned to be co-founder of the magazine; Miss Mayne (d. 1941) was one of its contributors.

Sir,—I have long had an uneasy feeling about my old neighbour in Kent, Mr. Ford Madox Hueffer. I knew that he was capable of imaginative reminiscences, and that in a small way he had been busy with my name. Fantastic biographical details have drifted round to me. I have heard how Mr. Hueffer gainsaid and withstood me about things I never did and answered neatly things I never said. He is now breaking into print with this stuff. It is a great pity. Mr. Hueffer has written some delightful romances, and he is a very great poet. Why does he make capital of the friendliness and hospitalities of the past to tell stupid and belittling stories of another man who is, by his own showing, a very inferior and insignificant person? This childish falsehood about my lecturing him, or anyone, on how to write a novel, is particularly incredible. 'How to do it' was the one topic upon which I never offered a contribution to my Kentish and Sussex neighbours. Only once did I lecture this drawling, blonde young man, as he was then, upon any literary matter. At our first meeting, he informed me that he had persuaded Mr. Joseph Conrad to collaborate with him. I tried to convey to him, as considerately as possible, what a very peculiar and untouchable thing was the Conrad prose fabric, and what a very mischievous enterprise he contemplated. That dead, witless book, *The Inheritors*, justifies my warnings. That and a second book, of which I forget the title—it was an entirely stagnant 'adventure' story, festering with fine language —were an abominable waste of Conrad's time and energy. For the rest, my conversations upon things literary with Mr. Hueffer were defensive. These endless chatterings about 'how it is done,' about the New Form of the Novel, about who was 'greater' than who, about the possibilities of forming a 'Group' or starting a 'Movement' are things to be avoided at any cost. There is a subtle mischief in this fussing about literary comment, this preoccupation with phrases and artificial balances in composition and the details of work, these campaigns to establish standard catch-words in criticism and to manipulate reputations, which affects nearly everyone who indulges in these practices. Literature is not jewellery, it has quite other aims than perfection, and the more one thinks of 'how it is done' the less one gets it done. These critical indulgences lead along a fatal path, away from every natural interest towards a preposterous emptiness of technical effort, a monstrous egotism of artistry, of which the later work of Henry James is the monumental warning. 'It,' the subject, the thing or the thought, has long since disappeared in these amazing works; nothing remains but the way it has been 'manipulated.' No beauty is left, no discovery. Here are no healing waters of thought, no fair gardens of invention, no distant prospects. The votary is invited to bathe in the pure sweat of the writer and rejoice. Sedulously I kept myself out of that talk—and it is no good for Mr. Hueffer to pretend that I ever came in.—Yours very sincerely,

H. G. WELLS

Dear Sir,—In Mr. Ford Madox Hueffer's very flattering reference to me in your July number, there is one passage which my sense of humour tells me is intended as the purest friendly 'chaff,' but which others might interpret seriously; and indeed a cutting received the other day is a proof that this has happened. I hardly supposed that it *could*, though I thought it might; if I had really anticipated such a thing I should have asked you sooner, as I ask you now, to let me say in your columns that all the reference in Mr. Hueffer's article to my 'influence' on the *Yellow Book* is simply *persiflage*. Mr. Hueffer knows as well as I know that I was the lowest of the angels. I contributed only twice to the Y.B. (to my sorrow), and I contributed under a very stupid *nom de guerre*—that of 'Frances F. Huntley.' (My reasons for that folly were as uninteresting as the pseudonym itself.) Certainly it *is* my greatest pride that Mr. Henry Harland was my first editor; that he 'discovered' me, as people say; but that did not make me anything but the humblest of his group of writers; for I was very young and wholly inexperienced —'off my head,' indeed, with pride and gratitude at being so included, but not so utterly besotted that I even for a moment imagined that anything I thought or said or did could influence him—as most certainly it never did. And I must say for myself that to attempt it never once entered my mind.

These sallies, which writers can enjoy among themselves, are sometimes ill-advised in print. I feel that this is an instance when a harmless joke might well annoy those to whom Mr. Harland's memory is dearer even than it is to me. Therefore I shall be very grateful to you if you will let me say these few words in the *English Review* for August. —Yours faithfully,

ETHEL COLBURN MAYNE

JOSEPH CONRAD: A PERSONAL REMEMBRANCE

39. Mrs. Joseph Conrad, letter to the editor of *The Times Literary Supplement*

4 December 1924, 826

If the 'Prothero affair' was limited to the *New Witness*, the reception of Ford's memorial volume to Joseph Conrad created widespread bad feeling against Ford. Reviews written by persons neither personally nor professionally connected with Conrad were non-committal or favourable, but when friends and associates began to write about the book, trouble began. Mrs Conrad in the role of outraged widow initiated a worldwide scandal: evidently having read the opinion of *The Times Literary Supplement* reviewer that Ford's book provided 'as clear and authentic a picture as we may hope to receive', she determined to set the record straight from her own point of view. The story of Mrs Conrad's long antipathy towards Ford and his first wife is complex (see *The Life and Work of Ford Madox Ford*, pp. 39–44, 83, 166–7), but there is no doubt that the letter printed below brought discredit upon Ford.

Sir,

Will you please allow me to correct a few of the most fantastic statements regarding my husband made in Ford Madox Hueffer's book, which was reviewed in your columns a few weeks ago!

If Mr. Hueffer intends a personal remembrance as a tribute to the dead friend with whom he claims to have had such close acquaintance, why endeavour on every page to show the vast difference between himself and his friend, and always to the detriment of that friend: his inferiority in intellect, character and ability? To those who knew Joseph Conrad personally these statements would have their real value, and to those who had also the privilege of even a slight acquaintance with Mr. Hueffer these few lines would be quite unnecessary. I deny most emphatically that Joseph Conrad ever poached on Mr. Hueffer's vast stock of plots and material in the fabrication of any of his (Joseph Conrad's) stories. A concrete plot, or detailed statement of fact, no matter now interesting, would never have been the least use to my husband. His books were, to my certain knowledge, based on a chance phrase, discovered in some old book of memoirs, or some few sentences culled from a book of history or travel. These few significant words were then nursed in that master-mind, full of personal experiences and rich with imagination, to emerge after a period of infinite care and real mental suffering as a finished masterpiece. In the matter of the *Arrow of Gold*, he often laughingly accused me of being the cause of the book. I came upon him one morning in despair as he had nothing in his mind on which to write. I suggested that he should make use of an episode he had once told me of, referring to his life before we were married. My suggestion was adopted and that book was the direct result.

During the years that Mr. Hueffer was most intimate with Joseph Conrad—between 1898–1909—Ford Madox Hueffer never spent more than three consecutive weeks under our roof, and when we returned the visit we always, with few exceptions, had rooms in a cottage close at hand. After 1909 the meetings between the two were very rare and not once of my husband's seeking. The author of *A Personal Remembrance* claims to have been Joseph Conrad's literary adviser, also his literary godfather! That claim is, like nearly everything else in that detestable book, quite untrue. I have heard my husband say more than once that he found Mr. Hueffer a mental stimulus, but that was in the early days—days before ever Ford Madox Hueffer himself became aware of the great dignity he claims—that of being the greatest English stylist.

    Yours sincerely,

JESSIE CONRAD

40. 'Romantic Biography': Edward Garnett, *Nation & Athenaeum*

xxxvi, 6 December 1924, 366, 368

One of the first reviews of *Joseph Conrad* was written by Edward Garnett (1868–1937), the man who first introduced Conrad to Ford. Publisher's reader and critic, Garnett edited volumes of his correspondence with Conrad and Galsworthy.

In his preface, Mr. F. M. Ford (Ford Madox Hueffer) declares: 'This then is a novel, not a monograph; a portrait, not a compilation. It is conducted exactly along the lines laid down by us both for the novel which is biography, and for the biography which is a novel.'

'Us,' if we are to take Mr. Ford's word for it, were Joseph Conrad and himself. But one suspects that the author's modesty has here misled him, and that he should take the credit of this concept of his biographical hybrid to himself. For Conrad, who had a passion for memoirs, personal and historical, and who searched them with a hawk-eye for hard facts and precise details, was the last man to give *carte blanche* to a biographical romanticist. To accept a fiction-biography would be to invite the three-card trick from every ingenious manipulator. In the magic name of 'impressionism' a man can magnify, distort, or suppress facts and aspects to his own glorification, he can dye everything with his own hues and belittle others, and then, on being brought to book, he can turn round reprovingly and protest, 'But this is a work of art!' This is precisely what Mr. Ford does claim for his *Personal Remembrance*, while he adds (one hopes with a sense of humour): 'It was that that Joseph Conrad asked for: the task has been accomplished with the most pious scrupulosity.' In the letter facsimiled in the present volume, Conrad remarks to Mr. Ford, 'You have a perfect right to say that you are "rather unchangeable." Unlike the Serpent (which is Wise) you will die in your original skin.' And when one surveys the lengthy list of Mr. Ford's literary works—fiction, poetry, and reminiscences—one perceives that the more he changes the more he is the same thing. He is a born Romanticist, born to write and propagate fictions, and it is significant that of the two novels in which he and Conrad collaborated one was called *Romance*, and the other was sub-titled 'An Extravagant Tale.'

I do not wish to be too exacting in respect to *A Personal Remembrance*, which, in its peculiar way, is quite a clever production, and does, with all its exaggerations and distortions of facts, contain many interesting picturesque impressions of Conrad as he 'revealed himself' to his collaborator. As I was a close friend of Conrad before, during, and after the period Mr. Ford writes of, as I introduced the two men to one another, had known Mr. Ford as a lad of eighteen, had sponsored his early works, was familiar with the 'atmosphere,' and am acquainted with certain circumstances not touched upon in *A Personal Remembrance*, I can speak by the card. To dwell on the favourable side, I can testify that Mr. Ford conveys excellently the atmosphere of The Pent, and Conrad's love for Kent and England, and that he hits off in a life-like way many of Conrad's personal ways and mannerisms. As a lively charcoal sketch of Conrad, approaching caricature but full of gusto, and as an impressionistic narrative of Mr. Ford's literary relationship with the great writer whose whole career was an adventurous drama, *A Personal Remembrance* has undeniable interest. Unfortunately, the simple truth is often not 'picturesque' enough for Mr. Ford's taste, and for the life of him he cannot help embellishing his 'portrait' with fantastic inventions. In his love of sensational colouring he cannot help distorting and exaggerating as he goes along, since 'facts' are simply the colours on his painter's palette to be mixed to get his forced effects and vibrating impressions. The story, for example, about Conrad's 'setting out from Stanford-le-Hope . . . to persuade an unknown writer of the pen, the finest stylist in England (viz., Mr. Ford), to surrender his liberty to a sailing partnership. . . . Conrad had expected to hear a reading by the finest stylist in England of a work far-flung in popularity as *Treasure Island*, but as "written" as *Salammbô*' this is merely moonshine. Mr. Ford's account of the collaborators' work over *The Inheritors* cannot be reconciled with a contemporary letter from Conrad in this reviewer's possession. It blows it into the air. Apocryphal also is the story that 'on that first night Conrad confessed to the writer that previous to suggesting a collaboration he had consulted a number of men of letters as to its advisability. He said that he had put before them his difficulties with the language, the slowness with which he wrote, and the increased fluency he might acquire in the process of going minutely into words with an acknowledged master of English.' Conrad had then written *Almayer's Folly*, and three of his finest books, *An Outcast of the Islands*, *The Nigger of the Narcissus*, and *Tales of Unrest*. He had attained to a complete mastery of the English tongue; he had composed *An Outpost of Progress*, ten thousand words, in five days, and *The Nigger of the Narcissus* in three months. Whereas Mr. Ford, in 1898, was the author of three or four works not at all remarkable in point of style, and he was then struggling along with little or no encouragement from anybody. Mr. Ford's fondness for blending himself and Conrad together as a species of literary Siamese twins is no doubt responsible for his statement that at the time when he and Conrad were collaborating in *Romance*, 'we were both extremely unaccepted writers.' Conrad's work had then been repeatedly eulogized by the leading reviewers, and he had been classed with Kipling by various critics, and had been serialized by Henley in the *New Review*; but his books in those early years had only attained a sale of about 2,000–3,000 copies.

It is no pleasure to me to set Mr. Ford right as to his more brilliant flights of fancy, but lest they be taken seriously and be propagated by others, I will annotate some of his characteristic improvizations. (1) The statement that 'Conrad entered the French Navy, remained there an indefinite time, leaving with the rank of Lieutenant de Torpilleurs de la Marine Militaire,' is, I believe, pure imagination. He simply served on French merchant ships, first as an apprentice and then as a junior officer. (2) Conrad, I believe, never spelt his name Kurzeniowski. (3) The statement that 'Conrad used to let drop that, as the writer knew, he had run through three fortunes in his life,' is perhaps about as true as the statement that Conrad's maternal uncle's name was Paradowski. Mr. Ford's romanticism wreathes itself in such a variety of picturesque exfoliations that it is hard to say from what misapprehensions they may have sprung. He has mixed up the Bobrowskis, Conrad's mother's family, with the Paradowskis, relatives only by marriage. The legend about a 'horridly aspersed' Polish gentleman travelling to Boulogne to challenge Conrad to a duel and committing suicide in a railway carriage on the way, is, no doubt, as *ben trovato* as the story that Conrad's uncle had 'secured to him the return of half the great confiscated estate of his father.' Mr. Ford loves to deal in superlatives. Quartos turn into 'elephant folios' at his touch; Mr. Galsworthy is made to 'confide shyly' to Conrad on the Torrens that he 'is writing,' years before he had set pen to paper. It is amusing, but irritating, to find Mr. Ford's 'mystifications' fathered on to Conrad, and the tall story, on page 93, about Conrad and Ratcliffe Highway is a genuine Huefferism. One cannot, of course, disprove such grotesque anecdotes as one meets on page 157, but one may note that there were no 'dilapidated motors' in the days when Colonel Marchand crossed the Sahara and arrived at Fashoda. Facts have never worried Mr. Ford, and Mr. Wells's statement that Mr. Ford had visited him and informed him that he had persuaded Conrad to collaborate with him is airily dismissed as 'a matter of no great importance.' Mr. Ford's trick of telescoping his impressions of early years into those of six years later may account for his confused statement about the few English writers 'that, acting as it were as a junta, we absolutely admired.' 'Acting as a junta' is good. 'Later there came . . . the work of Henry James,' says Mr. Ford. Whereas, in point of fact, Conrad had expressed his deep appreciation of Henry James's work to the present reviewer in a letter early in 1897. After this one is not surprised to learn that *Karain* was 'the one of his early stories that Conrad liked best,' whereas this reviewer possesses a letter from Conrad, in 1898, saying that it was the one he liked the least of all.

One need not press points such as these, or comment upon such curiosities as that Mr. Ford should have 'looked for woodcuts contributed by Ford Madox Brown through the pages of Dickens's *All the Year Round*,' when that journal published no illustrations! Sometimes Mr. Ford gets things right, and sometimes he gets things wrong, and sometimes he splices the head of one fact to the tail of another; sometimes he plays hide and seek with his amusing contradictory statements. However, the publication of Conrad's Letters will no doubt throw interesting light on various statements in *A Personal Remembrance*, and separate the wheat from the chaff. That there is genuine wheat in this book I should be the last man to deny, but if Mr. Ford throws on others the task of winnowing it, well, it is—his misfortune.

41. 'A Cross Section': Christopher Morley, *Saturday Review of Literature*

i, 27 December 1924, 415

This review is also affected by the controversy and literary discussions that accompanied the publication of the Conrad book. Its value lies in Christopher Morley's ability, as a creative person, to recognize the worth of a book that so irritated academic critics.

Morley (1890–1957) was a prolific novelist, critic and literary essayist. One of his best known novels was *Kitty Foyle*.

Ford Madox Ford's book on Conrad has aroused discontent among a number of people who had greatly looked forward to it. I feel incompetent to speak very helpfully of it as I haven't yet enjoyed second reading without which I find it difficult to talk intelligibly of any book. But the nature of the protests I have heard is such that I feel it well to set down my feelings. I sat late, three weeks ago, reading the book, and the thrill is with me still.

Mr. Ford calls his book *A Personal Remembrance*; it is not put forward, thank heaven, as an authoritative biography. But readers have complained that it is more about Ford than about J.C.; they object to Ford's allusions to himself as 'the finest stylist in the English language' (they forget that that is not necessarily the ultimate self-praise); they wonder whether all the anecdotes are precise.

The truth of the matter is that to readers who have never been held and sickened by the whirling emptiness of an artistic problem, who have never carried in their hearts the dead faggots of a dream that could not be ignited, the book may seem ill-advised or false. But I believe that to those who have any inkling of the kind of man Conrad was, or of the kind of furious inward life such a man must lead, this book will prove enormously valuable. It almost seems to me to break new ground in the art of biography. It gives us, as Ford says he hoped to, 'the subject in his scenery.' It is the story, told in fragments and glimpses, of a personal relation. It is easily misunderstandable to the reader who is deficient in guile. It is a kind of dream: the dream of one artist about another. To read it as one would read—for instance—a book I once read by Mr. Heinz (the great Pickler) describing a tour of Sunday School teachers in the Orient (a book that should be in every library of mental incunabula) would be (shall we say?) an error. It is always rash, even cruel, to say that a book is meant for a limited public; but it is often true. This book is meant for those who see that when Ford says Conrad was born in Gascony he doesn't mean he was *really* born in Gascony; that when he seems to say Conrad threw the tea-cups into the fire he means Conrad looked as if he'd like to. In Alice Brown's fine phrase, he refrains from unprolific truth. I dare say there were multitudinous Conrads; this is an etching of one of them. It may be granted that Ford plumes himself rather frankly on his intimacy with this particular Conrad: but why not? I believe that Ford, in doing this anthology of Conrad's moments, came sometimes measurably near being as 'acknowledged a master of English' as he tells us he was supposed to be a quarter century ago. And he is not without a graceful irony and self-mockery in so often alluding to the way in which J.C. was brought to him as a sort of pupil.

So first we must clear the hall of any possible readers who don't care for this kind of biography, or who don't quite savvy the way the intensely professional literary mind works. (It was lack of imagination in others that made Conrad want to throw the tea-cups into the fire.) It may as well be admitted that this is an utterly 'literary' book; it must be read not for any annotation of facts but for a sound of vanished voices. It might even, to the eye of statisticians, be gravely inaccurate; and yet be truer than any 'reality.' Perhaps it is a life of Marlowe. Certainly it is a life of two poets who didn't write poems. We should not forget that Conrad once said Keats was his favourite poet; and that he would like to have written *As You Like It*.

'When poems ripen into form,' says Grace Hazard Conkling in a charming verse, 'They must be harvested by a storm.' The mind of Conrad was a ripened strangeness that was harvested for us by storms. He was the perfect windfall, the greatest unearned increment recently enjoyed by England, always the luckiest of countries (as any Continental statesman will tell you). Looked at on the technical side, who can tell us more shrewdly than Ford (himself bilingual) how Conrad's mind concerned itself with its desperate task of triple translation: from dream into French, from French into English. Every thought of Conrad's comes to us at two removes. His books are like that work of fiction (still unidentified) in *Revelations*: 'a book written within and on the backside.' I don't suppose publishers have time to read *Revelations*, where their supreme happiness is so jovially suggested: as soon as the 'little book' was published 'seven thunders uttered their voices.' (Reviewers, perhaps?) But what I am thinking of is the passage (10th chapter):

I went unto the angel and said Give me the little book. And he said unto me, Take it and eat it up; and it shall make thy belly bitter, but it shall be in thy mouth sweet as honey.

Such are the books of Conrad: bitter to digest, for they are packed with the doomed nobility and folly of life; lovely to read for they chant with the grotesque cadence of a dream. In Mr. Ford's lightning flashes of divine anecdote we see the man himself, equally grotesque, and gallant, the 'gentleman adventurer who had sailed with Drake,' the man with increasing intensities of silence.

The real purpose of books is to trap the mind into doing its own thinking: to lull our outward restlessness with music so that the inner observation can break free. Much of Mr. Ford's rigmarole about style and writers' workshop talk may seem immaterial; and it may touch you little, since you have your own ideas about these things. But those topics were dear to Conrad: they were a part of his professional spirit, as sextants and soundings had been. If you don't know how Conrad and Ford felt, driving about the country trying grimly to get a word for the color of dark blue cabbages, this book is not for you. And it is lit up, too, by a color even more difficult to convey than the tint of cabbages: the warm tone of a great love and tenderness. The first night that Conrad spent with Ford in the latter's farm house, Ford felt 'as if a king were enclosed within those walls.'

'If Dirt was Trumps,' said Lamb to some grimy-nailed whist player, 'what a hand you would hold.' At a time when dirt has sometimes looked a good deal like trumps in literature, Conrad's books have been a *Torrent* flying the flag of beauty and terror. If you cut open any work of art you will find some sort of pattern, some contoured curve and looping, some sliced whorl or spiral or eddy, marking the lines of growth and tension. Some cross section of the exquisite filaments and designing structure that held it firm and fine. Even if you cut open (it takes courage) any given capsule of Time, you will find the cross-section shows a profile of Eternity. Ford, I think, has cut open, on a crosswise and oddly biassed slant, a segment of Conrad's spirit. And there we see a pattern and microcosm of great humanity and great art.

42. 'Instructive and Amusing': Edward Garnett, *Weekly Westminster*

14 February 1925, 473

It is unusual for a reviewer to publish more than one review of the same book. This second notice by Edward Garnett may have been prompted by Mrs Conrad's attitude. In any event, it generally substantiates the earlier article.

I have reviewed this book somewhat severely in another quarter. And in looking through it again I do not know whether to be more amused or irritated. It is just what I expected from Mr. Ford, and it is also just what Conrad would have expected—something between romance and record, fact and fable. It is difficult to assess it accurately, partly because it is an *olla podrida* of memory and imagination, partly because Mr. Ford has fathered his own literary methods, slips, mystifications and all, on Conrad himself, and steeped him in his own shifting fantasy.

Now Conrad was extremely clear and direct in his statements about his own life. Anything more unlike the style of his conversation than the nebulous, sensational, highly coloured anecdotes, retailed by Mr. Ford as droppings from Conrad's lips, cannot be imagined.

At the same time I can affirm that there is a good deal of true insight and clever description and of genuine atmospheric observation pervading these romantic pages. For Mr. Ford is a romanticist. He improvises, he exaggerates, he adds and suppresses, he lets his imagination run amok, and then he surprises you by telling you something really true, something that really happened.

Obviously, the temperamental gifts of a Tartarin are not those that any man of sense would demand in his biographer, and when Mr. Ford tells us that this 'portrait' 'is conducted exactly along the lines laid down by us . . . it was that that Joseph Conrad asked for,' one bursts out laughing. It is conducted exactly along the lines of Mr. Ford's temperament. Acute things and flashes of true discernment are sandwiched with Münchausen-like anecdotes and childish conceit. The book is in some aspects a work of art, being artfully written. It is inspired no doubt by deep admiration for Conrad and for his work, and by affectionate memories of the days of collaboration (1900–4), but we must take with a good pinch of salt many of Mr. Ford's statements about Conrad's literary methods and his attitude towards the younger man.

No doubt Mr. Ford's memory and imagination have misled him here. It is natural for the planets that circle round the sun each to believe that his orbit is of particular importance. It is important for the planet, but not for the sun, and whether the discussions that went on as to the shades of value in words, as to style, as to construction, structure, and development in a novel, helped Conrad or not materially may be studied by their effect in the collaborated novel *Romance* (1903). At any rate he was interested and stimulated by these 'endless discussions,' as well as by Mr. Ford's enthusiasm for Flaubert and Maupassant which matched his own. I can see Conrad raising his eyebrows in intent scrutiny over the disquisition that Mr. Ford develops, in forty pages, over the technique of the novel, bringing in Conrad at intervals to affirm or fortify the argument. No doubt Conrad did throw himself into these literary arguments with luminous comments and trenchant declarations, but the disquisition itself is Mr. Ford's creation.

I remember how, years ago, Conrad, on one occasion, after asking me why I had never written a technical study of the novel, such as Mr. Percy Lubbock has lately achieved, and receiving my answer that the subject was too complicated for my brain, remarked with a sigh: 'So it is for mine. I have never understood it.' This is not to say that Conrad did not make frequent experiments in those early years with the technique of the novel, but that he followed his instinct and had no sacrosanct plan when he commenced a novel. Or, if he had a framework, he chopped and changed it till it became something very different. However, on these technical points Mr. Ford has much to say, and one would like to hear Conrad's exclamatory comments.

As to the sketch of Conrad's life that Mr. Ford provides, punctuated with highly coloured anecdotes, it makes amusing reading; and though much of it is a travesty of the facts, still, a fair amount of it has a foundation of reality.

What makes it so difficult to criticise him seriously is that on every page he contradicts, or minimises, or softens, or qualifies his statements a few pages back. It was Turgenev who declared that he had an unbounded admiration for the German imagination and for the German Romantic faculty of day-dreaming, because it could transform anything into anything at its will or pleasure. Mr. Ford has certainly inherited the ancestral faculty. His book is both instructive and amusing, but it is more amusing about Conrad and more instructive about Mr. Ford.

43. 'The Conrad Wake': H. L. Mencken, *American Mercury*

iv, April 1925, 505-6

If Garnett's knowledge of the relationship between Ford and Conrad restrained him from making extreme statements, other writers felt free to exploit their ignorance and prejudices. One of these was H. L. Mencken (1880–1956) who at the same time as he cast aspersions on Ford recognized the great merit of his book.

For many years editor of the Baltimore *Sun* and later of the *American Mercury*, Mencken was famous as an outspoken social critic and student of the American language.

Now that Joseph Conrad is safely entombed in Canterbury, hard by the palace and golf links of the Most Rev. the Archbishop, we may look for a great gush of books about him, some of them judicious. The first to appear, so far as I know, is *Joseph Conrad: a Personal Remembrance*, by Ford Madox Ford, *geb.* Hueffer, a friend of early days and collaborator on two of the Conrad books, *Romance* and *The Inheritors*. This Ford, or Hueffer, has been a promising young man in England for thirty years. He got launched early through the fact that his grandfather, Ford Madox Brown, was much talked of in the nineties; he has made many gallant efforts, since then, to realize the high hopes of his sponsors and rooters, of which last group he has always been an ardent member himself. Once, with Douglas Goldring, he started the *English Review*. Another time he took to writing history and biography. Yet another time he consecrated himself to novels. Lately, apparently despairing of making a permanent go of it in London, he moved to Paris and started a *Tendenz* magazine called the *Transatlantic Review*—the sort of thing that Ezra Pound and his friends were doing ten or fifteen years ago, and that Young Aesthetes out of St. Louis, East Broadway and Rahway, N. J., still play with in the suburbs of Greenwich Village. Luck, I fear, is not with him; even his change of name has not got him anywhere. Half German and half English, he is a sort of walking civil war—too much engrossed by the bombs going off in his own ego to make much of an impression upon the rest of the human race. The high, purple spot of his life came when he collaborated with Conrad, and upon the fact, I daresay, his footnote in the literature books will depend.

In the present volume he makes as much of the episode as he can, and not unnaturally. Every drop of juice in it is squeezed out. The transactions between him and Conrad do not appear as exchanges between a young, pushing and extremely bad story-teller and one of the greatest masters of fiction of all time, but as friendly parleys between full equals, in which Ford, or Hueffer, usually gets rather the better of it, whether as artist, as literary business man or as English country gentleman. The fact seems to distress the English Conradistas, especially those who had places within the dead maestro's circle of intimates. The Widow Conrad herself, in an indignant manifesto in far from impeccable English, roundly denounces Ford-Hueffer as a cuckoo, shamelessly laying eggs in her late husband's nest. 'During the years,' she says, 'that Mr. Hueffer was most intimate with Joseph Conrad, between 1898 and 1909, Ford Madox Hueffer'—she seems to be unaware of his yet worse cuckooing of the patronymic of the Detroit thinker—'never spent more than three consecutive weeks under our roof, and when we returned the visit we always, with few exceptions, had rooms in a cottage close at hand. After 1909 the meetings between the two were very rare and not *once* of my husband's seeking.'

Have your way, Madame! I am too old and full of scars and bitterness to quarrel with widows, or even to question them. But the fact remains as plain as day that Conrad took in Ford, or Hueffer, as a collaborator on *Romance* quite voluntarily, that Ford, or Hueffer, provided the main outline of the story, and that the same Ford, or Hueffer, did his fair share of the writing. This last he proves, indeed, by a document over Conrad's sign manual. Conrad, in those days, was by no means the Eminentissimo he later became. His books were not selling, the reviews treated him stupidly, and he was so poor that he had to take a pension from the British Civil List. Ford, meanwhile, was a promising young man, very well connected, and full of plausible theories. Is it against the probabilities that Conrad took him seriously, and listened to him with respect? I don't think it is. Conrad, in fact, needed help. He was feeling his way, trying to formulate a programme, wrestling with the difficulties of a strange tongue. Hueffer, alias Ford, brought into the partnership all the high assurance of youth—more, a dogmatic positiveness of a powerful order. It steadied Conrad, and I believe he knew it.

At all events, Ford ben-Hueffer's account of those early years is surely not improbable on its face. What he says, even when he is most impudent, always has a well-greased reasonableness. He depicts a Conrad who is always plausible, and sometimes overwhelmingly convincing. The man emerges from behind his smoky monocle, and begins to take on the color and heat of life. How, at the start, did he happen to leave Poland and take to the sea—a matter almost as astounding as an archbishop's desertion of the sacred desk for Hollywood? The answer is found in the novels of Captain Marryat, read in the dog's-eared volumes of a French translation in a remote Polish manor-house. And how did he come by his peculiarly narrow but romantic philosophy, his reduction of all human virtues to one, his resolute fidelity to fidelity? The genealogy of that passion is traced back through generations of yearning and ineffective Polish squires, always under the shadow of the Russian eagle. Conrad, it must be obvious, was never the standard literary gent. There was always something remote and occult about him. He held himself aloof, and was a bit disdainful, even while he accepted patronage. Ford, I think, gets at the man within the cloak—perhaps not completely, perhaps not always accurately, but certainly more nearly completely and accurately than the rest of the Conradian exegeses. Himself in youth a blatant and hollow fellow, blown up by the gases of a preposterous egoism, he was yet sufficiently in the possession of sense to know that he stood in the presence of an extraordinary man, and sufficiently skillful to observe that man with sharp care. His book is affected and irritating, but full of valuable information. No matter how violently the Widow Conrad protests in her eccentric English it will be read with joy and profit by all parties at interest. It is packed with little shrewdnesses, and it is immensely amusing.

44. William McFee, letter to the editor of New York *Bookman*

lxi, June 1925, 500

William McFee's statement makes substantially the same point as Christopher Morley's (see No. 41). It had a special authority at the time, however, since McFee wrote of the sea and was thought of as a follower of Conrad.

Dear Mr. Farrar:

I've been about lately and had work to do so I have had no opportunity to tell you how glad I was to see Mrs. Conrad's letter reprinted in the *Bookman*. I had heard of it but had not seen it, so I was hampered and bothered by a lack of first hand knowledge. Because I had read F. M. Ford's book and thought, and still think, that it is a most fascinating and remarkable study. There has been much comment upon the flare up on the part of the Conradistas led by Mrs. Conrad, but the comment has been singularly lacking in imagination. The theory that a writer's wife is necessarily an infallible guide in matters concerning her husband's literary activities and friendships is novel and amazing. Mrs. Conrad's letter and her previous excursions into print lead one to suspect that had she not happened to be Conrad's wife, she would never have read Conrad's books. Her dislike of Mr. Ford has nothing to do with the case. Mr. Ford has written a brilliant study of Conrad. He premises at the outset that he is going to write a novel about Conrad. In doing this he has presented Conrad to us in an entirely satisfying and legitimate light. Because Ford has not had the luck or the cunning to secure an American public it is assumed that he is therefore small beer and of no importance. There are many writers in England who are just as legitimately the objects of our interest as Arnold Bennett, Walpole, Arlen, and others, and these fortunate writers would be the first to tell you so.

When Mrs. Conrad says that Ford's book is detestable she is expressing her own opinion, but it has no value beyond that of any other lady. Those devoted adherents of the Conrad cult are doing their hero a serious disservice in decrying Ford's book. It is a greater tribute to the dead master than most of the stuff ground out now by people who allowed Conrad's books to be pirated all over the place and were not even aware of his existence when he was not yet the vogue.

I am surprised no one has seen the amusing side of Mrs. Conrad's letter. I have personally known of married men who had affiliations and friendships unknown to their wives. I have known wives who were so prejudiced against men friends of their husbands that the husbands have soft pedalled those friendships.

But I am more interested in the reaction of the public lately to the Ford-Conrad squabble because I think most people underestimate *Romance*, the book Ford and Conrad struggled with for so long. To me it is one of the best of the lot. It is not Conradian in the sense that *Nostromo* and *Youth* are Conradian, but it is one of the best stories of the lot. It is so magnificently built, it seems to stand the strain of years and constant rereading. It owes much to Ford, and I for one wish some of the other books had had some Ford in them—*The Rescue* and *The Arrow of Gold*, for instance. Mrs. Conrad said a plot was of no use to her husband, which is true in one sense. But it is a sense that can be easily carried beyond reason. To say that Conrad was independent of plots is to misunderstand the whole business of writing. In Conrad's first book, written before he met Ford, *Almayer's Folly*, there is a very skilful and intricate plot structure. To say that Conrad could not use another man's plot means nothing. No writer can use the other man's plot as the other man hands it to him. But he can make it his own. As an example, I had a plot given me by another man. Indeed, he had made a story of it but it did not function. I took it. I agreed to use it. I stripped it to the bare bones. I even took the bones apart and reconstructed the skeleton. I provided new scenes, new characters, a fresh climax, and added several other improvements. But the idea came from the other man, and without his preliminary plot my story would never have been written.

This is explaining great things by small, but we are all human, I suppose. What I want to protest against is the *embalming* of Conrad in a grand tomb. Ford shows us the living man. Let us keep him living. Already publishers are beginning to advertise new books by authors who (strange to say!) resemble Conrad. Let us keep him human. He was a great man, but—correct me if I am wrong—only a mortal man.

WILLIAM MCFEE

LATER FICTION, REMINISCENCES AND CRITICISM

45. 'A Matter of Form': J. Middleton Murry on *Thus to Revisit*

Nation & Athenaeum, xxix, 28 May 1921, 328–9

Ford's decline as a novelist was compensated for by his criticism, reminiscences and topographical writings. From the beginning of his career he had written books in these genres, but later on he began to combine them in one work, using such fictional techniques as he could to give life and interest to what he was writing. Since the resulting books did not fit into a single category, as autobiography, literary criticism or sociology, they often irritated and bewildered critics accustomed to these neat, but often artificial, limitations. The suggestion that they represented whatever was important in contemporary letters also infuriated Middleton Murry (1889–1957), who had his own coterie to protect.

Murry was Katherine Mansfield's husband and a prominent critic and journalist. The material printed below is extracted from a joint review of two books, the other, *Poetry in Prose*, a collection of three essays by Aldington, Eliot and Frederic Manning not being immediately relevant to Ford.

Probably there are general conclusions to be drawn from the fact that the discussion of questions of literary form is becoming more frequent than it has been for twenty years. If there are, I do not know how to draw them. I merely register the hope that it does not mean that the young writers of to-day will appear twenty-five years hence to have been as ineffectual as their predecessors of the 'nineties. Then the form of the *conte* was continually discussed; the only short stories of that period which remain to-day were written by Mr. Kipling and Mr. Wells—for I reckon Henry James as before and Mr. Conrad as after the time—that is, by writers who held aloof from the discussion.

To-day the problem is different. If we are to take Mr. Hueffer's word for it, our modern preoccupation is with the form of poetry. Unfortunately, Mr. Hueffer is ever so little belated, in spite of his intense and resolute modernity. He imagines that the problem is solved by the invention, or the revival, of *vers libre*. Hardly has he written the final word of his apology pro *vitâ suâ*, which seems to have been one long immolation of himself upon the altar of free verse, than there comes a symposium on the merits and desirability of the prose poem. In this symposium—alas for poor Mr. Hueffer!—one of his own chosen young men, one of the writers of free verse upon whom he has been focussing an intense ray of artificial light, suddenly turns, and asks: 'May not poetry in prose prove an escape from the sterility and intellectual impoverishment of modern verse and the vulgarization of prose?' *Quousque tandem*. Poor Mr. Hueffer!

Mr. Richard Aldington, who asks the unkind question, is a very able young man, who steadily improves as a critic, and perhaps as a poet also, though his question would suggest that he finds himself in a poetical *impasse*. Probably that assumption best explains the nature of his argument to prove the existence and the desirability of the prose poem.

★   ★   ★

Now there may be sound reasons why we should apply ourselves at the present moment to the rendering of *choses vues*, isolated perceptions and emotions, in prose. If we do, they will be written in good prose or bad. But I see no reason why we should invoke the name of 'prose poem' to cover their nakedness. And on the previous question, there is undoubtedly the danger of being drawn into writing scraps. When I was a good deal younger than I am now I published a 'prose poem' (though I eschewed the name) in an 'advanced' magazine, and I waited, as we all did in those days, to see what Jacob Tonson would say about it in the *New Age*. He spoke. He said: 'Any fool can write a scrap.' I have since learned that the dictum is not wholly true. But it was the one piece of literary advice which has made a profound impression upon me. When I think back upon it, I realize how lamentable it is that there is no one nowadays to say to us and our younger successors the brutal and generous things that Mr. Bennett launched at our heads ten years ago.

If the 'prose poem' comes into vogue it will mean a pullulation of scraps. There are enough of them already. They have been cultivated as in a hotbed by that very fashion of *vers libre* which Mr. Hueffer has devoted himself to encouraging. Here, in so many words, is the seed of it all:—

> The trouble with nearly all poets was nearly always that, at any rate, the moment they took pen in hand, they were totally unable to forget that they were professionals, if I may so put it. For myself, I simply tried to get at myself in an absolutely 'unpoetic' frame of mind; I have always tried to get at that; I hope so to continue. If I have any value to the world it is simply the value of my unaffected self—and I daresay that any man's value in the world is simply that. For no man's views are worth very much; the facts that any man can collect during his short pilgrimage through life are ludicrously or pitifully few, and the only empire over which we can for certain reign, or for which we can assuredly speak, is the heart of man. And one's own heart is the heart one knows best!

Gott in Himmel! was für eine Poetik! Mr. Hueffer's mind is always in carpet-slippers, and sliding over a parquet floor. He is apparently quite unaware of the immense equivocation in the words 'unpoetic' and 'professional.' A writer, when he sits down to write, *must be* a professional: otherwise he is a jellyfish. To be a professional does not mean to have one's mind full of emotional and verbal *clichés*; it means to have one's mind alert, to be determined to construct, to create a vehicle for the individual emotion or perception that is within. 'Away with it all!' moans Mr. Hueffer, waving his hands—the same Mr. Hueffer who has been telling us for pages and pages that he was the only one (with one or two minor associates, like Mr. Conrad) to worry himself with problems of literary technique during the twenty-five years that separate us from the 'nineties! But he is gone and never shall return. Not art now, but heart! And Mr. Hueffer unbuttons his heart (which has a bad memory for dates) in two hundred pages of shocking garrulity, which culminate in this advice to the poet:—

> The poet then must seek to reproduce his actual vocabulary, his own characteristic turns of phrase, the exact cadence of his own usual sentences. The result will be himself.

I suppose that *Thus to Revisit* is Mr. Hueffer himself; perhaps it is also a poem in *vers libre*. I can see no reason why it should not be. It satisfies the definition. It is full of heart, also.

No, no, no! I am aware that in Mr. Hueffer's eyes I am the type of the young Academic critic, a viper nurtured in the breast of true Literature. But I think that the younger generation would be a great deal safer on my side than on his. Moreover, I wonder whether all those young men whom Mr. Hueffer so generously takes under his umbrageous wing are really there. Mr. Hueffer had better peep under and count his chickens. Perhaps they are only china eggs.

For not only is his poetic a wrong and misleading poetic, based upon an elementary confusion of thought; but it is also—unless I am utterly mistaken—a poetic that would be renounced by every single one of the poets whom he affects to champion. I do not profess to be in the counsels of Mr. Ezra Pound or Mr. T. S. Eliot, of 'H. D.' or Mr. Aldington. But I can judge their theories from their poetry and their criticism. However good or bad they may be as poets, they are at least intelligent, and they know that poetry is something more than a matter of heart, and something quite different from the reproduction of their own tricks of familiar speech and the exact cadence of their own conversation. Let me quote Mr. Aldington:—

A piece of writing is not poetry if it has not the word which creates an image, the unexpected and precise phrase rendering objects palpable to the senses, the art which creates in the reader emotions, perceptions, sensations similar to those of the writer.

That is not the whole truth; but it is true, and well and concisely put. And Mr. Aldington is one of the chief of Mr. Hueffer's chickens! Poor Mr. Hueffer!

46. L. P. Hartley, review of *A Little Less Than Gods*, *Saturday Review*

cxlvi, 24 November 1928, 692, 694

As a novelist, Ford was not able to maintain the reputation he had achieved with the Tietjens tetralogy. The first novel published after *Last Post* was *A Little Less Than Gods*, an historical novel which, he admitted, was written 'to stretch my arms a little'. Those expecting work of the calibre of the Tietjens books were naturally disappointed. Next came *No Enemy*, which in fact had been written before the tetralogy but, upon its publication in 1929, it seemed a tired extension of that series. After that came *When the Wicked Man* which dealt with the corruptions of the book publishing world in New York and consequently irritated a number of people. The reviewer for the Chicago *Tribune* undoubtedly spoke for many when she wrote of this book as '... the latest novel of the author of one of the greatest novels of our day, the tetralogy beginning with *Some Do Not*. One never would recognize the two books as the product of the same pen ...'

By the time *The Rash Act*, a distinctly better novel, was published, the reaction had set in to the extent that it received barely a dozen reviews; its sequel, *Henry for Hugh*, not even half that number. This decline in Ford's fortunes as a novelist meant that there were few interesting reviews of his later work. The one printed below is one of a handful that are still worth reading.

Mr. Ford Madox Ford is, of course, a considerable artist: everything he writes demonstrates this. He has evolved a method and a style and a point of view, all highly artificial, that are as second nature to him; his pen never rebels against the conventions he has dictated for it. It follows that his books have an interior harmony which cannot be disturbed, which resolves discrepancies and incompatibilities in a manner almost god-like. The disproportion, whether of fact, thought or emotion in which life abounds does not make itself felt in the novels of Mr. Ford. He is aware of it, certainly; he makes constant use of it for the raw material of his books. But he meets it always with irony; a surprised, rhetorical irony, sometimes indulgent, sometimes angry, that exalts the valley and lays low the mountain. Just as in an omelette several apparently unrelated ingredients meet together and achieve a unity, and we are aware, or should be, of one thing, not of many, so in the work of Mr. Ford the conflicting phenomena of life display one prevailing aspect. They do not contribute much to the books' variety; that is an affair of art, of studied sequences of mood and thought, of prose rhythms, sometimes of punctuation. Even the effects of spontaneity are calculated. Of course all artists arrange the raw material of life to suit their purposes; Mr. Ford does more, he cooks it.

Thus anyone who hopes to find in *A Little Less Than Gods* a coherent picture or even a vivid impression of France during the Hundred Days and the aftermath of Waterloo, will be disappointed. The book, Mr. Ford tells us, was to have been written in collaboration, presumably with Conrad, and Conrad's influence is as marked as if he had really had a hand in it. One sees how the central idea would have recommended itself to him. Marshal Ney, so runs an American legend, was not executed after Waterloo: a certain Baron de Fréjus suffered in his stead, and the Prince de la Moskwa took refuge in America. The intrigues and agitations that led up to this are seen through the eyes of a young Englishman who, in Elba and later in France, preserved an intense hero-worship for Napoleon and did not see eye to eye with his own country. A most romantic figure, this George Fielding, and one after Conrad's own heart. But Conrad would surely have simplified him, made him more obviously the sport of conflicting loyalties, drawn his portrait in firmer lines than those rhetorical flourishes which Mr. Ford weaves into the semblance of a human face. The narrative is confusing if it is not confused; it is overloaded with the ironical manner which Mr. Assheton Smith, an English *milor* fabulously rich, extended to all and sundry, even the Duke of Wellington. Just as Mr. Ford writes obliquely, inferring an important event from a concatenation of seemingly irrelevant and trivial details, so his characters seldom speak quite to the point. They must address the Universe, must protest their indignation, their innocence, their helplessness in the face of Destiny, before they can exchange an idea. Self-justification and self-pity are at the root of their characters; they are certainly less than gods, if indeed they are more than men.

47. 'The Career of Ford Madox Ford': Morton Dauwen Zabel on *Return to Yesterday*

New York *Nation*, cxxxiv, 6 April 1932, 403-4

Ford's numerous reminiscences and volumes of criticism produced a literary myth of his own creating, an interpretation which itself demanded critical assessment. One of the first of these was written by M. D. Zabel (1901–64), who was both professor at the University of Chicago and editor of *Poetry*. His interpretation accurately summarizes Ford's reputation in the early 1930s.

'The dubious pleasure of remembering analytically' is an indulgence which Mr. Ford has never been able to deny himself. Critics may question the worth of his historical analysis, but no one can deny the pleasure he takes in creating and patronizing literature, or in writing its annals. He has, in fact, returned to yesterday too often to permit great novelty or surprise in the present compendious record of his career. It will, however, be read with respect by anyone conscious of his service to contemporary literature and of the two abundant resources that have made that contribution possible—enthusiasm and a 'sense of the past.' One may marvel that in his eagerness to welcome new friends, writers, and 'movements,' Mr. Ford has had the luck to play so many winning hands. Yet 'luck' is a poor word for the perspicacity that took its lessons at the feet of veteran pre-Raphaelites and Henry James, accepted on petition the collaboration of the then obscure Conrad, befriended Stephen Crane, set the *English Review* and the *Transatlantic* afloat with their brilliant crews, and kept abreast of creative thought during many years of journalistic distraction and war service until the Tietjens tetralogy was produced. Through the four decades here chronicled (with scant attention, however, to post-war years), Mr. Ford has been at every point conscious of the program of events. He has profitably balanced his avidity for contemporary insurgence with a loyalty to the Victorian era, of which he remains, in many respects, an isolated survivor.

The past has been the lodestar of his career from its beginning. He started life as the inheritor of a circle of famous artists and writers who had survived the almost heroic rigors of Victorian fame. His literary ambitions were supervised by distinguished relatives to whom he paid the tribute of acting as their historian. The friendships and associations of his crowded later years have not encouraged him to relinquish these projects in reminiscence and memoir-writing. Whether in volumes of criticism and biography like *Ford Madox Brown, Henry James,* and *Joseph Conrad*; in books of historical or documentary motivation like the Katherine Howard trilogy (1906–08), the English series (1905–07), and the Tietjens group; in books on literary craft like *The Critical Attitude*; or in those volumes of pure reminiscence to which *Return to Yesterday* now acts as a pendant, *Memories and Impressions* (1912) and *Thus to Revisit* (1921), his work has been spurred on by a consciousness of temporal perspectives and of his own privileged existence among them. Disappointments in his public career have been accompanied by disorders in his domestic (he has spared his public the latter, but Miss Violet Hunt has not); yet through all the excitement, through all the collisions between external convention and personal independence, and in spite of a love of 'making things grow' which has made him desert literature for spasmodic excursions into agriculture, he has been intent on staying young and contemporary.

By his own admission he has had to struggle against the fatigue of setting words to paper, a statement which his sixty books and unnumbered articles of journalism would make difficult to credit were it not for his much-repeated and unquestionably sincere belief that the making of novels and poetry is the noblest occupation of man, worth the last ounce of his spiritual and physical energy. This same article of faith is the clue to his unbounded generosity for young talent. His books will have their value as 'mémoires pour servir à l'histoire de son temps' chiefly because of the courageous, and sometimes costly, support he gave to a succession of poorly appreciated authors. From Conrad, Hudson, and Crane, through Lawrence, Pound, and the imagists, down to some of the most original of current novelists, these beneficiaries of his editorial acumen provide a testimony to friendship which might pardon an even more repetitious and self-congratulatory record than Mr. Ford has written.

Generosity and enthusiasm are not, however, proofs of creative authority, and cannot enter into an account of Mr. Ford's claims to distinction among twentieth-century novelists. In the nineties he was hailed, as he frequently reminds us, as 'the most-boomed author in England' and 'the foremost English stylist.' With this beginning, his subsequent uninspired and aimless course must have come with the pain of distinct anti-climax. For about twenty years he wrote books which he can now call no better than 'worthless.' Admitting the pressure of financial necessity that kept him in journalism, one is reminded by the lives of Conrad and Hudson, and by the delineation of his own Tietjens, that another course was open to him and that some failure in purpose or integrity kept him from following it. The clue to this failure is discoverable in the present volume.

Facts are perhaps not, ultimately, of great spiritual significance, but the discipline required to master them is. Mr. Ford's happy unconcern about dates, sources, and authenticity in his anecdotes stands in no greater contrast to Conrad's tortuous search for words and data in preparing a novel than do the 'worthless' fictions of Mr. Ford's middle years to novels like *Lord Jim* and *Nostromo*. The garrulous self-esteem which can be as ingratiating as Mr. Yeats's or as tedious as Sisley Huddleston's, and which could condone in this book wholesale repetitions from earlier volumes as easily as it could tempt disaster for the Tietjens chronicle by yielding to a New York lady-editor's plea for a fourth volume, stands in sharp contrast to the rigorous self-effacement of W. H. Hudson or Stephen Crane. And the uncertainty of motive in Mr. Ford's projects may be traced at least partly to his inability to resolve and localize his aesthetic and civil morals. He is hospitable to revolt and insurgence in the creative order, yet confesses himself 'a sentimental Tory,' loving 'pomp, banners, divine rights, unreasonable ceremonies, and ceremoniousness.' Pitched less precariously than Henry James or Conrad between several national allegiances, he has tacked fitfully from German sympathies to English loyalties and ultimately to French enthusiasms. He has been in turn an heir of the Victorians, an arbiter among the Georgians, and a post-war *révolté*. His creative impulses have been centrifugal, his style in all but four books heavily damaged by exhibitionism, and his attention susceptible to almost every literary breeze in the air. His patronage has been spent wisely, but far too eclectically for his own good. One of his critics has wished for him 'less facility and more self-restraint.' It would be equally possible to complain of the irresolution which has denied his work conviction and a center. Given a host of personal acquaintances, intimately observed, he has produced novels of extraordinary perception and technique like *The Good Soldier* and *Some Do Not*. Left to his own devices he has written books whose excellent wit and enlightening anecdotes do not annul a sense of frustrated intelligence and misspent energies. On a life of such generosity and on books of such charm as Mr. Ford's this is an ungrateful reflection; but in his chapters on James, Conrad, and Hudson, no less than in his accounts of desultory literary adventure in London, New York, and Paris, Mr. Ford provides illustrations that make such a reflection irresistible.

48. V. S. Pritchett, review of *It Was the Nightingale*, *Fortnightly Review*

cxxxvi, July 1934, 122

Next to Graham Greene (see headnote to No. 49), V. S. Pritchett (b. 1900) was the English writer who seemed most interested in Ford's work during the late 1930s and who reviewed almost all of it as it was published. His affinity to Ford lies in part in their mutual attachment to specific characters and experiences, essential features in the temperament of a novelist. Pritchett is a prolific novelist, short story writer, critic and author of travel books. The review printed below also deals with Roy Campbell's autobiography.

These two autobiographies, one by a member of 'the old firm' and the other by a young poet, have little common ground but have certain common characteristics. Both are mixed in their Englishness and accept the English tradition with reservations—being, of course, most proud of the reservations. Both wheel themselves about like a Punch and Judy show, and proceed to thwack and declaim with gusto; and both have decided to defy foul chronology and to dress themselves up in the clothes of any event that pleases them as it comes along. This random literary garment Mr. Ford Madox Ford calls 'the time-shift'. 'You may think you do not like my "time-shift"', Mr. Ford says, 'when the truth is that you do not like me!' Mr. Roy Campbell is lordlier; if you don't like him—and he writes a deal of sentimental stuff about the necessity of Fascism—you are a pedestrian, the degraded creature whom all equestrians, jousters, troubadours and bull-fighters despise. You gather Mr. Campbell is a devil of a fellow and the show keeps up the appropriate pace. Now he is in his native South Africa, now on an island off the Welsh coast; he is back in Rhodesia hunting, then sailing down the Rhone on a barge, working a passage on a Mediterranean steamer—one of the jobs was loading cement over that perilous gang plank at Cassis—fighting bulls in Provence and twisting the tails of literary lions in London. Mr. Campbell hits hard when his Colonial scorn is roused; that is to say, his blows would be good if they landed, but they spend themselves in the air most of the time and the interest wanes. When he has real matter to hand, such as the coming of the sardines to his native coast, or the memory of some Rhodesian hunt, he can write those pages of clear and sonorous English prose which we expect from the most word-intoxicated poet of our generation. But from his random opinions, heaven protect us—and him.

Mr. Ford Madox Ford is much more the showman, a heavier and more festive fellow than Mr. Campbell, brilliant and laborious. He takes the floor—and this explains why a writer of his calibre, who can draw you an excellent young Galsworthy, a harassed Conrad, a suspicious George Moore and a fulminating Ezra Pound, becomes dull by being too brilliant for his own story. On the other hand, we get a picture of Mr. Ford protesting, enduring, denying, lauding, declaiming, parading and disarming and wandering on, which turns the rest of the circus into a side-show. And the reader will have the satisfaction of thinking that he has discovered things about the character of Mr. Ford which Mr. Ford himself has probably never suspected. An odd thing is autobiography. One of the odd things is his success in the little glimpses he gives of his mother. There has been (apparently) no elaborate working up to the incident—nor does the awful phrase 'and here is the point of the story' occur—but they slip out as if by accident, and each is perfect.

Post-war Montparnasse, memories of Kent, Sussex, Campden Hill and New York, pack the book. Most of it is good stuff and all good-humoured. I liked Mr. Ford's habit of attaching the names of his friends to his potato plants; and the gardener's bulletin: 'Mr. 'Enery James have picked up proper in the night, but Mr. Conrad do peek and pine and is yellowin'. Mr. Galsworthy's beetles 'ave spread all over Miss Austin ...' That might have been the text for a picturesque book.

49. 'The Landowner in Revolt': Graham Greene on *Great Trade Route*

London Mercury, xxxv, February 1937, 422–4

Ford's lack of commercial, or public, success was not matched by the neglect of fellow artists, for he was privately respected and a few young novelists were his disciples and admirers. Foremost among these was Graham Greene (b. 1904) who not only knew Ford's work intimately but also did what he could to call attention to it, in reviewing nearly all of his last books. Greene, who was influenced by Ford in the writing of his own novels, encouraged Penguin Books to reissue five of Ford's novels in 1948 and was responsible for the *Bodley Head Ford Madox Ford*, which he edited for publication in 1962.

Great Trade Route—that is Mr. Ford's personal dream of a past golden age, a huge oval belt extending from Cathay east and west of the fortieth parallel north through Europe up to the southern coast of England, a place of perfect peace and culture. 'The Sacred Merchants were at once civilizers, gift bringers, educators and the trainers of priesthoods.' It is never clear at what period this dream existed in fact; but that doesn't really matter, for to Mr. Ford the Great Trade Route means 'a frame of mind to which, unless we return, our Occidental civilization is doomed.'

Mr. Ford's genius has always been aristocratic. His flirtation with the Fabians was of the briefest; his real heroes were Tories and landowners, Tietjens and the Good Soldier. Perhaps that is why Mr. Ford, so incontestably our finest living novelist and perhaps the only novelist since Henry James to contribute much technically to his art, is not very widely read. The world, absorbed in the Communist-Fascist dog-fight, is ill prepared to listen to this Tory philosopher who finds the Conservative politician as little to his taste as any other. And yet men of Mr. Ford's character have much to offer: there is something disagreeably easy in the notion that only two political philosophies can exist and that we must choose between them. Mr. Ford is a Catholic, though he has seldom been in sympathy with his Church, and it is no coincidence that the subject of *Great Trade Route* is similar to that of the recent Pastoral Letter issued by the Catholic Bishops in this country. There must always seem something a little parvenu in the fierce self-absorption of the two new political creeds: an atmosphere of popular science, 'how wonderful this wireless, this electricity, this radium, this twentieth century,' to members of an international organization which has existed for nearly two thousand years.

Mr. Ford's solution, like that of the Catholic Bishops, is the Small Producer, as against the big individual capitalist and the small communist cog. He would have every man a part-time agriculturalist, because such a man is free in a sense unrecognized by either Fascist or Communist, free from the State ideal. 'I want to belong to a nation of small producers, with some local, but no national feeling at all.'

The inhabitants of the Great Trade Route to-day

never taste vegetables fresh from the beds, fruit fresh from the trees, bread from wheat not manured by chemicals, meats not rendered unassimilable by refrigeration and again by chemicals. . . . So their brains are for ever starved of good blood, their minds are incapable of reflection, courage or stability. . . . And, carrying on its back a screaming Mass Production the bronze bull that is the Machine Age charges the brazen wall called Crisis.

Mr. Ford defines the Small Producer:

He is a man who with a certain knowledge of various crafts can set his hand to most kinds of work that go to the maintenance of humble existences. He can mend or make a rough chest of drawers; he will make shift to sole a shoe or make a passable pair of sandals; he will contrive or repair hurdles, platters, scythe-handles, styes, shingle roofs, harrows. But above all, he can produce and teach his family to produce good food according to the seasons.

It is not a low ideal; it is the ideal of a country gentleman who knows his job; it is in the tradition behind Tietjens, and during this long and rambling journey, while Mr. Ford spots the villain Mass Production (little cellophane packets of corn sold at a high price on land where it had once been cheap as air), some readers will find their chief reward in vivid and dramatic asides which recall the novelist of the Tietjens series: Bismarck 'whom I remember to have seen walking along the Poppelsdorfer Allee after his fall, his head dejected and his great hound dejected also, following him, his immense dewlaps almost touching his master's heel;' the bourgeoisie of Flemington: 'extraordinarily silent men with harsh, hanging hands and Abraham-Lincoln-like faces who sat for hours without moving or speaking in rooms all shining linoleum, bentwood furniture, and tombstone-like sewing-machine cases.'

Their chief reward, because not unexpectedly the landowner with his appeal for 'a change of heart' is less practical than the ecclesiastic, who has the technique at hand for 'changing hearts.' He is a romantic. The enemy of the Great Trade Route was the barbarous North, and Mr. Ford still questionably stages his conflict in the terms of North and South, Yankee against Southerner, Lancashire against Kent. 'A clear, cold, tinny note of regions where food is not touched by the human hand—the note of grim peoples now and then trying to be cheerful in creditable circumstances—of regions where honesty is only a policy on a par with the other policy which leads septentrionals to recommend their raiding generals to leave invaded peoples only their eyes to weep with.' There may be truth in this picture of the barbarian North, but to its threat Mr. Ford presents only an unequivocal pacifism: he won't fight even for his small holdings, and he never answers satisfactorily the thoughts in all our minds, that Hitler is a southern Teuton and that it was Italy who first broke the peace in Europe.

50. 'A Veteran at Play': Graham Greene on *Vive Le Roy*

London Mercury, xxxvi, August 1937, 389–90

It came as a shock to me the other day to realize how long Mr. Ford had served literature. In the process of collecting copies of his complete works I found myself in possession of *The Shifting of the Fire*, published in 1892 in a precious period binding. And his service stretches further back into the Victorian age than that. On the title page—where the young author's name is incorrectly given—he is described as the author of *The Brown Owl*, *The Feather*, etc. So he retires into history evading capture, but if I snared the earliest book of all—that nameless Etc.—I should still expect to find Mr. Ford's unmistakable stamp—an outrageous fancy and a kind of pessimistic high spirits. Human nature in his books is utterly corrupt—but Mr. Ford is a Catholic and it doesn't surprise or depress him.

The stamp is there, for anyone sufficiently interested in our finest living novelist to do a little research, in *The Shifting of the Fire*, when the elderly Mr. Kasker-Ryves, reproving his son, whom scandal has driven from his regiment, drifts off into personal and lubricous reminiscence: 'Now, look here, dear boy, that was safe enough in those days—I mean to say no one made a fuss about it, but nowadays it is different, more especially as you want to sit for the borough . . . I remember,' he went on, 'I began when I was about twenty—a little less. . . .' And when the young man exclaims to himself, 'Good God! are all men in the world such villains?' we are aware of the half-humorous cry which breaks from all Mr. Ford's novels. The world is very corrupt, but Mr. Ford is not recognized by the official moralists because as a writer he finds the corruption so damnably amusing.

His latest novel is not one of his vintage growths—nor is it meant to be. It won't stand comparison with *The Good Soldier* or the Tietjens series: I wouldn't myself put it as high as *The Marsden Case* or *Mr. Apollo*. It is a thriller more on the romantic lines of his historical novels, although the scene is contemporary. When the story opens (if any of Mr. Ford's can be said to open: they usually break out unexpectedly half-way through) a Royalist *coup d'état* has taken place in Paris after an unsuccessful Communist revolution and a young American Socialist, Walter Leroy, is carrying a message and funds from the New York to the Paris 'comrades' hidden in the uncut leaves at the end of a French detective story—he is forced to go on reading the story day after day without ever reaching the end, and the message written in elaborate code and infinitely dangerous to the bearer is simply 'Courage! Standing by. New York county assn.' Meanwhile the King of France is assassinated and his chief minister, returning from a mission to the United States in the same ship as Leroy and detecting a strong resemblance between him and the King, decides to hush up the murder, kidnap Leroy, and maintain the Royalist regime by means of the Socialist, who is condemned to play the royal part for life.

It is amusing, romantic, exciting, full of ridiculous and irrelevant inventions (a retired Scotland Yard detective employed by the League of Nations turns out to be Leroy's 'illegitimate' father), and with one of Mr. Ford's most delightful heroines. Mr. Ford has the Victorian gift of being able to draw adorable women, but he can do what James and Hardy could not, convey immense sexual appeal. Listen to Walter Leroy's American mistress, a young painter from Seattle, full of loyalties and absurdities, criticize the Dubarry to the ex-inspector of Scotland Yard (she doesn't know at the time that she is to be a royal mistress herself). The dialogue in some mysterious way conveys physical desirability as well as charm. The secret is Mr. Ford's.

'Of course the Dubarry was too bosomy and fluffy and baby-ribbonish. And in certain ways she was ignoble. She came of poor people, poorer than I. So she ought to have known things. It was all right for Marie Antoinette to say: "Why don't they eat cake?" That was benevolence. But for the Dubarry to countenance it was ... low down. I forget what she was. Daughter of a baker or something in some provincial town. I'm the bastard daughter of you never knew who, from Seattle ... and if I were Dubarry....' She paused for a moment: 'Oh,' she went on, 'I could have all the canvases I wanted, and dozens of palette knives and ultramarine ground out of real lapis lazuli.... And some frocks, to keep Walter at my heels ... But, oh paradise, I'd do a little reforming on the side....'

51. 'Impressions of the "Impressionists"':
V. S. Pritchett on *Mightier than the Sword*

London Mercury, xxxvii, March 1938, 550-1

Ford's penultimate book, written originally as a series of articles for the *American Mercury*, was a survey, in the form of portraits, of a number of writers with whom Ford had been associated, especially in the early part of his career. Since Ford was one of the last survivors of that group, he was able to provide authentic portraits of them. His mastery of this form of literary criticism earned him due praise, particularly from fellow writers.

The effect of the Great War upon English life is only just being felt in literature, for we are only now beginning to see the work of a generation that was untouched by any serious pre-war memory. How very different that other world was a glance at Mr. Ford Madox Ford's portraits of men like Turgenev, Hardy, Hudson, Conrad, Stephen Crane, Henry James, Galsworthy and Lawrence will show. Impressionist, Mr. Ford calls his time. Rebellious, he says, against the moral purpose of the 'Victorian eunuchs and the elderly widow,' romantic but with due stress on the sinister side of things even in Mr. Wells. For if you are neither a Christian nor a reformer, original sin is released from its doctrinal bonds to grow and flower in the imagination in spectacular, hot-house fashion. Hardy has his stage Fates, James his unmentionable whisperers of corruption, as obvious to him as Blake's angels of darkness were to Blake, Galsworthy his haunting guilts, Wells his anti-human vapours, Conrad his impalpable betrayals. Even a writer appearing among this group, as late as Lawrence did, finds an exotic Satan in the mind of civilization itself.

They did not much care (not even Henry James) for civilization, except in so far as its corruption fascinated them. Losing Christianity, they believed in a kind of cultivated witchcraft, in which evil was still a principle, but unorthodox and relatively picturesque. Our psychological or economic theories of individual or social mechanism were despised, if at all known, when these men heard of them. Very properly they understood that art was not explanation; very naturally, thrown back upon themselves, they were content to elaborate imaginative personal theories which came to look more and more like a lot of words for luxurious private sensations that were not common coinage; like Byronism, something indeed dramatic but also to us somehow false. So it seems now that the far more spectacular and concrete evil of the war stands between us and has left us with the feeling that, for the moment, we have our hands full in preserving or reconstructing society and little time for thinking about the more grandiose but nevertheless speculative wilfulness of the cosmos. But if the 'little man, what now?' theme has been shoved aside, Mr. Ford's book is a valuable reminder that what matters is less the atmosphere of an age than the honesty of the work that was done in it. To this the judgment of posterity and even the kiss of fashion, sooner or later return.

Somehow Mr. Ford escaped the peculiar seriousness of his seniors in the period, and I imagine this is why his own mark has not been as strong as his talents warranted. It is always exciting to read Mr. Ford. He has that kind of quality which is easily underrated by the soulful world of English letters: a hard and brilliant originality, full of laughter, gusto, theories, digressions and asides. He is a festive and gregarious mind but not a heart. Stunned by a volubility in which every word strikes and starts a dozen echoes which distract him to further effects like a boy shouting under an archway, one sways giddily but enlivened. Before everything else a personality, he excels at recreating an impression of the personality of people like Turgenev, Hardy or James, by gathering together the least expected fragments. Bizarre as they may be, they are kept in place by an unusual common sense. The defence of Turgenev, for example, from the charges of expatriate rootlessness which are made against him strikes one as being very sound and shrewd. Turgenev was, indeed, working when all that educated Russia did was to talk.

The Hardy portrait, too, besides its irony, has several sound things in it: the observation, for example, that, whereas Hardy would alter a plot to suit any editor, he would not alter a syllable of his verse for anyone—with its obvious conclusion. There is a nice story of Mrs. Hardy begging the Garnetts to make her husband tear up the MS. of *Jude*, and another one of a visit to Max Gate where poetry was read at tea—Mrs. Hardy's poetry. But most delightful of all is the portrait of Henry James. This is a masterpiece of reminiscence and criticism. It is a model of Mr. Ford's method which is to plant an incident and then watch with glee its ramifications grow. A violent disillusion turned the later James into a man of infinite precautions, disastrous to his prose (unless it is read aloud) and yet an oblique stimulus to the immense patience and thoroughness of his investigation of any subject he was working on. Such, anyway, is Mr. Ford's theory, and with great wit he expounds it. The surviving impressionist of the Impressionists—and it is a typical effrontery, if I have not misunderstood him, that he can lump Turgenev, Wells, Galsworthy and Dreiser together under this egoistic term, with Hudson and Conrad—has brought the essence of them all to life in a manner which, outside his own earlier efforts, has not been equalled by any other writer.

52. 'Mightier than Most Pens': Charles Williams on *Mightier than the Sword*

Time and Tide, xix, 12 March 1938, 350

Like V. S. Pritchett, Charles Williams (1886–1945) was reminded by this book of the long history of contemporary letters of which Ford was a part. Thus at this late date there began to be an appreciation of what Ford had stood for over the years. Still, he never even approached the status of Grand Old Man. Williams was a poet and novelist and author of books with religious themes.

There is no other living writer whose work is more generally effective than Mr. Ford Madox Ford's. I have been aching for years, I now realize, to write that sentence. The method of his effectiveness is, to some extent, defined in a sentence in the present book. He says, of a certain period, that he was trying 'to evolve for myself a vernacular of an extreme quietness that would suggest someone of some refinement talking in a low voice to someone else he liked a good deal.' One recognizes there the development of a style, from (say) *Ladies Whose Bright Eyes*—and I cannot help it if Mr. Ford now despises that book, but I hope he does not—up to *Great Trade Route* and the present. The clauses of the sentence vary in application. In the Tietjens books the quietness and the accuracy were so extreme that the voice seemed to come from under one's own skin; if the experiences of those books were not one's own, yet the nightmare of them was. The reader was split; it was part of the nightmare. As Mr. Ford's description here of the Tsar reading Turgenev shows. In *Great Trade Route* and in this, the voice is raised by a little, by as much as, coming from one's brain, it would be more audible than coming from one's nerves. And as for 'of some refinement,' which might be evilly taken, there is no other word which suggests a certain clarity, an apprehension of history, an appreciation of proportion.

All these qualities are in *Mightier than the Sword*, which is a series of 'sketches of strong men who lived before today's Agamemnons.' They are Henry James, Stephen Crane, Hudson, Conrad, D. H. Lawrence, Hardy, Wells, Galsworthy, Turgenev, Dreiser, Swinburne, with a final note under the heading 'There were strong men.' It will be safe for any one to assume that Mr. Ford admires the owners of those names, but unsafe, without reading the book, to assume the particular quality of his admiration for each. He has known and been actively concerned with all. But here he has made them more than actual. 'I want them,' he says, 'to be seen pretty much as you see the characters in a novel.' *Tam antiqua, tam nova*; they are novel indeed. Mr. Ford has 'presented' them in such a way that the quality of his love is part of each figure, and since (as one would expect of the 'vernacular . . . of some refinement') he is aware that this must always alter and characterize the figure, he has in every sentence at once pressed and withdrawn that quality, now less and now more personal in his talk, at once conversational and classic, to the many, to the few, to the one, even to the one only imaginary reader whom he 'likes a good deal.'

Mr. Ford has never been without what, in any one else, would have been a touch of malice. There is a suggestion of malice without tears here, a faint flicker of something that might, elsewhere, be malice, and is no more than the extra sharpness of the pencil, the new ribbon on the typewriter. By love and by brilliant intelligence the book is full of the most thrilling things—Henry James talking to the housemaid, Lawrence appearing in the drawing room which was the office of the *English Review*, Hardy confessing that he was a practising and communicating member of the Church of England, Galsworthy at the dinner of the P.E.N. in Paris, Charlotte the housemaid and Mr. Swinburne, Hudson contradicting Mr. Belloc on Sussex, and so on. It is no less full of comments on our civilization which, also, come to one in a voice of some friendliness, some refinement, some quietness, some sense of danger and fate. This may be because, now, Mr. Ford is one of the very few writers who are not ignorant of our past. Sheer actual ignorance is the chief characteristic of most books today, and deliberate ignorance of most of the rest.

Mr. Ford may or may not remain as a part of English letters. But at least he has been steadily, admiringly, and pleasurably, read by some for a generation. The immortality of a generation for a generation. The immortality of a generation is perhaps the best working substitute for the absolute thing—if he will excuse the temporary offer.

53. 'A History of Writing': John Peale Bishop on *The March of Literature*

New Republic, xcvi, 26 October 1938, 339-40

Ford had hoped that his long *March of Literature*, his vast survey of literature 'from Confucius to modern times', would create a good deal of controversy, especially among academic critics, against whose influence it was directed. But the book was merely dismissed, at least in America, and given to second-string reviewers. The critic for the *Saturday Review of Literature* merely called the book 'a prolonged discourse by Mr. Ford. It has no other interest . . . It will exasperate anyone who knows the literature with which it deals . . .' For the critic of the *New York Times*, it was simply old-fashioned, 'a monument, possibly the last great monument, of the reading habits and education of the older generation, when to read was the beginning of literature'. The only American review that revealed an awareness of the book's intention was written by the poet John Peale Bishop.

'This is the book of an old man mad about writing—in the sense that Hokusai called himself an old man mad about painting.' So much, and no more, Ford Madox Ford claims for himself in his introduction to *The March of Literature*, and it would scarcely be possible for words more concisely to convey the personal and passionate quality of this history of the imaginative literature of the world. The book is tolerant, generous, large and, like the literature of which it treats, humane.

Written for the common reader, it will excite him alternately to admiration and annoyance. It can hardly leave him unmoved. He will find, whatever his complexion, any number of statements to cavil at; he will wonder at the inaccuracies, which are not many, but which when they occur seem due, never to ignorance, but always to a perserve invention. Why, for instance, should Mr. Ford, who was brought up at the knees of the Pre-Raphaelites and counts the Rossettis in his own family, assert against all conjecture that Guido Cavalcanti was forty years older than Dante? But of dullness, none will complain. And in the praise, all will, I think, concur. For Mr. Ford reminds us that it is the proudest privilege of the critic to praise, provided he can come on the proper words and reasons for his praise.

The reasons which Mr. Ford finds for praise are always his own. His preference is for order and restraint in writing, in content, for the ordinary; and hence, perhaps, he is least satisfactory among the great who, like Shakespeare, depend for the effects largely upon a penetrative passion and an excess of the sensual imagination. But Mr. Ford has read everything worth reading and much that is commonly considered unreadable by any but the specialist getting up a subject. At one point he says that he supposes himself to be 'the only man alive who can make the claim to have—in his hotter youth—read right through the voluminous and insufferable *Artaxerxes* of Mme. de Scudéry (1607-1701) or the even heavier and longer *Grand Cyrus*.' He knows Latin and Greek and has made French, Provençal, Italian, Spanish and German his own; where, as in Chinese, Russian and Hebrew, he has had to depend upon translations, he has always been in touch with someone who could command the classics of those languages in the original. He has read as only a man long mad about writing could read—without thought of extraneous rewards. He holds that the end of literature is to improve us, not by promoting this or that party, not by promulgating this or that opinion—though these are things which literature on occasion has done without ceasing to be itself—but by so increasing insight, by so sustaining with delight, that we are left more truly humane. The quality of literature is the quality of humanity, so that its history must, in the long run, become a history of what man has known and felt about himself.

To write his history, Mr. Ford returns to that method of narration which he worked out, a good many years ago, with Joseph Conrad for their common use in fiction. He has told us all about that before. But in the present volume he reminds us that they were not the first to discover it and that long ago Herodotus found it advantageous for history. Its great trick is the time shift. Its convenience is that it relieves the narrator from any necessity of following the temporal sequence of events; he can place them in what order he likes. It allows Mr. Ford to consider any writer at his choice, which may be to set him far out of his country and century. Thus, Homer is mentioned in his proper place in Greek letters; he is not discussed until Mr. Ford has come to Rome, where his masterly presence serves to show up the shortcomings of even the most famous Augustans. Voltaire is compared with Confucius. And the Spanish picaresque novelists are so portrayed that in time their salient features are seen to have been inherited, not by their compatriots, but by French and English grandsons.

That Mr. Ford would use this method with great skill and tact could have been foreseen. Here, it discloses an unexpected advantage. It allows him to show how the effort to make a man a creature more truly humane has been common to the whole of mankind. No one race has a hold on wisdom; there is none, now at least, which does not owe more to others than it can contribute. The conditions which make for great literature are not altogether clear; there have been long ages of agony and short periods of calm, and agony and calm have alike produced great writing; but this much it does seem possible to say: that only where there is a general effort to create for civilization circumstances more humane will the writer arrive who can succeed in saying with words what he has silently, and it may be unsuccessfully, done. Civilization and humanity, of course, are not the same; and when they conflict there is never much doubt where literature will be found.

The impressionistic method, however, is not without its weaknesses and these become more apparent as *The March of Literature* goes on. What happens to Mr. Ford's book, when it enters the nineteenth century, is very much what happened to impressionism in painting between, say, Manet's 'Olympia' and the 'Water Lilies' of Monet: discipline is lost and something, still skillful, but very like self-indulgence, takes its place. It is true that now the great streams he has long followed divide. But the currents still run and they are stronger and deeper than he lets us know. And the contemporary country is not so flat as he makes it appear on his map, from which he has removed nearly all the heights. It may be, of course, that he no longer finds any satisfaction in talking about it. But it is odd to find Mr. Ford writing a history of the literature that is closest to our own day and leaving out, not the names of its greatest writers, but in so many cases everything but their names.

54. 'The Good Life': Graham Greene on *Provence*

London Mercury, xxxix, December 1938, 217–18

Graham Greene's interest in Ford's books was primarily due to his admiration for his technique. In an earlier essay dealing in part with *Some Do Not*, he writes of methods which, as the review printed below indicates, were also employed in *Provence*:

> The novel covers more than ten years; the narrative does not proceed chronologically but leaps back and forth in time with an agility unknown to Conrad ... Mr. Ford is unable to write narrative; he is conscious of his inability to write, as it were, along the line of time ... The memory *is* perfunctory ... The trouble in a novel which follows the chronological sequence is that your events are never history. You are condemned to write of a perpetual present and to convey the shrillness of its emotions ... Mr. Ford does not ... simply leave out; he puts in the links in his own good time, but they are properly subordinated to what he can do supremely well, dialogue and the dramatic scene.

The title-page of this book is, I think, the first on which Mr. Ford has appeared as an LL.D. A small point, and yet to all lovers of Mr. Ford's work oddly endearing. He is an author who, like his old friend Henry James, has a personality which calls for both respect and mockery. A fine writer with traces of a most engaging charlatan. Who but Mr. Ford in a book written in 1915, with the patriotic title of *Between St. Dennis and St. George* and officially intended to fan the flames, would have casually claimed acquaintance with the enemy Emperor? He is the antithesis of Kipling's ideal—'If you can talk with crowds and keep your virtue,' how do the lines run? 'or walk with Kings nor lose the common touch.' Mr. Ford has walked with kings and has indubitably lost the common touch—his style swings like ribboned glasses.

In his non-fiction—a horrid library classification—he has painted a wonderful self-portrait (as he is or as he would like to be? for it has a daydream quality): the country gentleman, the Tory, the Tietjens, with old-fashioned ideals of honour and a touch of eccentricity (he is a Catholic, but he profoundly distrusts what Christianity has made of the world and would have fought beside the Albigenses against St. Dominic): a man with a large and easy acquaintance among the great (he would include the Emperor William, Mr. Ezra Pound, Christina Rossetti, the late Charles Masterman and the proprietors of various little-known restaurants) and among the poor (Kentish farm labourers, Paris taxidrivers, and peasants of Provence): a man who can grow his own vegetables and afterwards cook them—using garlic as it should be used—and who writes this book only because his money—changed into French paper because of the failure of American banks—has just been blown by the mistral into the Rhone. And now—we gather from the title-page—he is an LL.D., and this the first fruits of his doctorate.

In *Provence* he is back on the subject of the Old Trade Route (that dream of a past golden age), though much of it is written in discomfort from London.

I don't myself want a leader, but the spectacle of an immense city drifting not merely rudderless but as if she had never had a rudder is of a depression almost infinite. One asks: Is it for this that all the martyrs died? All the sufferings of Provence alone should have sufficed to give the world of to-day some light. But there is no light anywhere, and least of all between the lowering skies of Thames valley. I am not, you understand, a pessimist: I don't want our civilisation to pull through. I want a civilisation of small men each labouring two small plots—his own ground and his own soul.

This is a perfectly serious theme—back to the Dark Ages to be saved, but nothing in Mr. Ford's hands remains too serious. As in his fiction he writes out of a kind of hilarious depression. The world of to-day, with its Northern barbarians and its cellophaned foods, is a foul place, but there is always memory—and the book becomes an elaborate pattern of memories, historical and personal, called up not only by Provence, the province, but Provence, the idea: the Albigenses and the Troubadours and Lady Patrick Campbell: St. Louis, and Ellen Terry dropping her petticoat outside Winchelsea Post Office in the company of Henry James: the old and canny confessor advising the young Hueffer who couldn't digest the Third Person of the Trinity, 'Calm yourself, my son; that is a matter for theologians. Believe as much as you can': back to the Albigenses: the ill-doings of Clovis and Simon de Montfort: Pierre Vidal: the Tarascon café keeper who won a lottery: a bull fight: the Kaiser borrowing Mrs. Kennard's cook.

He (the Emperor) mightily embarrassed Mrs. Kennard by sending to her from places like Corfu and Valetta and Jerusalem telegrams signed only 'William' ... And Heaven knows, Mrs. Kennard used to say, what her village post office people might think! ... Innumerable telegrams saying what a good time William was having and how he blessed her and what perfect Heaven it was to eat day after day the cooking of a real English chef like hers.

There is one magnificent chapter called 'The Courts of Love' (the title is ironic and nostalgic) which is a geography of London memories described in a walk from the house in Fitzroy Square where Mr. Ford's grandfather painted his big assured historical pictures, through Charlotte Street and Soho Square, to Piccadilly Circus and the advertisements for liver salts—James and Gosse and Hudson and Christina Rossetti calling young Hueffer 'her dear young connection'—'with the air of one enjoying a holy joke. She had that in common in her aspect, with Henry James. Both used exact phrases with the air of savouring them, like a bull-finch cracking hemp-seed.'

The method, you see, has something in common with Mr. Pound's *Cantos*—simultaneity, but carried out with infinitely greater technical ability. And the subject, I suppose, is just the good life—as it was lived in the Dark Ages among the Albigenses (Mr. Ford's idealized Albigenses), as it can still be lived to-day in Provence by the man with a little ground to cultivate—as it should be lived by all the world.

55. 'A Bore to End Bores': Edward Sackville-West on *The March of Literature*

New Statesman and Nation, xviii, 4 November 1939, 654

The publication of *The March of Literature* in England occurred at about the same time as Ford's death, with the result that some reviews had an obituary overtone. That consideration, however, did not affect the critic Edward Sackville-West (1901–65) who attacked the book openly.

This intimidating tome is a comprehensive review of the world's literature 'from Confucius to Modern Times.' What is its object? To whom did its late author address it? The only answer I can find to the latter question is: uneducated and only fairly intelligent Americans. It is the kind of book which will enable a young man in a hurry to mug up the subject, with a view to a pass degree. In this respect it resembles Gustave Lanson's *History of French Literature*, with the important reservation that the French professor's judgment was very much less erratic, and his erudition less suspect, than Ford's. Histories of literature, with their straining after comparisons and 'tendencies,' so as to give to their wholes some semblance of unity, are quite useless to intelligent students of the subject and a positive danger to those whose own judgment is weak and diffident. Books like this lie about the centuries like so many puddings gone cold and uneatable. Mr. Stephen Potter played football with them in *The Muse in Chains*, and one hopes that in future they will become increasingly rare.

Ford's view of the function of literature (expressed on p. 323) is roughly that of Walter Pater, though he seems to qualify it on a much later page, when he speaks of 'the poet who, exactly observing the characteristics of his time, renders them with exactitude as did, say, Vogelweide, Dante, Heine or Villon.' Art which aspires to the condition of music never does that, and the step is long from Dante to Mallarmé or Valéry, whom, incidentally, Ford does not even mention. Where he seems to me at his best is in the filling-in of dark gaps—the 'dark' ages, or the nineteenth century in Spain. Information is always worth having; but one should beware, it seems to me, of Ford's expressions of opinion on writers of whom one has not read a word, simply because what he has to say of the others is often such as to make one fidget irritably in one's chair. For the fantastic shadow of Mr. Ezra Pound falls continually across these pages, and Ford follows him in the promulgation of enormous and paradoxical views. I append the following *sottisier*, chosen at random among 850 large pages:—

Villon (Mr. Pound's special pet) is described as among 'the great and omniscient (*sic*) works of humanity,' and later as 'the greatest of the great poets' (where are Aeschylus, Shakespeare, Dante, Homer?).

Shakespeare was 'the first Anglo-Saxon big business man'—on the strength of being an actor-manager!

Kleist's *Penthesilea* is bracketed with Klopstock's *Messias* for boring worthlessness.

Apart from Jane Austen there was no first-class English novel written in the nineteenth century—except perhaps *Framley Parsonage* and *Mary Barton* (the latter a charming book by Mrs. Gaskell—in case you've never heard of it).

Whistler is classed 'amongst the giants of all time.'

I Promessi Sposi (three pages are devoted to it) is considered preferable to all Scott, and Manzoni a much greater artist than Leopardi.

Ford 'would die' for a list of books (eccentric enough in all conscience! p. 664) which includes that poor old stuffed dummy, *Lorna Doone*.

'If actually you want to find fine, nervous, expressive vernacular prose in the 1820's you must turn'—to Hazlitt? Not a bit of it! to 'the *headlines* in the country newspapers in England and in the larger provincial towns in the United States' (italics mine).

Ibsen's plays are described, by allusion, as 'nearly formless outpourings of passion' (formless!—*The Wild Duck? John Gabriel Borkman?*).

Finally, a prey to one of those brainstorms which sometimes attack overworked and flurried writers, Ford, like the last of the bathwater hurrying down the waste, plunges slap through the nineteenth century to the present day, carrying everything with him. It is a piece of distorted perspective which, for sheer wildness, leaves the German Expressionist painters far behind. It must be read to be believed (p. 790); suffice it here to say that the paragraph ends with a final gasp in which Balzac is given 'the right to sit down beside the author of

Framley Parsonage.' Poor Trollope! I cannot believe that he would have cared for such gross adulation.

Ford's treatment of modern French literature is practically non-existent. Claudel, Valéry, Gide are not mentioned at all; Proust is dismissed in a single short sentence; and the only contemporary French writer of whom Ford will hear is M. René Béhaine, 'a novelist as to whom far from only I (*sic*) have pledged their words that he is the greatest of living French writers.'

Well, well! one lives and learns . . .

56. 'Last Journey': Graham Greene on *The March of Literature*

Spectator, clxiii, 17 November 1939, 696

Written in part as a reply to West, this review is a farewell by one writer to another and has special significance in so far as Greene is the leading exponent now living of the type of novel encouraged by Ford.

This enormous posthumous book of Ford Madox Ford is a kind of literary equivalent of Mr. Wells's *History of the World*: the work of 'an old man mad about writing,' it will probably offend a great many academic critics who know far more about Chinese, Hebrew, Italian or Spanish literature than Ford ever did. It cannot on those lines be reviewed at all, for you will not find a universal critic any more than you will find another writer capable of so vast a synthesis. It must be treated as a work of imagination, not as a text-book for American students, the excuse for its production. Ford wrote:

If we succeed in turning out a work of insight and imagination and one couched in clear, uncomplicated and not harsh prose, we may make ourselves see the great stream of literature issuing from its dark and remote sources and broadening through the centuries until it comes to irrigate with its magnificent and shining waters, almost the whole of the universe of today. If we succeed in that, we too shall have produced . . . a piece of literature.

For the first third of the book he has splendidly succeeded. We are back on Ford's great trade route, but this time it is not caravans of food and spices making from the East towards his beloved Provence; it is civilisation itself swaying like a camel, harried and hunted by vandal tribes, sometimes settling down in the desert sand to die, getting up on its knees again and goaded on. . . . There is no happy ending—any more than there was to *Great Trade Route*: he sees 'the doctrines of humaneness going, coiling as it were, from Sardis and Lydia to Babylon and again to Jerusalem and coming thus to us who sit here in times so infinitely more ferocious, to be to us at once a cause of shame and enlightenment.'

One can only jot down notes on the progress of the immense journey: how freshly, for example, Ford writes of Xenophon in terms of soldiering, as if he were a general under whom he had served (it was a theory of Tietjens' creator that most great writers have seen military service); the breadth of his references, so that Aristophanes puts him in mind of Leon Daudet, Pindar of a certain regimental roll call in the French Army, Athens of the atmosphere of Paris during the Press strikes; the novelty and excitement; he brings to the consideration of the too considered names in Latin literature.

With the death of Virgil and the birth of Christ the magnificent poetic range, the wide comprehension of this curious Catholic, breaks abruptly off. He explains it himself, 'It was as if, then, divinity passed at once from the figures of emperors and poets to light up figures vastly different—to St. Simeon on his pillar, to St. Joan on her faggots, and say to the late Mr. Spurgeon of the City Temple . . . except for Dante and of course Goethe, world poetry was at an end.' So Shakespeare is oddly (and interestingly) minimised as a national dramatist, and it is in Donne alone in English literature that Ford finds the otherworldliness which is the mark for him of greatness: Villon, Dante, Isaiah, St. Augustine—he finds in them and in Donne 'an overtone that can only be reached by those whose nature has been purged by the contemplation of supreme horror.'

But we have reached nationalism, and with no leaders the caravan is going astray. This is the Balkanisation of literature; it is necessary to follow in too much detail too many literatures; sometimes we get bogged in a mass of minor German novelists. It is as if the attack on the caravan had at last succeeded (Ford would have said when St. Dominic destroyed the Albigenses, for whom he had a blind attachment). We get the figure of a camel-driver hunting his beasts here and there rather frantically: a good many have been lost altogether: no mention of Camoëns: only passing references to *Paradise Lost*, Baudelaire: no Proust or Rilke. Dryden gets a savage blow from the goad (nobody, it seems, can get any aesthetic pleasure from 'The Hind and the Panther,' and Ford speaks of his 'quite unreadable plays'). Judgements become wild, the time sequence hopelessly confused, until we stagger at last into the unsatisfactory caravanserai of the nineteenth century. Then our enjoyment of the book, which has never—even at times of extraordinary confusion—faltered, becomes rather different. Here is the Ford of the autobiographies, of the astounding anecdotes which he never pretended were strictly accurate (even the year of his own first novel is wrongly given): we hear of Stevenson seeking adventure round Seven Dials dressed as a railway ganger; Thackeray coming on board his liner at Leghorn in the early morning, striking his forehead in repentance and exclaiming, 'I am a hoary lecher!'; Zola waiting for the author in Hyde Park, 'seated on a park bench almost in tears over the quantity of hairpins that with the end of his cane he was counting on the ground.' So this great writer takes his bow—as one of our finest prose writers, as a poet, and—it would have been incomplete else—as one of the scamps of literature.

57. 'A Literary Banqueter: With Madox Ford Through the Ages': unsigned review of *The March of Literature*

The Times Literary Supplement, 9 December 1939, 716, 721

The Times Literary Supplement was one of the few journals in England or America to give adequate space to Ford's last book. The opinion of their reviewer may be taken as generally representative of Ford's literary reputation at the time of his death.

This is not a posthumous publication because Ford's book was printed and published in America last year, and he died in June of this year. It is not possible, therefore, to follow the natural impulse to acquit him of careless proof-reading, which has left many little mistakes, and of less excusable carelessness which has left more serious mistakes. That 'almost every year the Greek play given at Westminster School—which is one of the great social functions of the London season—will be one of Aristophanes's dramas adapted to the denunciation or ridicule of prominent English politicians, members of the clergy or educationalists'; that 'the late Mr. Kipling, before the late War, never spoke of the French save as the *Bander-Log*—the chattering little people, thus monkeys'; that Ben Jonson was accounted the best actor of his day; that Purcell set Shakespeare's songs to music while 'the Tudor manor houses were going up all over' the 'broad acres' of England; and, later, that Purcell's songs were sung by Colonel Hutchinson, who died when Purcell was five or six years old—these are errors in matters familiar to most of Ford's English readers which counsel wariness in accepting all he says in strange fields; and three whopping howlers in the quotation of George Herbert's lines (known and hated by every housemaid) about sweeping a room do not inspire confidence in quotations from poets less generally known.

In so large, so vehement, so manifold a book as this, such mistakes are, no doubt, inevitable; but there is another kind which could ill be spared because they throw so much light on Ford's own mind and on the results of this aldermanic way of devouring books. One of Ford's odd ideas is that, to make good literature, a man must live a hard life and be dependent on it, or, in milder form, that the man of action—'the writer who has lived'—writes better than the man who has only read. To illustrate this he shows two groups descending from his great hero, Chaucer—Otway has somehow managed to get into both—but because Richardson was one of Ford's great writers a place must be found for him among the 'writers who had lived.'

It is evident by the example of great writers that a man must have lived a full life of action, danger and even despair before he could render the life that surrounded him. For how can you estimate the real values of life unless you have fought to preserve your own with rapier and dagger, unless you have faced, with Villon, starvation, or unless you have at the very least learned the value of mere money, like Richardson, who supported himself as a printer before he ever thought of feeding the presses.

That passage is enough in itself to send a hundred readers in haste to a book that can offer them such exciting surprises, such gaily defiant literary acrobatics. And indeed Ford's prejudices, and his ingenuity in the gallant defence of them, are one of the most alluring qualities of this joyful book. But soberer persons must give and take warning. Among the writers who were not men of action but mere readers comes Fielding. Ford loathed Fielding. Another is Addison; and just to prove how the mere readers, Addison among them, drift into affected Latinisms, he quotes a piece from the *Spectator* by Steele and another piece by Addison (the Steele paper is No. 11; the Addison No. 26; both are numbered wrong in Ford's footnote). We are asked to contrast the prose of the officer of Horse Guards with that of the mere reader. But it so happens that Steele's sentences, a piece of direct and simple narrative, are peppered with words of Latin origin.

Addison's offence was that in meditating over the tombs in Westminster Abbey he called certain tombstones 'Registers of Existence.' What is more, he quotes, in the original Greek, out of Homer, and in the original Latin, Virgil's literal translation of them. Addison, then, 'cannot even meditate a moment among the homes of the dead without showing that he was acquainted with Greek and Latin.' But Steele could not tell his readers about Mr. Thomas Inkle of London without putting a Latin tag at the head of his essay; and Addison had a very particular purpose in quoting out those names from Homer and from

Virgil as well. 'A "tombstone,"' writes Ford, 'is a disagreeable reminder; a "register of existence" could not unpleasantly still the bosom of a Sophia, a Narcissa or an Olivia.' It is better, no doubt, to use one's imagination wrongly on an author than not to use it at all; but the truth is (as all who know that limpid and lovely essay have long understood) that 'register of existence' is the simplest, most precise, the least affected statement of what Addison meant. He is writing of the tombs of people unknown. Their tombs are their only memorial; like the parish register, they are the only evidence that such people ever existed. Like the three heroes mentioned by Homer, they are unknown outside that reference; so unknown that Virgil had nothing to tell about them but their names. And 'registers of existence' is more than a clear, precise piece of English compared with Steele's 'preventing the natural impulses of his passions, by prepossession towards his interests'; it has a reason for existence which Ford's own 'homes of the dead' has not. Ford, to adapt a phrase of Shylock's, was a huge reader; but the hugest reader could scarcely miss so plain a point if he were not blinded to it by what Steele would call a prepossession to his interest, a point that he wants to make. This form of blindness befell Ford more severely still when he came to write about Cervantes. The simplest explanation of his criticism would be that he had never read *Don Quixote* through, and knew nothing of the care that Cervantes takes to show the Don's natural nobility of soul and wisdom of judgment, and nothing of Sancho's rulings when he sat in judgment as governor of his 'island.' But it is much more likely that Ford had read the whole book, but with slight attention to the parts of it which might modify his preconceived idea of it, and without pausing to reflect that what he saw as 'a vulgar kick in the behind' to the departing ideal of chivalry was an attempt to give true chivalry room to grow by cutting away dead rubbish.

Something, perhaps too much of this. But this extraordinary and life-giving book will be thrown away on anyone who accepts it as an authority, as most histories of literature are accepted by the ingenuous student. Nothing would make Ford himself more angry—Ford with his insatiable contempt for all men, opinions and bodies academic. There is inconsistency in the very title of his book—*The March of Literature*. A march is a combined, regulated, prescribed, involuntary movement. The march of which Ford writes is about as regular, organised and predictable as the flight of a butterfly. 'From Confucius to modern times'—nothing less than that is the subject which this 'old man mad about writing,' as he calls himself, purposes to set before us; and if the progress had been indeed a march, a duller writer than he could have followed it in a duller book than this. Something of the scope and variety of the theme may be learned from the first section of the fourth chapter of the first part of the first book; but a compacter statement of the theme will be found in the second chapter of the first part of the second book—that which brings us on from Shakespeare and Marlowe to 'the most English of all writers—the Donne, Herbert, Crashaw, Marvell, Vaughan, Dryden constellation.' He has been considering (with his favourite device of significant dates) the nature of the literary intercourse of Spain, France and England, and leaving his reader entirely free to accept or not to accept certain suggestions—among them the idea of 'the influences of Ronsard and Du Bellay and the rest of the Pleïadists as being wafted across the English skies as pollen is showered on the winds by the opening buds of May.' But these speculations, he goes on, are worth weighing privately; they enlarge the mind, and

point to the fact that our beloved art is the product of all humanity from the beginning of time. It is unnecessary to insist minutely on the derivations of Richardson from K'ung-Fu-Tsze or Po-Chu-I, with whom we began these histories, though we have already chased out influences of the Sage of the Middle Kingdom to Voltaire. But it is as well from time to time to take the eye from the printed page and to consider that it is, our art, an immense stream, coming from the dawn and spreading its eddies for thousands of years and half the globe over, as an immense, an overwhelming, proof of the fact of the unity of humanity and of the products of the human mind.

Literature, he says elsewhere (and in his very first chapter he has fallen over himself in his eagerness to explain what he means by literature):—

Literature, the humaner letters, has been an immense river that, starting from Cathay and Nile sources, spread through Palestine, Greece, Rome and then, broadening out as the West mentally broadened, went lapping away in an immense, slow, boundless, tide, not merely towards Ultima Thule but into the inmost recesses of the Teutoburger Wald.

Starting from Cathay and Nile sources—our author begins with folk-songs of Egyptian peasants and fishermen of more than two thousand years B.C.—he ends with writers still alive. The huge reading, in many languages, which went into this work alone commands respect. True, Ford was given a good start. With Francis Hueffer for father and William Michael Rossetti for uncle by marriage he was cradled in artistic and literary enthusiasms; and among the many personal touches that enliven his book he lets out that as a child he read John Lyly, Novalis, Schopenhauer, *Celestina*, *Lazarillo de Tormes*, *The Grand Cyrus* and goodness knows what else in their original tongues. So large an appetite for reading, not for duty but for the love of it, rarely finds the strength of thought to support it. Ford's enthusiasm never flagged; and perhaps the most engaging page in the whole book is that (p. 664) in which he talks about the books which are 'almost universally beloved and before which criticism suspends itself.' He had at hand, then, good store of matter for the exhibition of literature from ancient Egypt to modern New York: and he had also the breadth of vision which could hold the course of his 'immense river' from the source to the flats over which he saw its waters at last expanded.

In estimating some books it would matter much whether the central theory was sound or not. In this book of Ford's it matters not a jot. It may be partly true, or wholly untrue, and the quality of the book remains unharmed. In details, an expert in any one of Ford's many periods and subjects will pretty certainly find plenty to correct; clear knowledge of all that carelessness or prejudice or ignorance has distorted will not diminish the pleasure of reading in the book. That pleasure comes of swinging along at a very rapid pace in company with one who has considerable knowledge of the whole country and, more important still, can communicate his passionate likes and dislikes and give at any rate plausible reasons for them. Some sort of principle suggests them. We stand, he writes ('we' meaning himself and the reader who is in agreement with him):—

We stand for Homer and the Greek lyricists as against Virgil and the Augustan Romans; for the Middle Ages as against the Renaissance; for the seventeenth as against the eighteenth century; for the Realists as against the Romantics; and, above all, for the conscious literary artist as against the inspired person,

who, he goes on to say in his most torrential manner, only writes when he is drunk. That profession is fairly sound. The core of it is the conviction that the writer's duty is to write of life as it is about him, and his worst crime is to shut himself up in an ivory tower or romantic aloofness. Most of Ford's vehement dislikes, and some of his even less easily explicable omissions, can be traced back rather faintly to that, with some little impatience and insensitiveness to help. Fielding, the Decameron, Goldsmith, Schlegel, these he detests mainly on moral grounds; and, when he writes of the drama which 'with Congreve and

Wycherly and the rest finally abandoned the literary art,' we cannot but wonder whether he had ever read Congreve's prose with care, and who 'the rest' may be that can thus be lumped in with him. But Ford's great hatreds—his denunciations of Plato, of the Virgil of the Aeneid (to the beauties in which he is utterly blind because the poem had a political and courtly purpose), of Scott and, in some measure, of Dante—these seem to depend sincerely upon some test in his mind or instinct which rejected the faintest taste of romance. These outbursts are almost as stimulating as his admiration; but they lose a little through their tendency to annoy. It is when Ford's enjoyment is the enjoyment of liking, not of disliking, that he is at his best. When he praises Chaucer, or his beloved Provence, or *I Promessi Sposi*, or Henry James, he reveals at its noblest his passion for beauty.

The quality that is necessary for the production of the Art of Literature is simply that of a personality of wide appeal. An art is the highest form of communication between person and person. . . . The more attractive the personality making the communication the wider in extent, the deeper in penetration and the more lasting will be the appeal. What the subject may be is of no importance whatever.

That is one of his initiatory shots at defining literature. And near the end of the book he is vowing that the first duty of the author is to keep himself out, not to intrude. It is a melancholy decline from the assertion of personality to a literature in which every one must try to write exactly like every one else. But the reader of Ford's book will have an exhilarating journey from the one point to the other.

GENERAL ARTICLES ON FORD

58. 'Ford Madox Ford: A Portrait in Impressions': Herbert Gorman, New York *Bookman*

lxvii, March 1928, 56–60

The success of the Tietjens novels in New York created a considerable amount of interest in Ford, and Herbert Gorman's article constitutes the first extended treatment Ford and his work ever received, apart from some of the early reviews of his poetry. Gorman's description of Ford in his Parisian milieu must have been of special interest to Americans, many of whose authors were then living abroad as expatriates.

Herbert Gorman (1893–1954) was a New York journalist and author of several works of literary criticism and biography.

I

The taxi, its impertinent little horn squeaking blithely, slurs about the corner on two wheels. Behind it the Panthéon—where Jean-Jacques Rousseau lies in his sepulchre and where Voltaire does *not*—looms in a cloudy mist. It is dark in the rue du Cardinal Lemoine except for the tiny flashes of light from the few *brasseries*, dark until the taxi—its engine heaving breathlessly—draws up before the narrow entrance to the *bal musette*.

Then, as the door opens, a thin shaft of light spurts across the pavement. We enter to the high whining moan of an accordion and the measured thump of a drum. The music resolves itself to the eternal tune of Parisian *bal musettes* this season as we press by the tiny zinc bar.

Valencia!
Terre exquise
Où la brise
Effeuille les fleurs d'orange!

We dispose ourselves at a long wooden table, call for champagne, and turn our attention to the small square of dancing-floor in the rear, a square that is now crowded with figures hopping up and down in a peculiar rhythmic fashion. Above these syncopating puppets is a small balcony fastened like a bird's nest to the wall and in it are seated two perspiring nonchalant musicians, one of them pressing an accordion and the other pounding on a drum.

These musicians are the last word in ennui. Their eyes are partially closed and their hands move like hands in a trance. José Padilla's bastard Spanish music flows down through the smoke and dust from their automatic hands and curls about the feet of the dancers but it means nothing to these blasé figures in striped shirts and unabashed galluses. They will come to life presently when the music stops and two large glasses of atrocious French beer are hoisted to them by the tiny bar-maid. Then, with moustaches snowy with froth, they will discourse learnedly with one another. What do *bal musette* musicians talk about between dances? If we knew that we could possibly throw more light on the perplexed problem of the French franc.

We drop our eyes from the two-man orchestra, sip our champagne, and observe the hopping figures. At first these men and women, these boys and girls, crowded on the small square of dancing-floor are a kaleidoscopic medley. We recognize the young French labourers in highly colored shirts and with caps clutched in their hands. We recognize the young women and wonder if it would be literary pomposity to call them *grisettes*. Then, as our eyes become accustomed to the smoke and dust and lights we begin to perceive individuals, to fasten our eyes upon them, to conjecture about their personalities. It is while we are indulging in this purposeless and impossible pastime that we notice what at a first glance appears to be a behemoth in gray tweeds. He turns in the dance and we recognize him immediately. The blue eyes, the blond hair, the bland cherubic expression, the open mouth—we rise up from our champagne and shout, 'Hey, Ford!'

It is the Leviathan of the Quartier Montparnasse, the gentle Gargantua of Lavigne's, the sophisticated Doctor Johnson of Notre Dame des Champs, Ford Madox Ford. He plods happily and with a child-like complacency through the dance, his partner swaying like a watch-fob before him. After the music stops he will amble over breathing a trifle heavily in memory of the poisonous gas during the Great War and sit down and invite us to join his party. And then, at another table much nearer the dancing-floor, we see Stella and Olga and Jean and Ernest and Bill and realize that this is Ford's Night at the *bal musette*.

So we change our places and there is dance after dance, bottle after bottle, laughter, bursts of song, and, finally, a string of taxis bearing us back to the Quartier where there will be more liquor and more music and much conversation. The stars will shine down on the Luxembourg Gardens and the quietude of Montparnasse cemetery and Saint-Sulpice and the deserted street-crossing before the Café du Dôme but we will continue to sit and talk of the right word in the right place and dear Ezra—now in Rapallo—and Joyce and Ernest's new novel and the winding roads of Provence and expatriatism and what is the best brand of cognac and all those immeasurably important things that make life on the Left Bank worth living. And through our conversation we hear faint echoes of an accordion and a drum.

Valencia!
Fleur perverse
Qui nous verse
Tous les parfums tour à tour—
Je t'aime
Car j'eus le bonheur suprême
Dans ton paradis d'amour!

II

Ford occupies a curious place in the life of the Quartier and to understand it we must differentiate between surfaces and depths. The casual visitor will observe no more than a glancing surface, a series of social forays, a flow of conversation liquidated with Biscuit and stabilized with *pain français*. Around that notorious street-corner, which, after all, sees so little of Ford, the purposeless expatriates swirl, repose in wicker chairs before tiny tables, gulp endless *apéritifs* and *bocks* and *liqueurs*.

These people are the people of Ernest Hemingway's *The Sun Also Rises*, Gertrude Stein's 'lost generation'. Where they are going and what disastrous culmination of circumstances set them in motion is a theme that has no place here. It is enough to point out that these *enfants perdus* do not entirely possess the Quartier Montparnasse; they are but a small whirlpool in the great and placid river of life in that section of Paris. Their antics have become a topic of conversation in two countries but they are not representative of the sixth *arrondissement*. They are the noise of the Quartier, the idle, drinking, lost regiment of careless fatalists.

Montparnasse has its depths, however. Ford, himself, suggests them in *A Mirror to France*, where he writes:

> In a post-war world I have come to believe that the indigent alone are the only persons worthy of respect—or at any rate those who are frugal and undispendious, and it seems to me that the young men who work their passages from Cardiff or Indiana and, arriving in Paris without knowledge of the language or money for taxis, at dead of night make somehow their way to the Luxembourg Gardens round which they wander seeking an entrance, till dawn—these Young are the salt of the Anglo-Saxon. (They do this because of Remy de Gourmont's 'Night in the Luxembourg', which makes them imagine that you can sleep on a bench beneath the statue of Verlaine.) And there are enough young men like these to make the Montparnasse district almost worthwhile of themselves. So, if one adds the several distinguished practitioners of all the arts who work there (I *can't* work there myself), it really does assume a very marked aspect of worthwhileness. I should imagine (again I remark that I don't work there myself) that the most vital work in the Arts that is now being produced is the work of artists living somewhere in the square of territory included between the Luxembourg Palace, the Lion de Belfort, the place du Maine and the bottom of the rue de Rennes—or at any rate by workers very familiar with those *parages*. I am of course talking of non-French artists who are there in the immense majority.

The reader, therefore, must remember that for every man lolling in a chair before the Café du Dôme, Le Select, or La Rotonde there are five working in high studios. These workers do drop into the cafés at times, some of them every day, but they loaf with the pleasant realization that they have accomplished something or are, at least, in the heat of some creative labor.

It is from the hordes of these ambitious and serious young men that Ford draws his entourage. His *Transatlantic Review* (now unhappily defunct) was a rallying point for them. Many of them were (and are) 'Ford's boys'. There are reasons for the paternal place which Ford occupies in their midst. He is, after all, 'the good soldier' of literature, the understanding officer who encourages, suggests, and pushes his men forward. He is a man of sensibility, if the word may be used, and he is, in himself, a living example of the literary tradition.

It would be gratuitous to point out again Ford's literary antecedents and life-long contacts. Specifically it means nothing that he is related to the Rossettis or that he was a collaborator with Joseph Conrad. These things, again, are unimportant. But they predicate a something in Ford, a flowering of the mind, an immersion in the 'right' river, a being 'in' and a partaking 'of' that makes the born and fully-developed literary man. He emanates an atmosphere of authenticity in letters that influences those about him. Whether he is sitting quietly and talking of literature, telling tales out of school, as it were, about movements and men whose names are now a portion of the English heritage, or whether he is plunging with a delightful wholeness of mind and being into his beloved French life, he always suggests the intellectual life.

There is no way of precisely putting it. One can but suggest his sanity of purpose and his literary self-assurance. Younger men, therefore, feel that in touching hands with him they are touching hands with the vital force of literature and when they converse with him they are dipping their minds into the expansive stream of quickened and alert impulse. This is provocative and it sends the young man back to his manuscript with renewed perception and confidence in himself. He is 'set right', as it were, because of the indefinable aroma of the born writer that emanates from Ford.

Ford has never hurried himself. He decided that he could not write a really fine novel until he was forty years old and therefore it was not until he was forty that *The Good Soldier* appeared. And it was not until nearly a decade after that *Some Do Not* saw the light, to be followed in due course by *No More Parades*, *A Man Could Stand Up* and *The Last Post*. He had been in the thick of the mêlée long before *The Good Soldier* was published, however, and the row of his early books is long and impressive. A deal of this work was *pastiche*, the ebullitions of an inordinately clever young man, and it comprehended novels (an admirable story like **Ladies Whose Bright Eyes**, for instance), reminiscence (witness *Revolving Lights*), poetry (half a dozen excellent little books, the cream of which may be found in the *Collected Poems*), and monographs, nature essays, critical commentaries (his *Henry James* is a sensitively understanding introduction), travel (there is *New York is Not America* for a recent example), and political discussion.

In other words, he has touched the intellectual life of his times at all angles, has been intrigued by all facets, has been an inveterate foe of narrow specialization. Most of this, at least until we reach *The Good Soldier*, may be regarded as a brilliant preparation for what was to follow. He was achieving that high state of comprehension and intuitive artistry that flowered so finely in *Some Do Not*.

III

This, however, is not a biographical account of Ford. Neither is it a critical study. It is impression merely and to delve too deeply into his specific works would defeat the object of these paragraphs, which is to suggest the nature of the man. If he has done so much he has not failed to play agreeably when the opportunities to do so presented themselves. So we have the varying pictures of Ford wandering through Toulon, of Ford swimming in the Rhone where the Palace of the Popes looms in the distance, Ford dancing at the *bal musette* or in his capacious studio, Ford brewing a hot Regency punch in the supposed Sahara of New York, Ford descanting on the vagaries of Welsh soldiers in the back dining-room of Lavigne's, Ford advising a gloomy friend to have a nice hot cup of *tilleul* in the Closerie des Lilas, Ford meandering up the Boulevard de Montparnasse with a string of friends pursuing him, and Ford meticulously ordering the best dinner that ever was at the Grille St. Michel.

He is unhurried in all of his actions and this tranquillity of being immediately sets him apart from those young men with whom he enjoys tasting the various bits of life. They, with years to spare, are still rushing about, ruffled in demeanor, uncertain of purpose, and exasperated with trifles; Ford, having passed the mid-point of his career, moves more sedately, contained and poised, quite certain as to his objective, and unannoyed by peccadilloes.

He comprehends the younger generation (a generation which he preceded in maturity but which he has made peculiarly his own) with a singular astuteness and humor. In his hours of slippered ease he may imagine himself a Tory but if he is that almost extinct species he yet whiles his Tory hours away with Ezra Pound's latest poem. He is a Roman Catholic, too, and yet he was one of the first to recognize the genius of James Joyce and the greatness of *Ulysses*.

He is, first of all and always, a champion, a stout St. Paul for such enthusiasms as Henry James, Stephen Crane, Ezra Pound, or Ernest Hemingway. Wherever distinguished individuality in letters appears we may be sure of finding him, a ready fighter in a good cause, an unenvious ally. New forms do not displease him and neither do new thoughts; but he insists on the purity of the literary instinct, the absolute sincerity behind the experiment.

He admires a distinguished precision of utterance. Was he not, for years, concerned with *le mot juste*? In his own later work, in *Some Do Not*, in *No More Parades*, in *A Man Could Stand Up*, in *The Last Post*, he has given ample evidence of his love of precision, of his love for an essentially modern approach, of his love of the fastidious capture of nuances. His gods are obvious—pure thought and the Arts.

Although no one can be more English than Ford (there are even times when he looks and talks like a very epitome of all English squires) it is impossible to dissociate him from France. He has been accused of having written the finest French novel in the English language and this kindly accusation gives a hint of the Gallic lucidity and precision in his mentality. France has influenced his literary personality almost as much as England. The two countries stand for those things for which alone he considers life worth living. He delivers his dictum on this matter straight from the shoulder in *A Mirror to France*.

And what stands out in our world of Thought and the Arts is this: It is only England and France that matter to our European civilization of today—England for all the finenesses that she has produced and ignored; France for all the glories that would have been forever hers had she not owned Provence. On the fate of England, trembling in the balance, and on the destinies of France, hang the hopes of all the European world.

Let us, for heaven's sake, be insular and —as long as we include France—bold, bad, remorselessly exclusive. We are not now in a world that concerns itself with international commerce, sham diplomacies, politico-economics; hardly even with military good-fellowship. These are not the concerns of Thought or of the Arts; they are the games of savages who out of ham-bones, skins, beef-tins and dyed potato sacks make gods for themselves. Did you ever talk to a diplomat? I have talked with one, almost omnipotent, about international affairs when he happened to be rather drunk and I was very angry. If you had heard that conversation you would know why the world of great industries is staggering to its ruin amidst imprecations.

So let us, for heaven's sake, say that it is only these two countries that matter. Imagine the bottom of the sea falling out and, into the cavity, England going down. There would be a considerable whirlpool. Imagine France to follow; there would be no more world—not any world of Thought and the Arts. Not anywhere. Its backbone would be gone.

This is possibly thin comfort for the embattled young American who perceives in the Republic a vast future for both Thought and the Arts. It must be remembered, however, that Ford is moulded and shaped by England and France, that—immersed in that European civilization—he draws all his vitality from British and French springs. For him the bottom *would* be out of the world if his two nations were to disappear. And, perhaps, there would be very little pure Thought and unalloyed Art for any of us left if France and England were to fail us.

The white dusty road overlooks the Rhone and where I stand I can see the old ruined bridge thrusting forward like a finger in the calm current. Behind me that great desolate heap of masonry that once was the Palace of the Popes rears itself on the height. It is very quiet in Avignon, very hot, and the sunlight burns upon the white battlements. Far away, in one direction, lies Paris where in the rue du Cardinal Lemoine a blasé accordion-player starts feet dancing in a tiny *bal musette*; and not so far away, in another direction, lies the breathlessly blue Mediterranean Sea under a cloudless sky. That ancient water laps softly against tawny shores. It is full of mingled voices, faint cries, and ancient objurgations. Disconnected vocables seem to whisper on the shingle, Phoenician, Roman, Spanish, French. This too, is the land of Ford, perhaps the dearest of his lands. He, himself, has said: '. . . From the very beginning of life—and no doubt in my ante-natal blood, I have always been subject to the feeling of a pressure towards that Southern magnetic Pole which lies in the region between Avignon, Arles and Nimes'. He knows that civilizations are born of gaieties, paganisms, riches and lazinesses and he knows that Provence was the home and cradle of all these things. Therefore he goes back every summer and steeps himself in an old magic that is fashioned from sunlight, laughter, memories, ruins, and leisure.

If our first meeting with him was in the *bal musette* where he was dancing to the strains of an accordion and the thumping of a drum our last glimpse, perhaps, should be one of him swimming in the Rhone with the hot sun hovering over him like a golden hawk. For there he is merged in the contentment of an impalpable atmosphere formed of historical memories and forgotten urges. And after he comes out of the glittering water he will make a nice hot cup of English tea for us while the gracious Stella will put us at ease and we will talk of Bertran de Born and the Courts of Love and the Fair of Beaucaire and—oh, yes!—pure Thought and the Arts.

59. 'Ford Madox Ford—A Neglected Contemporary': Granville Hicks New York *Bookman*

lxxii, December 1930, 364–70

A year before this article was published, Hugh Walpole noted the disgraceful critical neglect Ford had to endure: '. . . there is no greater literary neglect of our time in England than the novels and poems of Ford. Consider only the diversity of it from the Henry VIII Trilogy, through the fine austerity of *The Good Soldier* to the nobility of the War novels! Why doesn't some one write a proper critical article on Ford? Here is a subject crying out to be used' (*New York Herald Tribune Books*, 24 November 1929). Whether Granville Hicks's essay was written in direct response to this suggestion is unknown, but it certainly fulfilled a need as the first general critical survey given Ford's work and career as a whole. Hicks (b. 1901) is a well-known American critic, biographer and literary essayist.

It would not, I imagine, please Mr. Ford to be called neglected. He has written more than sixty books, and he has seen the Shelleys of the last half-century very plain indeed. When he was in his twenties he was called the most perfect stylist in the English language; Joseph Conrad sought him as a collaborator; and more recently, his war tetralogy has led to his being compared with Proust. He has not, obviously, been neglected in any ordinary sense. This is not a tale of a lonely genius, left to starve in the conventional garret, bequeathing to the world a slender manuscript of exquisite verse or a few pages of miraculous prose. It is a much more puzzling story, the story of a man who has been in the thick of every literary fray and yet is ignored by the literary historians, a man whose individual books have, as they appeared, been greeted as unusual achievements but whose work as a whole has made little impression on the contemporary mind. In several rather detailed studies of modern literature his name is not even mentioned, and no one, so far as I know, has ever made an effort to estimate his importance. Everyone knows he exists—it would be rather hard, all things considered, to ignore the fact—but there are few people who could accurately tell you what he has done.

Ford was born in 1873. His was a pre-Raphaelite boyhood. In the home of his grandfather, Ford Madox Brown, he looked upon Holman Hunt, Edward Burne-Jones, William Morris, and the Rossettis, one of whom, William was his uncle. Ford's father, South German by birth and a Doctor of Philosophy from Göttingen, was music critic for *The Times*; he was an ardent Wagnerian, an admirer of Schopenhauer, and a foe to Prussianism. Young Hueffer—the surname was changed to Ford after the war—grew up in the literal shadow of late Victorian genius, and his first words must have been spoken shrilly in order to be audible above the argumentative rumblings of poets and painters.

Pre-Raphaelism furnished Ford with subjects for two biographies, a critical monograph and a book of reminiscences. More important, however, than any literary material that his early environment gave him was the stimulus that it must have provided. Whether such stimulus was altogether beneficial is a question. Constant contact with genius might inculcate in a youth a feeling that he must assert himself, that he must vindicate his right to associate with the great. A youth in such an environment might become arrogant and patronizing, might develop the familiar traits that compensate for a sense of inferiority. That such a development took place in Ford cannot be demonstrated but it may be suspected. What is sure is that some stimulus or other led him to begin his literary career when he was in his 'teens. His *Collected Poems* contains verses written, he tells us, when he was fifteen and published in *The Torch* in 1891. It must have been at about the same time that he published his first book, for its appearance was made the excuse for dismissing him from the school he was attending. Other books followed; he had at least four to his credit when, at the age of twenty-two, he began to write his grandfather's biography. His first volume of poems, *Poems for Pictures*, appeared in 1879.

It appears, then, that Ford was what might be called an established writer, though he was only twenty-five, when Edward Garnett brought Joseph Conrad to Limpsfield. Garnett was always, Ford writes, bringing the 'Great New' to see him. Conrad had only recently published his third novel; compared to Ford he was a mere beginner.

In the course of the conversation Ford mentioned a bit of local history, and at their next meeting Conrad proposed that they collaborate in writing a novel around this affair. Conrad, conscious of the inadequacies of his English style, was seeking some master of the language with whom to work, and Henley, he said, had told him that Ford was incomparably the best stylist extant. Ford, though by no means eager for such an undertaking, agreed, and *Romance* was begun.

Romance was not published until five years later. Difficulties arose and the book was dropped. The collaborators began and finished *The Inheritors*, which was published in 1901, and then, in 1903, completed *Romance*. The only other fruit of their collaboration was *The Nature of Crime*, published in the *English Review* in April, 1909, signed with the extraordinary pseudonym Baron Ignatz von Aschendorf, and reprinted after Conrad's death in 1924. *Some Reminiscences*—the American title is *A Personal Record*—was written for the first issues of the *English Review* at Ford's suggestion and was in part dictated to him.

In his *Joseph Conrad* and in an appendix to *The Nature of a Crime* Mr. Ford has fully recorded the details of this collaboration. He put himself, so he says, entirely at the service of Conrad, not only in the composition of the books they wrote together but also in the development of the novels that Conrad was at the same time writing independently. That Conrad may well have profited by Ford's assistance is not to be doubted, for Ford's fluent and colloquial style has qualities that Conrad's lacks. Their joint achievements, however, are not altogether impressive. *The Inheritors*, a kind of political satire, is thin and almost unreadable. *Romance*, though more substantial and not without excellent pages—both in the sections attributed to Conrad and in those allotted to Ford—certainly displays neither the characteristic Conradian virtues nor yet Ford's more admirable qualities. Though their theories of fiction were much the same, their temperaments were very different, and it is doubtful if either could have profited from a prolongation of their alliance.

After the appearance of *Romance* each man turned to the independent development of his talents. For Ford the next five years were chiefly spent in two enterprises, a trilogy, of books on England, a trilogy of historical novels concerning Katherine Howard and Henry VIII. *The Soul of London*, *The Heart of the Country*, and *The Spirit of the People*—the three were published in the United States in one volume entitled *England and the English*—are impressionistic, even at times arbitrarily so, but they are pleasantly written and have an air of plausibility. *The Fifth Queen, Privy Seal*, and *The Fifth Queen Crowned* led Conrad to write to Galsworthy, 'The whole cycle is a noble conception—the swan song of Historical Romance—and frankly I am glad to have heard it.'

It was not with an unenviable reputation and after a varied career that Ford undertook, late in 1908, the publication of the *English Review*, the principal of his colleagues being Arthur Pearson Marwood, the original of the Christopher Tietjens of the war tetralogy. The legend is that they founded the magazine because Thomas Hardy could not find a periodical that would publish his poem *A Sunday Morning Tragedy*. Certainly the poem may be found in the first issue, where it is the leading contribution and is followed by a story by Henry James, the first installment of *Some Reminiscences*, the first installment of *Tono-Bungay*, and stories and articles by Galsworthy, W. H. Hudson, and Count Tolstoy. Cunninghame-Graham, Anatole France, Norman Douglas, W. B. Yeats, Arnold Bennett, H. M. Tomlinson and Ezra Pound wrote for subsequent issues. Ford contributed a series of editorials, later published in a book called *The Critical Attitude*.

Under the editorship of Ford and Marwood the *English Review* was perhaps as distinguished a periodical as twentieth-century England has seen. Ford's connection with it was, however, brief, for Austin Harrison became its editor in 1910. From 1910 to the outbreak of the war Ford's career seems rather desultory. He was, it is true, writing and publishing many books. When *Memories and Impressions* appeared in 1911 he could observe that it was his thirty-seventh volume. But one has the feeling that he was gathering his forces for some more memorable exploit than any of the thirty-seven books could be said to represent. In 1913 he used a book on Henry James not only to acknowledge his indebtedness to that master but also to state his views of what the novel should be. In 1914, as part of a tidying-up process, he published his *Collected Poems*.

The truth is that Ford was meditating retirement from literature. As he tells the story in *Thus to Revisit*, various critics had announced that he was dead, and he was willing to take their word for it. He had however, one task to do. It seemed to him that not until one was forty could one expect to write a novel of force and originality. He tossed off sundry historical romances, but they scarcely counted. Now that the requisite term of years had expired, he proposed to write his novel. His literary demise would, therefore, have to be postponed until he had finished *The Good Soldier*.

The Good Soldier was not published until 1915. It is one of some half-dozen books that the war cheated of due recognition. By the time it appeared Ford was engaged in non-literary activities far different from those agricultural endeavours that he had planned for his retirement. Trained in devotion to France by his grandfather and in hatred of Prussia by his father he immediately threw himself into the war, giving to the country his services both as soldier and as propagandist. In the latter capacity he wrote *When Blood is their Argument* and *Between St. Dennis and St. George*. Men of more ardently pacifistic principles wrote in those days, far more bellicose books, and it is idle to single out Ford for special condemnation. It may, however, be recorded that *When Blood is their Argument* was widely distributed in the United States, and anyone familiar with our own 1917–18 contributions to the discussion of war guilt will recognize it as a primary source of local opinion on Teutonic culture.

The two pieces of propaganda, a volume of poetry, and *Zeppelin Nights*, written in collaboration with Violet Hunt, were the only violations between 1914 and 1921 of Mr. Ford's total abstinence. For that reason he felt justified, when he undertook to write a book on the literary scene, in calling it *Thus to Revisit*. It is of Ford's many books, the most amusing and the most irritating. Ostensibly a treatise on contemporary writers, it concerns itself primarily with one Ford Madox Ford. This Ford, we learn, has 'the faculty of absolute indifference to my personal fate or the fate of my work.' He is often hailed as the greatest living critic, novelist, and poet. When he is attacked or slandered he merely shrugs his shoulders.

It is, no doubt, that Ford's way of talking about himself has prejudiced many of his contemporaries against him, and it is quite possible that his tone is such writings is the partial cause of his being neglected; it is difficult to take seriously a man who so recklessly exposes himself to the charge of asininity. There must be those who, when *Thus to Revisit* appeared, sincerely regretted, on Ford's own behalf, that the pledge of retirement had not been kept. But if the vow had not been violated our literature would be considerably the poorer, for it is since 1921 that Ford has written his remarkable series of war novels.

The development of the war tetralogy has been accompanied by a determined plunge into the troubled waters of contemporary literature. One of the ventures of this latest period was the *Transatlantic Review*, which gave Ford the opportunity to abandon himself once more to what he regards as an inherited characteristic—'the hope of discovering new, beautiful talents.' Paul Valéry, Nathan Asch, E. E. Cummings, Ernest Hemingway, James Joyce, Glenway Wescott, Gertrude Stein, and Ezra Pound were among the contributors to this periodical during the year of its existence. An Englishman of partly German parentage living in France and frequently visiting in America, Ford has become a kind of international nursemaid to the arts in general. His attempts at national interpretation—*A Mirror to France* and *New York is Not America*—may be regarded as by-products of this phase of his career. He has also turned again to the historical novel.

There Ford stands, with one trusts, considerable of a career before him, but certainly with enough behind him to warrant the attention of the critic. Perhaps it is because there is so much of a career behind Ford—so many books and in such a variety of forms—that critics have hesitated to try to define his position among his contemporaries. The task is not, however, so difficult as it appears; examination of his work shows that we may legitimately confine our attention to his novels. Even in his non-fiction Ford is primarily the novelist and should be so judged. His books about France, England, and America have the merits of a novelist's note-books; quickness and accuracy of observation, an interest in the precise rendering of physical and mental qualities, a sense of the dramatic possibilities of situations that are only hastily and fragmentarily seen. His criticism also, though Ford lacks the patience to rear that structure of hypothesis and generalization towards which the judicial critic aims, does show the sensitiveness and discrimination of a thoughtful novelist to whom no phase of his craft can be uninteresting.

One might even, without extravagance, go on to say that Ford's poetry discloses his talents as a master of prose fiction. He has said that the conventional forms of verse are either too easy or too difficult to be worth bothering with, and certainly his own experiments in these forms are little more than the exercise of a bright student. In 'vers libre' his performances are more individual, but even here the level of intensity is usually low and the diction often careless. The imagery is fresh, but it is involved and leisurely; usually it could be transferred to a page of prose without the reader's being conscious of any incongruity. Ford probably does not lack the qualities of imagination that are essential to poetry, but he has never made the effort to master poetic expression. The writing of verse seems to be for him a kind of recreation, whereas the writing of fiction is a matter of careful artistry.

Ford has, in short, tried his hand at all sorts of things, and his brilliant resourcefulness has always stood in the way of complete failure; but there is only one literary form that he has taken the trouble to master, and that is the novel. Only the novel has been sufficiently attractive to persuade him to subject his facility to a thorough discipline, and, though his work in other fields is never discreditable, it is his novels alone that entitle him to serious consideration. Perhaps, indeed, the best one can say is that in whatever he undertakes there are evidences of a first-rate talent for the novel.

In examining the novels we come first upon the historical romances. Whether Ford's disparagement of this type of fiction is purely 'ex post facto' we cannot tell, but we are not likely to disagree with his judgment. The historical novel seldom permits the full expression of a rich mind or a scrupulous technique, and it may even be that some of the qualities we think of as necessary for the creation of first-rate fiction are for the historical novelist only handicaps. The historical novel should have a clear and fast-moving plot; it should contain plenty of incident; its characters should be boldly presented. In Ford's *Henry VIII* series these qualities are not to be found. The author's interest, on the contrary, is centered in the presentation of states of mind and the rendering of sequences that are largely psychological. Lacking the animation, the pageantry and the simplicity of the true romance, they derive their interest almost altogether from virtues not ordinarily discoverable in works of their kind. Conrad was not far wrong in calling the series the swan song of historical romance; the 'genre' cannot flourish long in an atmosphere of sophistication, analysis and artifice. What Ford was clearly working toward was the psychological novel. Difficult as it is to accept his statement that, while waiting for the crucial fortieth year to arrive, he consciously devoted himself to the writing of 'divertissements,' one cannot deny that his earlier work was, though not in any obvious way, a suitable preparation for the tasks assigned to his maturity.

On his fortieth birthday Ford began writing *The Good Soldier*. The subject on which he chose to 'extend himself' was one that, he says, had been hatching for a decade and to this period of gestation the novel doubtless owes both sureness of conception and strength of construction. The aim is to present a situation in the lives of five persons, and for method Ford selected one that, though it had certain great advantages, offered towering obstacles. The narrator is one of the major participants in the story. During the several years in which the situation was developing he was completely ignorant of what was going on; and yet at the moment he tells the story he is, of course, aware of all the facts. Since he is conceived as a naive person, he could not be allowed to withhold facts for the sake of effect; and since he is supposed to be telling the story as it recreates itself in his mind, he could not be allowed to develop the narrative in simple chronological order. He must present the characters at first in one light and afterwards in a quite different light, but he must not do this consciously. Ford's problem was to maintain the consistency of his narrator and at the same time reveal the situation with complete accuracy and with careful consideration of climactic effect.

To test Ford's success all that is necessary is to read the novel a second time. Though you know how the story ends, though you have seen the characters as they really are, you cannot find a phrase that is misleading nor can you discover any withholding of facts that the narrator could justly be expected to give. On the other hand, you discover in the early chapters references and allusions that carefully prepare the reader for his final impression. It comes close to being a flawless book, remarkable for its sustained inventiveness and its sound, unfaltering progress. There was justice in calling it 'the finest French novel in the English language.'

With all its technical virtuosity, however, *The Good Soldier* is not merely a 'tour de force.' There is no disproportion between the technical skill and the solidity of the work. As a revelation of life the book is worthy of the technique, and every formal subtlety adds to the accuracy and force of that revelation. With the utmost tenderness Ford pushes deeper and deeper into the minds of his characters, disclosing realms of passion and agony and meanness. Conrad never attempted to present so complex a situation, and James never ventured to explore emotion so intense and volcanic. When the book reaches its terrifying close, one realizes that only such formal perfection as Ford exhibits could bear the weight of this tragedy.

If Ford had kept his vow of literary nonparticipation, *The Good Soldier* would have been a magnificent climax to a not undistinguished career, but, standing so far above its predecessors, it would have had something of the appearance of a happy accident. Fortunately the vow was not kept, and we have the war tetralogy to set beside *The Good Soldier*. This group of novels has suffered because of its subject.

There are, it appears, special standards by which war books are judged, and according to those standards *The Good Soldier* and its sequels fall short. But this is patently unfair, for they are only incidentally war books and are primarily psychological novels, to be judged precisely as one judges *The Good Soldier*.

Considered in this way, they show the originality and clarity with which Ford can create characters and the force and logic with which he can present situations. How faithfully Tietjens is modelled upon Arthur Marwood we cannot know, and it does not matter. He is, with his omniscience and his strange suggestion of being Christ, one of the most unusual figures in recent fiction, and at the same time one of the most credible. Sylvia, quite as far removed from the commonplace of life and literature, is equally real. None of the other characters—Valentine, Duchemin, Macmaster, Campion, Mark Tietjens—is ordinary and none is implausible. These strongly individualized characters Ford takes and marshals into such amazing scenes as the Duchemin breakfast, the celebration of the Armistice in Tietjens's room, or the descent of Sylvia upon the Tietjens *ménage* the day Mark dies. Only a strong grasp of structural principles could control such inventiveness as Ford displays in these works.

The style in which the tetralogy is written is a kind of diluted stream-of-consciousness method, a report in indirect discourse of the thoughts and impressions of the various characters. At times the method becomes a little monotonous, and there are moments, especially in *The Last Post*, when the reader feels that Ford can go on this way indefinitely and fears that he has taken it into his head to do so. On the whole, however, the method serves to reveal precisely those mental states that it is necessary for the reader to understand in order to catch the dramatic values of the climactic situation. Like Conrad, Ford takes the reader forward and backward, hither and yon, but in the end the reader finds that he has progressed to the goal the author has appointed for him.

If all four of the Tietjens books seem to have been a little hastily written, and if none of them attains to the formal perfection of *The Good Soldier*, their cumulative effect, the greater vitality of certain sections, the brilliance and especially the variety of character portrayal, and the intimations they offer of a changing social order, all demonstrate that Ford's creative powers have not weakened. They definitely show that he has a place in what he is fond of calling the main stream of European literature.

It is chiefly with the five novels just discussed that any attempt to evaluate Ford's work must be concerned. In thus limiting the Fordian canon we are following the method that would have to be pursued by the serious critic of Wells, Galsworthy, or Bennett; few of Ford's contemporaries have 'extended' themselves in all their books. In these five books Ford reveals himself as the principal psychological novelist in England, the chief contemporary representative of the school of Henry James, and Joseph Conrad. In the twentieth century the English novel has been predominantly in the Fielding tradition; the aim has been to give a cross-section of English life and the method has been biographical. In the latter decades of the nineteenth century James broke away from that tradition, occupying himself with situations rather than social orders and imitating the compact organization of the French novel instead of adopting the sprawling leisureliness of the English. James left few followers. His greatest disciple, Conrad, was so much more than a disciple that his indebtedness was obscured. Other novelists—Joyce, Mrs. Woolf, Miss Richardson, for example—triumphantly carried the novel into new fields and devised new methods. The characteristic Jamesian approach—as formulated, for example, in Percy Lubbock's *The Craft of Fiction*—has, for the most part, been neglected. Fortunately there has been Ford. He has not departed in any fundamental way from James's aims and methods, yet he has done certain sorts of things that James could never have done and would not have attempted. Thus he has demonstrated the vitality of the Jamesian novel in our day.

It is, among other things, including the temperamental eccentricities to which I have alluded, the distance that separated Ford from his contemporaries that has led to his comparative neglect. His books have neither the sociological interest of the novels of Wells and his associates nor the experimental interest of the works of Joyce and his followers. However, as the sociological novel continues to decline in favor, and as the experimental novel reveals its limitations, Ford's work may receive more attention. The past few years have brought an increased interest in problems of form, but there still exists, especially in the United States, an unhealthy dichotomy. For the most part we have life and passion on one side, with formal perfection and sound writing on the other. If one must choose between the two, one would, surely, prefer the strength of *Look Homeward, Angel* to the symmetry of *The Woman of Andros*. But the choice is unnecessary. Ford's work not only shows that formal excellence may be combined with vitality and vigor; it reminds us that the sole justification of formal excellence is its effect in enhancing the vitality of the work in question.

The burst of novelistic energy released by the publication of *Ulysses* seems, at the moment, to have been dissipated. Many of the more talented young writers content themselves with sleek and plausible imitations of the successful novels of the last hundred years. As a result, almost the only novelists one can watch with any pretense of interest are the few radical experimenters. Dos Passos, for example, one studies eagerly—but also with a certain amount of trepidation. He may, of course, succeed; but even if he does, it will still be true that not many novelists are capable of such an enterprise as he has begun in the *42nd Parallel* and that not all worthy subjects could be treated by such a method. It seems clear that there must be some kind of novel less amorphous and less fully exploited than the sociological novel, at the same time less perilously difficult than the experimental novel, whether of the Joyce or the Dos Passos type. Perhaps the Jamesian novel offers the best solution of the dilemma. But the Jamesian novel, if it is to serve our purposes, must break away from the limitations of subject matter that James himself submitted to, and it must develop the ability to portray more aspects of human character than he was interested in. That it can transcend the original limits Ford has already demonstrated; he has shown that it has greater possibilities than James attempted to exploit; it remains for other novelists to indicate how great these possibilities are. No one can predict the course that the novel will take, but at this moment of uncertainty, we can afford to neglect no method that offers promise for the future. It would at any time be a pleasure to call attention to the excellence of certain of Ford's books; at the present time there may also be some importance in indicating their possible significance for the development of the novel.

60. 'Portrait of an Editor': Douglas Goldring, *English Review*

liii, December 1931, 820-9

For many years, Ford's most important contribution to literature was thought by a number of people to have been his editorship of the *English Review*. His achievement there was remarkable, and numerous writers and critics acknowledged that magazine's supremacy among its fellows. Douglas Goldring (1887-1960), who was later to be Ford's first biographer, had served as Ford's sub-editor, and his account of the early days of the review undoubtedly added to its reputation.

I had not been more than a week in New York when I was one day summoned to the telephone, and heard a rather drawling voice that seemed familiar and was certainly English. 'Is that you, Goldring? Why didn't you tell me before that you were in New York? Look here, won't you come and dine with me tonight at the Arts' Club . . .' The voice was Ford Madox Ford's. I was next door to the Arts Club when I received this message, in the hospitable 'Players,' for which I had been put up on arrival by a friendly publisher, and I was fortunately free.

The first thing I noticed about Ford, after we had greeted one another, was the fact that he seemed as completely at home in New York as he is in Montparnasse. The club was very full of people of both sexes, women perhaps predominating, and the arts were much in evidence. Pictures of all kinds covered the walls, and in two large rooms on the ground floor were displayed all the season's publications—a really admirable idea, this. We browsed among the new books for a few minutes, and then went in to dinner. No sooner had I opened my napkin than a strange thing happened. From the rather unduly talkative man 'in the forties,' which I know myself to be, I found myself suddenly changing, slipping back into my own past, becoming once again a shy and tongue-tied youth, 'having dinner with the editor.' Filled with amused astonishment, I devoured my blue-fish, failed to eat my first 'alligator pear' (because there was none left), and to the accompaniment of Ford's agreeable monotone sent my thoughts travelling back to the far-off days when he actually *was* my Olympian chief. And after dinner, while Ford was writing letters and I was alone with my cigarette, all sorts of memories came crowding in upon me.

When I was a boy of twenty-one, just beginning to earn my living on the staff of *Country Life*, after a few terms at Oxford, my Editor introduced me one morning to Mr. Ford Madox Hueffer. Ford at that time—it was, I think, the summer of 1908—was already making his preparations for launching the famous first number of the *English Review*, and, much to my delight, he appointed me his sub-editor. I had at that period and—despite appearances to the contrary—have never entirely lost it, a large amount of respect for the real heads of my profession, who, I need hardly say, are not necessarily those who make the most money or receive the largest measure of publicity. Ford then, in those far-away days, struck me as one of the most awe-inspiring figures I had ever met; more awe-inspiring even than the captain of the 1st XI had been, when I was a new boy at school.

My first spell of duty for the *English Review* took the form of a week-end at his house in Kent. (As an employer Ford was always characteristically and incorrigibly hospitable.) The place was somewhere on high ground, with a view across green marshlands to where Rye and Winchelsea stand dreaming by the sea. I seem to remember a longish, low house with various outbuildings, in one of which I slept and in one of which I remember taking down in long-hand, at Ford's dictation, the most graceful letter, to accompany a substantial cheque, which I imagine that any editor has ever written to a contributor, however distinguished. The letter was to Thomas Hardy, to thank him for the poem called 'A Sunday Morning Tragedy,' which, subsequently, appeared at the beginning of the first number of the *Review*. From it I got my first glimpse of how, in an ideal world, the old and great should be addressed by their younger *confrères*.

The next incident which I can recall with any vividness was also a week-end, this time with Joseph Conrad, who was then living in a gloomy old farmhouse near Luton. I don't exactly know why Ford took me down there with him, unless it was that in those days he was amusingly 'baronial' and regarded me as his suite or retinue. Anyway, editor and 'retinue' arrived at Luton on a dripping-wet afternoon, and got into a stuffy fly which very slowly splashed its way along the country lanes to Conrad's door. The house was surrounded by trees and seemed to me unutterably melancholy. After dinner, Ford, Conrad and the 'retinue' went up to Conrad's big candle-lit study on the first floor, and there my elders talked while I sat in a corner and listened. And how they talked! Tirelessly, endlessly, and in a mixture of French and English, they discussed the job of writing in general, and the composition of the first number of the *Review* in particular. They discussed the technique of the novel and the short story, and quoted long passages from *Madame Bovary* and *Un Cœur Simple* at one another, with ever-growing excitement. I can see before me now Conrad's short, broad-shouldered, long-armed figure and his dark, pointed beard and dark eyes, as he stood in the candlelight in front of the fire, with Ford, tall, blond and blue-eyed, by his side; and I can hear again Ford's light-pitched, drawling tones mingling with Conrad's deeper, more staccato notes. What I chiefly remember about the conversation, apart from the references to Flaubert and to the contents of the first number of the *Review*, is that it hinged on the necessity for English writers to follow the example of the French and learn how they got their own effects. Too many even of our best writers, the inference was, have been artists by accident as it were, instead of as a result of deliberately disciplining their talents and learning 'how.' And I got an inkling, during that endless discussion which prolonged itself far into the night, of just what the *Review* was intended to accomplish for English letters. It was going to set up and maintain a standard of literary values, of *real writing*. And, in the first gallant year of its existence, despite incredible difficulties and unimaginable turmoils of which at the time I knew little, no one can now say that it failed in its purpose.

Ford, it must be admitted, made an original and slightly eccentric editor, nor could it well have been otherwise. One single individual could hardly be expected to combine a pure love of good letters, unusual critical insight, admirable gifts as poet and novelist, and the most incorrigible sociability with those hard-faced commercial and administrative talents which produce the 'paying concern.' A 'paying concern,' the *English Review*, during the year of Ford's editorship, certainly was not. It was a gallant adventure nevertheless, and has well earned its place in our literary history. Difficulties and turmoils there were in plenty, during the agitated twelve months in which Ford occupied the editorial chair, though I was far too excited, far too youthfully self-centred and too inexperienced to appreciate them. For me that year was one long thrill: in a literary sense it was the *real thing*, at last.

The little group of Oxford poets I had met in my undergraduate days and after—James Elroy Flecker, J. D. Beazley, Trelawney Dayrell-Reed and several others—had cast a glamour for me over the profession of letters. We all turned out verses, some of us with great facility, and dreamed of dying young and famous, though Flecker was the only one of our little group who was destined to turn this dream into a reality. But we were all contemporaries and beginners; and even for Flecker the magic of print was at that time hard of achievement. Ford's flat at 84, Holland Park Avenue, where the *Review* was edited, was, on the other hand, filled daily to overflowing, not with aspirants but with the tried, the tested, the acknowledged! The Beverly Nichols type of young man (which I am not yet too old to appreciate) scarcely existed twenty years ago. Perhaps, if I had been endowed with some of the hard modern insouciance and disillusion I should have noticed in these, to me, august figures only their queer clothes, their odd personal habits and idiosyncrasies. As it was, they were the only sort of 'great' for which I had any respect. And I contrived to keep my two worlds entirely separate—the world in which I danced more or less efficiently and in which no one knew one end of a book from another, and the world in which I sat demurely in a corner and listened to my betters. Only once or twice did the water-tight compartments fail to act, and I shall never forget the shock I had at a dance at Kent House in Knightsbridge, when I heard my hostess ask Mr. Rudyard Kipling to take Mrs. Humphry Ward down to supper, and thus identified them! Nowadays, I'm afraid, I take but little interest in encountering the writers whose works I admire, in the flesh: and I have come to think the 'public personage' about as cheerless as the public library. Age creeping on, I suppose.

The manuscripts that were sent in to the *English Review* were housed in a very beautiful old inlaid Spanish cabinet, in Ford's study. When I arrived in the evening—for I sub-edited *Country Life* during the day, and usually did not appear at Holland Park Avenue before 6 p.m.—I was generally despatched at once to the Shepherd's Bush Empire, to secure a box or two stalls for the 'second house.' After dinner, we chartered a hansom and Editor and 'sub' drove down to the music-hall, with the manuscripts which had been sent in during the day. During the performance, or rather during the duller turns, Ford made his decisions and I duly recorded them. But when somebody really worth listening to, the late Victoria Monks, for example, appeared on the stage, the cares of editorship were for the moment laid aside. After the theatre we usually went back to the flat and worked on, sometimes till 2 a.m. And that was, more or less, the way in which the most distinguished English literary periodical of the present century got itself into print.

After all, there must have been a good deal to be said for the Shepherd's Bush Empire, from Ford's point of view. The atmosphere was conducive, there was no one to worry him and he could think undisturbed. In the flat, on the other hand, apart from the endless parties, stray callers seemed to arrive at all hours of the day or night, all of them, no doubt, bursting with advice, suggestions or complaints. By contrast, the music-hall must have seemed a haven of peace.

At one of Ford's tea-parties I remember seeing a little quiet, gray old man who turned out to be Thomas Hardy. I was standing next to Hugh Walpole, at the back of the room, near the tea-table. The conversation among the lion-cubs in our neighbourhood was no doubt very brilliant and very 'literary,' but suddenly there came the usual inexplicable hush. It was broken by Hardy, who, turning to an elderly lady by his side, remarked, 'And how is Johnny's whooping-cough?'

Conrad was, of course, frequently in the flat during the first months of our existence. I remember once being deputed to stay in after dinner and keep him company, until Ford returned from some party or other. Alas, on this occasion I missed an opportunity. For, as it happened, I had an assignation that evening with a young person of the opposite sex, and my inability to keep it must so have preoccupied my mind that I cannot now recall one word of a prolonged conversation.

Of the younger writers whom Ford, I will not say 'discovered'— for that is a word which, in my experience, invariably arouses rage— but whose gifts he was, at all events, quick to appreciate, the most outstanding figures were P. Wyndham Lewis and Ezra Pound. Both of them, at that period, in clothes, hairdressing and manner, made no secret of their calling. Pound contrived to look 'every inch a poet' (and still does), while I have never seen anyone so obviously a 'genius' as Wyndham Lewis when, after his return from a sojourn abroad, he first appeared at Ford's parties.

The story (no doubt apocryphal) of Lewis's first call at the *English Review* office formed one of the many legends which collected round that singular flat. Lewis, tall, dark, and with romantically disordered hair, wearing a long, black garment buttoned up to his chin, arrived one morning at Number 84 with the MS. of 'The Pole' in his inside coat-pocket. Getting no answer to his ring, he walked into the flat and searched the first-floor rooms, in vain, for an occupant. Undeterred, he climbed another flight of stairs, and hearing at last sounds of human life, he knocked at the door through which they came, and walked in. It happened to be the bath-room, and there, reclining on his back in the bath, in two feet of hot water, with a large sponge in one hand and a piece of soap in the other, was the missing editor. Quite disregarding any unconventionality in his surroundings, Lewis at once proceeded to business. After announcing in the most matter-of-fact way that he was a man of genius and that he had a manuscript for publication, he asked if he might read it. 'Go on,' said Ford, continuing to play with his sponge. Lewis then unbuttoned his coat, produced 'The Pole,' and read it aloud. At the end Ford observed: 'Well, that's all right. If you leave it behind we'll certainly print it.' And the interview terminated. The literal truth of the whole or any part of the above story, of course, I cannot guarantee. All I can say is that if it didn't happen, it ought to have done.

Other distinguished figures who came to the flat were R. B. Cunninghame Graham, who looked like a Spanish hidalgo (and wrote the most illegible hand it has ever been my lot to try to decipher), W. H. Hudson, Edward Garnett, Edward Thomas, Stephen Reynolds and the late Percival Gibbon. Gibbon was a merciless practical joker and used constantly to rag me about my efforts to get my poems published, once pretending that he had just heard that an eminent firm had decided to issue them in a limited large-paper edition. Alas, how eagerly did I allow myself to be deceived! On one occasion he played a joke on Ford with equal success. He arrived at the flat, late one snowy night, in a state of well-simulated horror and consternation. 'Ford, what d'you think has happened?' he gasped. 'I drove here in a fourwheeler, and just as we got near the Tube station the cab stopped suddenly. I got out to see what was up, and found the poor old cabby *dead on his box*. We *must* go out and do something about it.' A wave of humanitarian emotion swept over Ford and his companion. Murmuring 'doctor . . . brandy . . . cold and exposure . . . poor old fellow' they hurried into their coats and rushed forth into the icy street, followed by the chuckling Gibbon.

Soon after Ford and the *English Review* parted company, a small legacy came my way, which, with the unwisdom of youth, I promptly 'put into a paper' and became, in my turn, an editor. It was an illustrated monthly magazine, which quickly swallowed all the capital invested in it, and died, after a not altogether inglorious existence, within a year. Subsequently, I became connected with a firm of publishers which issued at my instigation, James Elroy Flecker's *The Golden Journey to Samarkand*, and also an edition of Ford's *Collected Poems*, which, out of natural *pietas*, I produced in as beautiful a form as I could contrive. It must now be a rare book, and I wish I possessed a copy of it myself.

I was just wondering where the dickens my copy had got to when Ford finished his letters and suggested that we should go along to one of his addresses—in New York, as in Paris, he defends his working-hours by having several retreats—where a party of young people were expecting us. It was November, but we were in the midst of a heat-wave, and the night was warm and starry. The theatres and movies had already begun, and the streets were pleasantly deserted, so that, as rarely happens in New York, we were able to stroll in comfort. As we passed into Washington Square, Ford pointed out to me the window of the room in which Henry James was born. And somehow, after that, it didn't seem quite so singular that Ford and I should be strolling about together in New York, after having, but a few months before, strolled about together in Paris. For the great Henry was not the least august of the contributors to the *Review*. Although I never met him, it fell to my lot to read his proofs, and I remember once drawing Ford's attention to a passage, in a story whose name I have forgotten, which struck me as odd. It was a question as to whether a gentleman wearing a top-hat *could* put his head, conveniently, through a carriage window and kiss its occupant. The point was submitted to the great man, who, I believe, with plans and diagrams and the utmost elaboration, explained precisely how the deed was done.

When we arrived at our destination, it turned out to be a house in a street which Londoners would call 'Early Victorian.' It might easily have been a London street, for it had a name and not a number, and there were none of the usual New York fire-escapes disfiguring its façades. We entered by a basement door, which looked exactly like the entrance to a 'speak-easy,' and making our way into a small back sitting-room, we found awaiting us round a deal table a group of two or three young poets and a literary critic, not one of whom could have been more affluent than his opposite number in Paris or in London. But it was easy to tell that they were all of them interested in writing for its own sake. Soon the conversation became critical and technical —real literary talk, a little in the big bow-wow style—of a kind I hadn't heard for nearly twenty years. For in England, somehow . . .

I don't know. Most of the young English writers I have come across have been elegant and moderately affluent personages who try to give the impression of stooping from Mayfair to conquer Bohemia. Their living is complicated rather than plain; and their 'high-thinking' is done 'off stage.' If they want to discuss literature, they either give public lectures or write essays or middles. But here, in New York, was a group of young people who were talking quite easily and naturally about the subject which interested them most. Ford, of course, was very rightly encouraged to hold the floor. And for about an hour, with elbows on the table, he talked about books and their writers with a judgment, penetration and depth of knowledge which few men in that city of lecturers could have equalled. I suppose he knew perfectly well that he was talking to men who took their jobs seriously, that the atmosphere was right. And it was entirely in keeping with the Ford of the *English Review* days that, with an engagement-book that could easily have been filled to overflowing, he should elect to spend an evening at his ease, in a basement sitting-room in a back street, talking about writing.

61. Graham Greene, *Spectator*

cxliii, 7 July 1939, 11

This obituary article, written partly to correct errors in other accounts, was later included in *The Lost Childhood and Other Essays*.

The death of Ford Madox Ford was like the obscure death of a veteran —an impossibly Napoleonic veteran, say, whose immense memory spanned the period from Jena to Sedan: he belonged to the heroic age of English fiction and outlived it—yet he was only sixty-six. In one of his many volumes of reminiscence—those magnificent books where in an atmosphere of casual talk outrageous story jostles outrageous story

—he quoted Mr. Wells as saying some years ago that in the southern counties a number of foreigners were conspiring against the form of the English novel. There was James at Lamb House, Crane at Brede Manor, Conrad at The Pent, and he might have added his own name, Hueffer at Aldington, for he was a quarter German (and just before the first world war made an odd extravagant effort to naturalize himself as a citizen of his grandfather's country). The conspiracy, of course, failed: the big loose middlebrow novel goes on its happy way unconscious of James's 'point of view': Conrad is regarded again as the writer of romantic sea stories and purple passages: nobody reads Crane, and Ford—well, an anonymous writer in *The Times Literary Supplement* remarked in an obituary notice that his novels began to date twenty years ago. Conservatism among English critics is extraordinarily tenacious, and they hasten, on a man's death, to wipe out any disturbance he has caused.

The son of Francis Hueffer, the musical critic of *The Times*, and grandson, on his mother's side, of Ford Madox Brown, 'Fordie' Hueffer emerges into history at the age of three offering a chair to Turgenev, and again, a little later, dressed in a suit of yellow velveteen with gold buttons, wearing one red stocking and one green one, and with long golden hair, having his chair stolen from him at a concert by the Abbé Liszt. I say emerges into history, but it is never possible to say where history ends and the hilarious imagination begins. He was always an atmospheric writer, whether he was describing the confused Armistice night when Tietjens found himself back with his mistress, Valentine Wannop, among a horde of grotesque and inexplicable strangers, or just recounting a literary anecdote of dubious origin—the drunk writer who thought himself a Bengal tiger trying to tear out the throat of the blind poet Marston, or Henry James getting hopelessly entangled in the long lead of his dachshund Maximilian. Nobody ever wrote more about himself than Ford, but the figure he presented was just as dubious as his anecdotes—the figure of a Tory country gentleman who liked to grow his own food and had sturdy independent views on politics: it all seems a long way from the yellow velveteen. He even, at the end of his life, a little plump and a little pink, looked the part—and all the while he had been turning out the immense number of books which stand to his name: memoirs, criticism, poetry, sociology, novels. And in between, if one can so put it, he found time to be the best literary editor England has ever had: what Masefield, Hudson, Conrad, even Hardy, owed to the *English Review* is well known, and after the war in the *Transatlantic Review* he bridged the great gap, publishing the early Hemingway, Cocteau, Stein, Pound, the music of Antheil and the drawings of Braque.

He had the advantage—or the disadvantage—of being brought up in pre-Raphaelite circles, and although he made a tentative effort to break away into the Indian Civil Service, he was pushed steadily by his family towards art—any kind of art was better than any kind of profession. He published his first book at the age of sixteen, and his first novel, *The Shifting of the Fire*, in 1892, when he was only nineteen—three years before Conrad had published anything and only two years after the serial appearance of *The Tragic Muse*, long before James had matured his method and his style. It wasn't, of course, a good book, but neither was it an 'arty' book—there was nothing of the 'nineties about it except its elegant period binding, and it already bore the unmistakable Hueffer stamp—the outrageous fancy, the pessimistic high spirits, and an abominable hero called Kasker-Ryves. Human nature in his books was usually phosphorescent—varying from the daemonic malice of Sylvia Tietjens to the painstaking, rather hopeless will-to-be-good of Captain Ashburnham, 'the good soldier'. The little virtue that existed only attracted evil. But to Mr. Ford, a Catholic in theory though not for long in practice, this was neither surprising nor depressing: it was just what one expected.

The long roll of novels ended with *Vive le Roy* in 1937. A few deserve to be forgotten, but I doubt whether the accusation of dating can be brought against even such minor works as *Mr. Apollo*, *The Marsden Case*, *When the Wicked Man*: there were the historical novels, too, with their enormous vigour and authenticity—*The Fifth Queen* and its sequels: but the novels which stand as high as any fiction written since the death of James are *The Good Soldier* with its magnificent claim in the first line, 'This is the saddest story I have ever heard'—the study of an averagely good man of a conventional class driven, divided and destroyed by unconventional passion—and the Tietjens series, that appalling examination of how private malice goes on during public disaster—no escape even in the trenches from the secret gossip and the lawyers' papers. It is dangerous in this country to talk about technique or a long essay could be written on his method in these later books, the method Conrad followed more stiffly and less skilfully, having learnt it perhaps from Ford when they collaborated on *Romance*: James's point of view was carried a step further, so that a book took place not only from the point of view but in the brain of a character and events were remembered not in chronological order, but as free association brought them to mind.

When Ford died he had passed through a period of neglect and was re-emerging. His latest books were not his best, but they were hailed as if they were. The first war had ruined him. He had volunteered, though he was over military age and was fighting a country he loved: his health was broken, and he came back to a new literary world which had carefully eliminated him. For some of his later work he could not even find a publisher in England. No wonder he preferred to live abroad—in Provence or New York. But I don't suppose failure disturbed him much: he had never really believed in human happiness, his middle life had been made miserable by passion, and he had come through—with his humour intact, his stock of unreliable anecdotes, the kind of enemies a man ought to have, and a half-belief in a posterity which would care for good writing.

62. Ezra Pound, *Nineteenth Century and After*

cxxvi, August 1939, 178–81

Ford's fullest obituary, among the few scant references his death occasioned, was written by his old friend, Ezra Pound. Although the two men saw much less of each other after Pound's move to Rapallo in the late 1920s, there was correspondence between them, and each was well acquainted with the other's mind and habits. This essay, then, has exceptional authenticity.

There passed from us this June a very gallant combatant for those things of the mind and of letters which have been in our time too little prized. There passed a man who took in his time more punishment of one sort and another than I have seen meted to anyone else. For the ten years before I got to England there would seem to have been no one but Ford who held that French clarity and simplicity in the writing of

English verse and prose were of immense importance as in contrast to the use of a stilted traditional dialect, a 'language of verse' unused in the actual talk of the people, even of 'the best people,' for the expression of reality and emotion.

In 1908 London was full of 'gargoyles,' of poets, that is, with high reputation, most of whose work has gone since into the discard. At that time, and in the few years preceding, there appeared without notice various fasciculae which one can still, surprisingly, read and they were not designed for mouthing, for the 'rolling out' of 'ohs.' They weren't what people were looking for as the prolongation of Victoria's glory. They weren't, that is, 'intense' in the then sense of the word.

The justification or programme of such writing was finally (about 1913) set down in one of the best essays (preface) that Ford ever wrote.

It advocated the prose value of verse-writing, and it, along with his verse, had more in it for my generation than all the retchings (most worthily) after 'quantity' (i.e., quantitative metric) of the late Laureate Robert Bridges or the useful, but monotonous, in their day unduly neglected, as more recently unduly touted, metrical labours of G. Manley Hopkins.

I have put it down as personal debt to my forerunners that I have had five, and only five, useful criticisms of my writing in my lifetime, one from Yeats, one from Bridges, one from Thomas Hardy, a recent one from a Roman Archbishop and one from Ford, and that last the most vital, or at any rate on par with Hardy's.

That Ford was almost an *halluciné* few of his intimates can doubt. He felt until it paralysed his efficient action, he saw quite distinctly the Venus immortal crossing the tram tracks. He inveighed against Yeats' lack of emotion as, for him, proved by Yeats' so great competence in making literary use of emotion.

And he felt the errors of contemporary style to the point of rolling (physically, and if you look at it as mere superficial snob, ridiculously) on the floor of his temporary quarters in Giessen when my third volume displayed me trapped, fly-papered, gummed and strapped down in a jejune provincial effort to learn, mehercule, the stilted language that then passed for 'good English' in the arthritic milieu that held control of the respected British critical circles, Newbolt, the backwash of Lionel Johnson, Fred Manning, the Quarterlies and the rest of 'em.

And that roll saved me at least two years, perhaps more. It sent me back to my own proper effort, namely, toward using the living tongue (with younger men after me), though none of us has found a more natural language than Ford did.

This is a dimension of poetry. It is, magari, an Homeric dimension, for of Homer there are at least two dimensions apart from the surge and thunder. Apart from narrative sense and the main constructive, there is this to be said of Homer, that never can you read half a page without finding melodic invention, still fresh, and that you can hear the actual voices, as of the old men speaking in the surge of the phrases.

It is for this latter quality that Ford's poetry is of high importance, both in itself and for its effect on all the best subsequent work of his time. Let no young snob forget this.

I propose to bury him in the order of merits as I think he himself understood them, first for an actual example in the writing of poetry; secondly, for those same merits more fully shown in his prose, and thirdly, for the critical acumen which was implicit in his finding these merits.

As to his prose, you can apply to it a good deal that he wrote in praise of Hudson (rightly) and of Conrad, I think with a bias toward generosity that in parts defeats its critical applicability. It lay so natural on the page that one didn't notice it. I read an historical novel at sea in 1906 without noting the name of the author. A scene at Henry VIIIth's court stayed depicted in my memory and I found years later that Ford had written it.

I wanted for private purposes to make a note on a point raised in *Ancient Lights*; I thought it would go on the back of an envelope, and found to my young surprise that I couldn't make the note in fewer words than those on Ford's actual page. That set me thinking. I did not in those days care about prose. If 'prose' meant anything to me, it meant Tacitus (as seen by Mackail), a damned dangerous model for a young man in those days or these days in England, though I don't regret it; one never knows enough about anything. Start with Tacitus and be cured by Flaubert via Ford, or start with Ford or Maupassant and be girt up by Tacitus, after fifty it is kif, kif, all one. But a man is a pig not to be grateful to both sides.

Until the arrival of such 'uncomfortables' as Wyndham Lewis, the distressful D. H. Lawrence, D. Goldring, G. Cannan, etc., I think Ford had no one to play with. The elder generation loathed him, or at any rate such cross-section of it as I encountered. He disturbed 'em, he took Dagon by the beard, publicly. And he founded the greatest Little Review or pre-Little Review of our time. From 1908 to 1910 he gathered into one fasciculus the work of Hardy, H. James, Hudson, Conrad, C. Graham, Anatole France, the great old-stagers, the most competent of that wholly unpleasant decade, Bennett, Wells, and, I think, even Galsworthy.

And he got all the first-rate and high second-raters of my own decade, W. Lewis, D. H. Lawrence (made by Ford, dug out of a board school in Croydon), Cannan, Walpole, etc. (Eliot was not yet on the scene).

The inner story of that review and the treatment of Ford by its obtainers is a blot on London's history that time will not remove, though, of course, it will become invisible in the perspective of years.

As critic he was perhaps wrecked by his wholly unpolitic generosity. In fact, if he merits an epithet above all others, it would be 'The Unpolitic.' Despite all his own interests, despite all the hard-boiled and half-baked vanities of all the various lots of us, he kept on discovering merit with monotonous regularity.

His own best prose was probably lost, as isolated chapters in unachieved and too-quickly-issued novels. He persisted in discovering capacities in similar crannies. In one weekly after another he found and indicated the capacities of Mary, Jenny, Willard, Jemimah, Horatio, etc., despite the fact that they all of 'em loathed each other, and could by no stretch of imagination be erected into a compact troop of Fordites supporting each other and moving on the citadels of publication.

And that career I saw him drag through three countries. He took up the fight for free letters in Paris, he took it up again in New York, where I saw him a fortnight before his death, still talking of meritorious novels, still pitching the tale of unknown men who had written the *histoire morale contemporaine* truthfully and without trumpets, told this or that phase of American as seen from the farm or the boiler-works, as he had before wanted young England to see young England from London, from Sussex.

And of all the durable pages he wrote (for despite the fluff, despite the apparently aimless meander of many of 'em, he did write durable pages) there is nothing that more registers the fact of our day than the two portraits in the, alas, never-finished *Women and Men* (Three Mountains Press, 1923), Meary Walker and 'T.'

63. Sherwood Anderson on Ford Madox Ford

'The Legacies of Ford Madox Ford', *Coronet*,
viii, August 1940, 135-6
New Directions Number 7, 1942, 458-9

Like Dreiser, Anderson (1876-1941) was an almost exact contemporary of Ford and although the two were never close, they were friends and shared similar temperaments. The first of the two statements was a published obituary, later included in Anderson's *Memoirs*; the second appeared in a symposium in Ford's honour and memory printed by James Laughlin in his *New Directions Annual* for 1942. Anderson's best known book is *Winesburg, Ohio*.

Ford Madox Ford was a true literary man. He was always generous, particularly to young writers, often too generous. A thin trickle of talent became to him a flood. A talk with Ford would send a young writer floating away into feathery clouds. Publishers and editors would clamor for his work. When he awoke in the morning there would be a dozen of them camped on his doorstep.

Indeed, in Ford's imagination they did camp there. I once heard him tell a tale of such an incident. He had found a young writer. He had proclaimed him. Now there were a dozen publishers waiting for him. Ford was telling the tale as a fact, and to him it was a fact. Later I saw the young writer and spoke of it. A sickly smile came to his lips. 'You see Ford wanted it. He wanted it so much that it became a fact to him,' he said. At least he understood Ford, the depth and sincerity of his generosity.

Once, in the city of Paris, I met Ford at a party. It was before disease had begun to punish his poor body. He took my arm and led me into a corner.

'You are just the man I have been waiting to see.' He began to speak of a house he had in the hills of Pennsylvania. There it was. He described the house, the view from a terrace at the front, the garden, the apple trees that grew on a nearby hillside. The house was beautifully furnished and there was a retinue of servants. The pity was that he had built the house, intending to go there to work, but had never been able to do so.

And what was a man to do? He could not bear the thought of discharging the servants and closing the house. And why should I not take the place, go there to live, Ford wanted to know? It would cost me nothing. The house had been built having in mind some writer who wanted to retire to some such quiet and secluded spot to work.

'Please,' he said, 'you take it. You go there. At least promise me that you will spend your summer there.' His voice was rich with fervor. There was an eager light in his eyes.

Only those who knew Ford well will understand how sincere the offer was, how real and tangible the house had become to him.

At the time I did not know Ford well. 'He is a rich man who has houses scattered about the world,' I thought.

During the course of that evening, Ford offered me two other houses, one in Florida and another in California. They were there waiting. 'A man can't go about discharging servants. It upsets him too much, gets his mind off his work.'

As I was nearly broke at the time, I took all of this with entire seriousness. Now I know that, in offering the houses, Ford was himself entirely serious. The houses existed for him. He was a man who lived in a splendid world, created in his own imagination, and the world he had created was gloriously real to him.

It gives me real pleasure to have this chance to say a word about the significance of a man we both know and sincerely respect, Mr. Ford Madox Ford. We shall never have enough Fords. They don't appear often. There is too much confusion in the minds of most of us regarding our craft for most of us ever to get into the clear. We are, too often, business men who write, publicity seekers writing, money and fame hungry men writing. The real meaning of the job we undertake in becoming writers gets lost, isn't understood.

And also there is a kind of moral strength needed that too many of us haven't got.

Ford had it. He understood what a man undertakes in becoming a writer. He understood the obligation taken on. There was a real aristocracy in Ford. He was a professional writer who didn't soil his tools. He was unashamed, firm, a real workman, a man who understood what it is that gives a man's own life some significance. We do mighty well, here at Olivet, to set aside a day to do him honor.

Ford Madox Ford was a rich man. He was rich in a way in which we would all secretly like to be rich. He was rich in good work done, in self-respect. He didn't go about in an over-commercialized world being half apologetic because he was the very type of the artist man.

He was a sophisticate. He had seen the wheels go around, knew something about how they turned, a man who had seen life closely in many places, in many kinds of people, a fellow of ours who knew truth from nonsense. The man was equipped with a full-bodied imagination and knew how to use it. He never used it to hurt anyone. He used it to give joy.

The man and his name are both now a part of a fine tradition. It is an old tradition. He knew what it was. He kept the faith. I take it as an honor to myself that I am asked to say these few words in honor of such a man.

64. John Gould Fletcher, *New Directions Number 7*

1942, 472-4

Although never a close friend, John Gould Fletcher (1886–1950) knew Ford at various quite different periods of his life. They first met in London when Ford was most concerned with young poets, just after ceasing to be editor of the *English Review*. They were again associated in the 1930s, when Fletcher, along with Allen Tate and others, was a member of the Agrarians. He was a poet, novelist and author of books on Japan.

The first time I was to see Ford Madox Ford was on a day early in July, in England; and the year was 1913. It was Ezra Pound who shepherded me by bus, through the western parts of London to where Ford was then living, in a house near Holland Park Road. I recall the day perfectly—an exceptionally clear and warm one, for that latitude; and I recall also the aspect of my host's study, with its innumerable pipes on a table, its special machine for cutting tobacco, its books, and its air of comfort. Although I had, at that time, lived in London for four years, I was still, as regards authors and authorship, a greenhorn; and I had little to say. Ezra and Ford had an animated discussion, I recall, concerning Henry James or Hudson or Conrad, who were then Ford's favorites, or perhaps concerning Yeats, Joyce or the Chinese who were then Ezra's. The pair played a game of tennis on the court which was in Ford's garden; and I watched them.

Ford was then forty. What struck me then about him was his intense and unchangeable Britishness, a quality no less manifest in his bulky masculine aspect, as in his mind. The British tradition—for there is a British tradition, no less manifest though far less clear and defined, than the French tradition—contains in its essence a certain element of purely personal and individual rebelliousness. Ford, from the standpoint of the British tradition, was a rebel; as he grew older, he became more so—but never to such an extent as, for example, such a rank 'outsider' as D. H. Lawrence. He had been very much on the 'inside' at the time when the Pre-Raphaelite Movement was carrying much before it, and in close contact with its leaders. Like them, he hated and despised the gods of the Victorians: Dickens and Thackeray, Tennyson, Matthew Arnold, all were tainted with the hypocrisy, the sentimentality and the snobbishness of the public-school system and the Empire. His early gods were not even English: Turgenev and Tolstoy, Flaubert and Henry James were some of them. A born novelist and essayist, he had come to maturity as one of the 'discoverers' of Joseph Conrad, and of Stephen Crane; and had already made his mark on the stodginess of British literature by becoming, five years before I met him, the editor of the *English Review*, which had attempted to broaden the basis of that literature by printing, not only Conrad, but Tolstoy, Hardy as poet, and even D. H. Lawrence, in his earlier prose.

Now here he was in the flesh, very different in his bovine slowness and impressiveness from the quick, nervous, jumpy Ezra, a writer of historical romance in the more or less established Maurice Hewlett tradition, and with his solider work as a war-realist far in the then invisible future. He was scrapping with Ezra about something in Rossetti or in Yeats, whom he undoubtedly and justly regarded as un-English, and whom he charged Ezra with failing to understand. Ezra, for a wonder, seemed disposed to listen to him with deference; and I did not disagree, because—although not born to the British tradition—I was content to leave that tradition alone.

It was circumstance, not choice, that made of Ford an upholder, not of British centralisation and narrowness, but of the wild diversity of American regionalism. Born half-a-German, and, I suspect, a very Saxon sort of German, the reaction of this slow-moving, concrete, thorough-going craftsman, when confronted by the war, was to change his name and to proclaim himself unalterably an Englishman. It was only under pressure of the worst kind of domestic trouble that he took the path of exile, so easy for us Americans. And once in Paris, his task was to repeat, in wider compass, in the pages of his *Transatlantic Review*, the cosmopolitanism of his earlier *English Review*. He had all the American emigrés then in Paris, to draw on for this effort. It was probably the wild stimulus of their presence that persuaded him into coming, at last, to this country and that made him—a sober serious, craftsman of the older sort—into a champion of experimental, utterly new writing.

He was Ford Madox Ford—that is to say something quite apart from all the clamor of the schools—imagist, unanimist, dadaist, surrealist, and proletarian—that went on continually about him. Fundamentally, he believed in only two things: in every writer's privilege to express what was the core of himself, and in good writing. He was broadminded enough to champion other kinds of writing; but was himself a realist of the Flaubert sort, though less able to conceal a vein of sentiment than Flaubert had been. The vein came perilously near to the surface sometimes in his poetry, the least important part of him, but the part which was possibly nearest to his own heart. The last time that I saw him, at the Baton Rouge Conference of 1935, he sat and talked to a hundred people for an hour, reminiscing over his own experiences and quoting in the end a poem of his own—in Yorkshire dialect—as an example of regionalism. We, products of an unpredictable, undirected, spasmodic and undisciplined country, were all fascinated with his discourse, coming from a source so alien to us; and somewhat amazed, as well, at the generous mistake by which he confused the honest narrowness of British provincialism with the far wilder and more confused claims of American regional writing.

65. Katherine Anne Porter, *New Directions Number 7*

1942, 478-9

Katherine Anne Porter (b. 1890) knew Ford best during the years when he lived mainly in Paris, during the late 1920s and early 1930s. Miss Porter is one of the most distinguished writers of short stories in America.

Several years ago Ford Madox Ford remarked to a friend, with a real pride and satisfaction, that he had a book to show for every year of his life. Now he knew as well as any one that no man can write sixty *good* books, he said himself there were books on that list he was willing to have out of print for ever. But at the time of writing them, he had believed firmly each book was going to be good; in any case, each book was as good as he was capable of making it at that moment, that given circumstance; and in any case he could not have stopped himself from the enterprise, because he was a man of letters, born and bred. His life work and his vocation happened to be one and the same thing. A lucky man, in spite of what seems, sometimes, to the onlooker, as unlucky a life as was ever lived.

His labors were constant, his complicated seeking mind was never for one moment diverted from its speculations on the enduring topic of literature, the problems of creation, the fascinating pitfalls of technique, the moral, psychic, esthetic aspects of art, all art, any one of the arts. He loved to live the life of the artist, he loved to discover, foster, encourage young beginners in what another admirer of his, Glenway Wescott, has described as 'this severe and fantastic way of life.' Towards the end, when he was at Olivet, Ford described himself as 'an old man mad about writing.' He was not really an old man—think of Hardy, think of Tolstoy, think of Yeats—and his madness was an illuminated sanity; but he had, when he wrote this, intimations of mortality in him, and he had always practised, tongue in cheek, that 'pride which apes humility.' It pleased him to think of himself in that way; and indeed, when you consider his history, the tragic mischances of his life, his times of glory and success alternating with painful bouts with poverty and neglect, you might think, unless you were an artist, that he was a little mad to have run all the risks and to have taken all the punishment he did take at the hands of fortune,—and for what? I don't think he ever asked himself that question. I doubt greatly he ever seriously considered for one moment any other mode of life than the life he lived. I knew him for twelve years, in a great many places and situations, and I can testify that he led an existence of marvelous discomfort, of insecurity, of deep and pressing anxiety as to his daily bread; but no matter where he was, what his sufferings were, he sat down daily and wrote, in his crabbed fine hand, with pen, the book he was working on at the moment; and I never knew him when he was not working on a book. It is not the moment to estimate those books, time may reverse his own severe judgment on some of them, but any of you who have read the Tietjens Cycle, or *The Good Soldier*, must have taken a long step forward in your knowledge of craftsmanship, of just what it takes to write a fine novel. His influence is deeper than we are able to measure, for he has influenced writers who never read his books; which is the fate of all masters.

There was in all something so typical, so classical in his way of life, his history, some phases of his career, so grand in the old manner of English men of letters. I think a reading of his books and a little meditation on his life and death might serve at once as guiding sign and a finger of warning to all eager people who thoughtlessly, perhaps, 'want to write.' You will learn from him what the effort really is; what the pains, and what the rewards, of a real writer; and if that is not enough to frighten you off, you may proceed with new confidence in yourself.

66. Allen Tate on Ford Madox Ford

New Directions Number 7, 1942, 487–8
'Random Thoughts on the 1920s',
Minnesota Review, i, 1960, 51–3

Allen Tate (b. 1899) and his then wife, Caroline Gordon (see headnote to No. 71), were probably Ford's closest friends and admirers among writers in the United States. Although indebted to Ford in many ways, as the accounts printed below indicate, they also helped to gather round Ford a group of admirers, especially in the South, who gave Ford a real sense of connection with American letters during the last decade of his life. Mr Tate is widely respected as a poet and critic.

Perhaps Ford knew in the winter of 1939 that he was going to die soon, for he went to France in the spring to spend the summer, as he had not done for several years; he had been going over in the autumn and coming back to America in the spring. It was well that he died in France, a country that he not only loved but that he represented far more than he ever did England, his native country. It is not too much to say that he was a French man of letters who wrote his principal works first in English, and then rewrote them in French. He was a man of letters too, on the French model of the mid-nineteenth century: a man of enormous 'culture' who had survived into an age that no longer assumed the autonomy of the arts but had gone off into varieties of neo-primitivism or into 'politics.' As the heir of Flaubert and the avowed disciple of Henry James, Ford believed passionately in the novel as work of art, a distinct *genre* to be explored and developed in terms of form, not of social ideas or of mere subject matter.

This point of view went into an eclipse at the end of the last decade, giving way to the cruder social-political novel, or even cruder than that, to the personal or expressionist novel of the sort written by the late Thomas Wolfe. And Ford's reputation, after a brief rise in the middle twenties, declined.

But it seems to me that if the novel is to survive the heresies of mere ideology and reporting, it will have to return to the great tradition of Flaubert and James—and of Ford Madox Ford, in whose three or four great books that tradition is most immediately available to us. If the future does not go back to this masterful tradition, it will have to learn its lesson all over again, at great cost of energy and of time. The other, temporarily dominant school purports to teach us about life, and that is perhaps what the public reads for. But it is fatal for a literary artist to get life out of novels; what he must look for is the lesson of form.

Ford touched more phases of contemporary literature than any other man of our time in the Anglo-American world. It was inevitable that he should make innumerable enemies. He will make no more enemies, and the great distinction of his service to literature can now be assessed.

I cannot end this tribute to Ford without some comment upon his qualities as man and friend. In the fifteen years of our friendship I saw in him—as he doubtless saw in me—great faults of character, which seemed to me to proceed from a special romantic sensibility. One fault he did not have: I shall call it the artist's cowardice. He had, as man of letters, an immense courage; through poverty, through prosperity, through the complications of his personal life, he *wrote*; and in writing he never ceased to explore his medium for new effects or to learn wherever he could. One day he brought me a sentence, and like a young beginner he asked me, a beginner: 'Do you think it will do?' He could ask this because the dignity and the unremitting demands of his art came first.

When I arrived in Paris in 1928 some of the old friends of the New York period were there—among them, Ford Madox Ford and John Peale Bishop. Ford had come to the United States—he had made many visits before—but when he came in 1925, just after he had published one of his great novels, *Some Do Not*, I had the privilege of meeting him: we became friends and remained friends until his death fourteen years later. Through Ford and Bishop I became a member of a clique. Americans abroad always get together. They might as well be in Harlem, or Minneapolis, because they all get together and don't see anybody else. It's like living in a small town. Everybody knows what everybody else is doing. By the next fall, the fall of 1929, I was going every Sunday to the bicycle races at the Velodrome d'Hiver with

Ernest Hemingway. I never thought I'd like a bicycle race, but he had the gift of imparting enthusiasm for anything that he was enthusiastic about. I wish I had gone to bullfights with him. It would have been much the same thing, I'm sure. And almost every Sunday night I went to the Boeuf sur le Toit with the Fitzgeralds. They had to make 'appearances.' It was a kind of social obligation. And almost every night I was at the Café des Deux Magots because it was my duty to attend the Master, Ford Madox Ford, who had to play Russian Banque at least three hours every evening and drink four brandies before he could go to sleep.

Ford was one of the great men of the Twenties. He had had a great literary career before the Twenties but he came into his own at that time. He had been born in London in 1873 with a formidable and rather suffocating background to deal with. He was the son of old Dr. Hueffer, an Alsatian who had come to London as the music critic on *The Times* and had married the daughter of the pre-Raphaelite painter, Ford Madox Brown. Algernon Charles Swinburne was Ford's godfather, his uncle was William Michael Rossetti, and a more impossible background a poet-novelist could scarcely have. Ford told me that up until the time he was twelve years old he had to wear one purple stocking to show that he was a pre-Raphaelite. But there were certain advantages in this background, and Ford acquired an immense literary culture—through the pores of his skin, so to speak. When I knew him he was a man in his fifties. He was the last great European man of letters. They don't produce them anymore—anywhere. He knew everything, Latin and Greek literature, French literature, Italian and German. He was tri-lingual—English, German, and French, and read Italian. When his perhaps greatest novel, *The Good Soldier*, was brought up for translation into French in the late 1920's, the publisher asked Ford to suggest a suitable translator. Ford said, yes, I'll find one. Six weeks or two months later, Ford produced the manuscript. He had rewritten the novel in French himself without referring to the English text. If you compare the two versions, the English and the French, they are sentence-by-sentence identical.

Ford was not only a great writer. He was a great teacher. He believed in literature, in its dignity and value to civilization; he spent hours encouraging young writers and helping them—not merely encouraging them but going over their manuscripts, and getting them published. I could name dozens of writers from Ernest Hemingway to Katherine Anne Porter whom he helped. He helped me a great deal and I'm still grateful to him. He was also, of course, a great editor. In 1908 he founded *The English Review*—he used to say, rather plaintively, to publish a poem of Thomas Hardy's that nobody else would publish. People like Wyndham Lewis and D. H. Lawrence were first brought to the public through Ford, and he was one of the first editors of Ezra Pound. He was at the center of international literary life for some thirty years.

LATER EVALUATIONS

67. Edward Crankshaw on Douglas Goldring's *The Last Pre-Raphaelite*, *National Review*

cxxxi, August 1948, 160–7

For the first decade after his death, a period largely occupied by the Second World War, Ford's reputation went into a complete decline. This is an experience common to many writers, but to Ford's admirers it seemed to indicate the eclipse of a name that had never become firmly fixed in English letters. Then, in 1947, came Douglas Goldring's biography, and a year later, the Penguin paper-back edition of *The Good Soldier* and the four Tietjens novels. These events prompted a certain amount of critical attention in England, of which Edward Crankshaw's piece is probably the most thorough and distinguished. Crankshaw (b. 1909) was one of the 'two friends' he mentions in his second paragraph as attending Ford's lonely funeral in France; prior to that, he succeeded in convincing George Allen & Unwin to publish all of Ford's last books.

For some years, Mr Crankshaw has been the London *Observer*'s Russian expert and has written widely on that subject.

It is characteristic of the sad story of Ford Madox Ford that even now, nine years after his death, he is more often remembered by his life than by his work. This would not have surprised him. Throughout most of his career he had to watch his contemporaries not only engrossing themselves in his private affairs, but also attributing to his work undesirable qualities said to be found in the man. The most agonisedly reticent of human beings, there was nothing he could do to stop it. His silences provoked still wilder imaginings; his forlorn attempts to throw a smoke-screen round himself produced through the distorting haze the apparition of a monster, like a pink elephant, absurd, bizarre, immense. And the more, once committed to the public gaze, he struggled to produce a fictitious personality, the more extravagantly coloured the world's image of him became. When at last he simply went away and was forgotten, his work was forgotten too.

He died three months before the outbreak of war, at Deauville, on the journey from America to Provence. Two friends, one of them English, attended the funeral of the man who had once been almost suffocated by the weight of his friends and who throughout his life had poured out time and energy, as well as the practical wisdom he so completely failed to apply to his own affairs, for the unstinted benefit of any new writer of any promise whatsoever who cared to apply. Even this death in tawdry exile was not the end. Any other man could have counted on resting in peace on the Normandy cliffs among the acres of rusting metal crosses and hotly glittering glass domes of the municipal cemetery. But not Ford.... Before the year was out his grave was a site for German anti-aircraft guns protecting an advanced dive-bomber station. It has not yet been re-visited. The whole of Ford's life is in the story of his death and burial, separated from England by the breadth of the sea, in surroundings representing everything he held detestable, unhonoured.

Of all men he held most firmly to the idea that an artist's private life belongs to him and to nobody else. This was not a consequence of his own humiliations; it was a settled principle. In one of his earliest books, a small monograph on Rossetti, he says at the outset:

Again, the most profitable method of criticism is that of paying attention to a man's work.... The artist should be allowed to live out his life in peace. If he is not, if the censor of manners must for the public good be called in to say: 'This man was a good citizen and saved money; this a Bohemian who worked after supper,' our view of his art becomes generally less clear.

It is time someone said this for Ford.

But the muddles of his own private life continue to pursue him after death. At the very moment when the four novels of the first World War (*Some Do Not...*, *A Man Could Stand Up*, *No More Parades* and *Last Post*), at the very moment when these volumes reappear as Penguins, offering a new generation which is not interested in Miss Hunt the chance to rediscover a neglected master for itself, Mr. Goldring comes forward with a discussion of the celebrated private life, and the whole sad, dreary business starts up again. Certainly the new generation stumbling across *Some Do Not* . . . will want to know what possessed its parents to leave out of consideration the work of so consummate an artist. The possible justification for Mr. Goldring's book is that it offers part of the answer to that question. On the other hand it might have been better had Ford's own expressed wish for no biography been respected, at any rate until all concerned are dead. For it is really impossible to do justice to Ford without wounding others. It is probably impossible to do justice to Ford in any case. And when it comes to the Tietjens novels Mr. R. A. Scott-James' warm and eloquent little introduction is all that is really required to 'place' them.

It is necessary to touch on this matter because Mr. Goldring's book is about little else. Mr. Goldring was Ford's assistant in the office of the *English Review*, and saw little of his subject in his latter years, which, in a way, were the happiest of Ford's life. His book is offered as an act of piety; but there is only one way to make up for the wrongs done to a dead writer in his lifetime, and that is to clear the ground about his *work*. This Mr. Goldring does not do. Instead he gives us the image of the man who so bewildered his contemporaries that they rejected him. One day there will emerge from the tangle of misapprehensions the figure of a man whose whole life was his work—as a poet virtually unknown, as a prophet ignored, as a novelist neglected—and in his unending struggle to persuade society to recognise the artist. In this struggle he threw all his energies into the causes of others, forgetting to count in his own magnificent achievement. But that will remain.

The important truth about Ford as a man is that he was afflicted with an ungovernable integrity. The great public scandals of the Third Republic, all of which contributed to the break-down of France, were commonly taken by censorious Anglo-Saxons as proof of a peculiar corruption. Corruption certainly existed as a normal component of human society. But corruption exists elsewhere without provoking moral crises intense enough to split a modern state from top to bottom. What caused the scandals was not the corruption but the ungovernable integrity of certain Frenchmen, who, like Clemenceau in the Dreyfus case, found it intolerable that wrong should be allowed to strangle right, even if the publishing of a secret crime meant the disruption of

France and the dishonouring of her army. The absence of a Dreyfus case from the annals of recent British history is not a reflection of our national integrity, but of what we like to call our sense of proportion. This sense of proportion Ford, with the French incorruptibles, totally lacked. Add to this deficiency, or quality, an exacerbated sensibility caused by the lack of several outer skins, wall it round with a studied and sometimes offensive manner (excusable only in the invulnerable, who would have no use for it), and by the misleadingly assertive glitter of a bogus personality projected to distract the eye from uncertainty within, and you have the essentials of the great Ford mystery, or muddle, which is important only in so far as it is reflected in Ford's work (his chief characters, for example, also lack a sense of proportion, or common sense). No child could have been taken in by Ford; but, to his own undoing, many adults were.

The remarkable aspect of the Ford case is not that the man was misconceived by his contemporaries, but that this misconception was allowed to obscure his manifest gifts. These in any case would have had a hard struggle to make themselves felt, if only because Ford produced his best work at the worst possible time, while his literary 'references' had the worst possible associations for that time. That is to say, in brief, that apart from *The Good Soldier* which appeared in 1914, and was immediately swallowed up by the first German war, his masterpieces did not begin to appear until the publication of *Some Do Not . . .*, in 1924. Ford by that time was already dated as the associate of Henry James and Stephen Crane, who had been dead for several years and who were both then overlaid by later novelists. What is worse, he was known as the friend and collaborator of the early Conrad; and Conrad died in that very year, plunging steeply into temporary oblivion. Thus, although both *The Good Soldier* and the four Tietjens novels were received by diverse critics with the startled and somewhat flurried homage accorded evident masterpieces which are unexpected and cannot easily be placed, nobody at that time wanted to read the sort of book they thought Ford must be writing. The co-author of *Romance* and *The Inheritors*, the adviser of Conrad in his *Nostromo* period, the late editor of the *English Review* and champion of the Vorticists, the gifted dilettante critic and poet who had somehow touched an unexpected summit of accomplishment in the limited field of the historical novel, with the astonishing *tour de force* of the *Fifth Queen* and its two successors, the familiar, not-to-be-taken-seriously figure of Edwardian London who had gone off to the war under a cloud and never, apparently, come back—this was not the sort of man to have anything to say to a generation which was gulping Lawrence and Proust and waiting hungrily for Eliot and Joyce. To crown the situation, *Some Do Not* . . . and its successors were largely about the war, and people were not yet prepared to read about the war. When they were so prepared they wanted it neat; the cataclysm to which they owed their disorientation had to be magnified into a monstrous negation of everything that had ever happened. Ford, intent on showing the Flanders battle as one aspect of contemporary history, did not fulfil this need.

Even those who read him, full of admiration for his talent, were puzzled. All the past of Ford, all Hueffer, in a word, belonged to a ruined epoch; and yet these novels did not belong to that epoch. All the present belonged to Joyce and Proust and Ezra Pound, whom he advertised loudly as he had once advertised Conrad and James; but they were not in these novels. All the future belonged to the young, the tongue-tied generation of Hemingway, the dumb ox, whom Ford himself caught and bullied into articulateness. But these novels were not dumb. They were neither past nor present nor future, as these abstractions were so sympathetically defined by Ford himself. Evidently, then, he was a failure, one of those artists of marked talent who never make the grade, a sort of forerunner, a Baptist of *Les Deux Magots*. And so effectively did this selfless genius preach the supremacy of his chosen swans, or geese, that it never occurred to anyone that all the time he was tenaciously and stubbornly pursuing a line of his own, not faltering somewhat timidly in the footsteps of Conrad, James, Lawrence, Proust, Joyce, Hemingway, or what have you. The artist and the connoisseur of the new in art are rarely found in one person; in Ford, though they rarely met, they existed side by side, and the reputation of the one was killed by the reputation of the other. 'Watch Conrad!' he would murmur confidentially, gasping for breath between the syllables. 'Watch Lawrence—Watch Béhaine—Watch Joyce— Watch Faulkner—Watch Greene. . . .!' But never; 'Watch me!' Indeed, driven by what compulsion, he sought persistently to divert attention from his own work as a novelist by parading himself as a cook, a horticulturalist, a composer of symphonies at the age of sixteen. His own work as a novelist, nevertheless, though little known to the general reader and ignored by the critic and the public assessor of tendencies and trends, has, like the air we breathe, quietly found its way, either directly or through others, into the work of many of the best contemporary writers. So that when he opens the latest offering of Mr. Greene, *The Heart of the Matter*, the first thing that strikes the attentive reader is the unseen presence of Ford.

How that presence makes itself felt, or what, in a word, Ford's contribution to the English novel really amounts to, is far from easy to define. He was not a breaker of new ground in the normal sense of that image. Rather, he was the supreme cultivator. If he had a theory of the novel it was an entirely commonsense theory. Indeed, poetically, all the commonsense missing from Ford's transactions as a member of society went into his approach to art, to literature. For what, above all, he gave was, precisely, a sense of proportion. He combined, for example, a rigid structure with extreme flexibility and range of expression. The range and flexibility to which he aspired had to be firmly anchored. Anchorage could be supplied only by the clearest and strictest terms of references. The precision of his constructions was not arbitrary; it arose from the precision of his conceptions. Thus, *The Good Soldier*, the most perfect of his novels, is in every way a text-book novel; but it is not what is understood by a novelist's novel. The precision of the machining, the high polish of the surface of this extraordinary narrative, which plumbs the obscurest chambers of the human soul with about as much fuss as a black boy diving for pennies, is simply a reflection of the articulation of the story, which cannot be analysed apart from the story. Here the novel seems to grow as, in Conrad's word, the style of Hudson grew, 'like the green grass.' It is all invention, and yet, in the words of Miss Rebecca West, 'behind it is a force of passion which so sustains the story in its flight that never once does it appear as the work of man's invention.'

Nowadays almost the last repository of good fiction is the detective story. This may distress, but need not surprise. The writer, the artist of any kind, is only free when he is quite sure of his subject, whether it is a Madonna or a murder. Given that fixed point, that anchorage, he can range where he likes. The detective novel has such an anchorage; a fixed, a static point, upon which all the action must converge, however remote and peripheral; 'Who did it?' This centripetal structure is the foundation of all the novels of Ford, in which all the actions of all the characters bear down on a single, fixed point. His plots, that is to say, turn not upon what the hero does but upon what happens to him as a result of what he does. There is nothing revolutionary in this approach. Euripides and Shakespeare both used it. But in the novel it had no place until Henry James and, above all, Conrad developed it as the supreme method, the only method, indeed, for getting the last ounce of meaning from a given spiritual crisis. Ford, taking over from them (and having a great deal to do with the development of Conrad's architectonics so splendidly revealed in *Chance* and *Under Western Eyes*), thus was far from inventing the centripetal construction, as opposed to the centrifugal construction (if you can call it that), instinctively resorted to by past novelists of the English tradition, including some distinguished foreigners, such as Tolstoy himself. But he developed it past belief, and in two distinct aspects. It is this development which makes itself felt in much of the most accomplished fiction of to-day, as, for example, in the work of Mr. Greene.

James and Conrad, revolting in their various ways against the loose panoramic construction with its great weakness of diffusion and its multiplicity of offshoots leading nowhere, sought to focus the reader's attention on a central crisis which would colour the mood of the book throughout and towards which all the action would point. Conrad himself expressed this preoccupation when introducing Marlowe in *The Heart of Darkness*:

'To him the meaning of an episode was not inside like a kernel but outside, enveloping the tale which brought it out only as a glow brings out a haze, in the likeness of one of those misty halos that sometimes are made visible by the spectral illumination of moonshine.' The whole narrative apparatus of Conrad, including Marlowe himself, is called up to answer this very preoccupation, which was shared, in rather different terms, by James. These two, intent on focussing all their gifts on the central affair, or crisis, were driven to various forms of isolation. James isolated his characters from humdrum society by ignoring that society; Conrad, with a far wider range of experience and finding his characters in many walks of life, still isolated his central affair by steeping his stories, even *The Secret Agent*, in a strong romantic dye. Both, that is to say, in achieving concentration, unity, and perfectly expressive form, abandoned more or less what had hitherto been the exclusive field of the novel; portrayal of the life and manners of society. They exalted the novel for the first time in English to the level of the highest art by forcing certain aspects of it, at the expense of others, in a hot-house temperature.

But Ford, sharing completely the ideals of Conrad and James, was nevertheless equally concerned with the novel as a mirror of society. In his eyes the aim of the novelist must be to illuminate the human heart in terms of contemporary experience. This purpose he achieved by turning the very methods perfected by his seniors as instruments of exclusion into a gigantic apparatus of inclusion, and without sacrificing any of their effectiveness in the task for which they were evolved. Thus, in the Tietjens novels, and subject only to the limitations of his genius, he combined the intensiveness of the new school with the extensiveness of the old masters.

On the other hand, by taking the reader straight to the heart of the matter, the permanent crisis arising from what Tietjens had done (his marriage with Sylvia and his refusal to divorce her for adultery), by allowing the past to appear only in terms of the present, thus automatically excluding everything that lacks a direct bearing on the present (*i.e.*, the subject), by allowing no character to appear or to speak except in so far as he contributes to the Tietjens crisis and by never for a moment letting the reader forget that crisis (the stories of Sylvia, Mark and Valentine being in no way digressions but rather inward-pointing arrows)—by attending to all this, he achieved a concentration and unity equal to that achieved by Conrad in *Chance*. Indeed, his strategy was identical with Conrad's though his tactics are entirely individual.

On the other hand, by standing his chief character in the very centre of contemporary life, instead of well off-centre (which is the normal position for the hero in the novels of Conrad and James and other novelists of the human spirit), by bringing into his orbit wave after wave of common humanity from all ranks and all stations, and always converging on the centre—indeed, pulled towards the centre, Tietjens, as the tides are pulled towards the moon; by, above all, abjuring lay figures and giving full value to every subsidiary character, from the unseen banker's son who tries to ruin Tietjens with an R.D. cheque, to 09 Morgan who stumbles into a dug-out to die all over Tietjens' feet (absolutely full value; there is not an atom of difference between the treatment of Tietjens in four volumes and 09 Morgan in scattered lines)—by attending to all this, Ford is able to weave his chief characters into the fabric of society as a whole and thus achieve the panoramic sweep of the traditionalists.

This combination, this synthesis of opposed developments in the novel, is one of the things we have in mind when speaking of the presence of Ford in the work of his more interesting successors. It has to do with the structure and therefore the content and expressiveness of the novel as a whole. The other thing has to do with the structure, the content and expressiveness of the individual scene, or paragraph, or sentence. For just as in the architecture of the novel every scene, every action, every character, is subordinated to the laws of the moon, so, in the detail, every paragraph, every sentence, every word shows the same subordination. It is not simply that there are no purple patches; there is scarcely a quotable sentence throughout the four Tietjens novels. And yet every sentence is finished. In memory these novels are rich in palpable impressions of things seen; in fact there is scarcely a single description of a scene or even a mood. The impressions, take shape and group themselves as one reads by means of a word here, a phrase there, as the story requires. But what one is reading is always the story. This is more than the subordination of impressions to a central theme, as in Conrad and James; it is the atomisation of life and its re-creation by rearrangement of minute components—and with the uninhibited use of every conceivable technical device in the novelist's armoury.

Thus beneath the smooth surface, which does not look like invention, lies the most arduous and finished experimentation. *The Good Soldier*, the four Tietjens novels, and their successors, have none of the disarming floundering and lack of balance which we associate with experimentation; they have the faultless lucidity of the habitual. It would be truer to call them revolutionary prototypes than experiments; all the tears and striving lie behind them. It is unfortunate for the original artist if his work is not immediately recognisable as such. Because a concealed novelty strikes obscurely, sounding inexplicable overtones of unease. This happened to Ford, who was rejected not, as so many thought, because he had nothing new to say, but because he had too much and with new accents which most readers took for the old.

68. R. A. Scott-James, preface to the Tietjens novels

Coincident with the Douglas Goldring biography was the publication by Penguin Books of the four Tietjens novels and *The Good Soldier* in 1948. Since paper-bound books are rarely reviewed, there were few important critical notices of these books. In any event, the best critical statement about them was contained in the preface written by R. A. Scott-James, who had known Ford as a contributor to the *English Review*. This essay traces the development of Ford's literary development up to the mid-1940s; and the literary temper of the times is suggested in the necessity Scott-James apparently felt to compare the tetralogy to the *Forsyte Saga* of Galsworthy.

In 1928 there was a sudden revival of interest in books about the Great War. It was then that Edmund Blunden's *Undertones of War*, and many other books of war reminiscences achieved success. At last the public was willing to recollect or study emotional experiences which for eight years it had been trying to forget. But Ford Madox Ford's *Some Do Not*, *No More Parades*, *A Man Could Stand Up* appeared in 1924, 1925, and 1926—too soon. People were not yet willing to re-live the painful years of the Great War or ponder the social conditions at home which were associated with it. The Tietjens novels were praised by the reviewers and of course had a measure of success—greater, I believe, as is understandable in the circumstances, in America than in war-weary Britain. But it is perhaps significant of the period that the great public was much more willing to acclaim the *Forsyte Saga* of Galsworthy and study characters which peered back into the last century than fret itself with the fretful recent happenings with which Ford was concerned. And anyway, who was this Ford dealing in so tragical a manner with the painful experience of yesterday's all too gruesome world? Was he not that dexterous, fanciful, almost dilettante writer who had trifled so attractively and non-significantly before the war? What was he doing in this galley?

But that earlier Ford Madox Ford (or Hueffer, as he was till he elected to change his name) was not really so insignificant or even non-significant. He was not by any means distressed or even fully aware of the fact that during the first forty years of his life he was seldom taken seriously by any but the frivolous or the young. He liked to declare—doubtless with his usual exaggeration—that as a boy he had been looked upon as the fool of the family. 'Fordie,' as he had been called, had been indulgently patted on the head by his father, Dr. Hueffer, the musical critic, and by all the members of that circle— the Rossettis, Madox Brown, Swinburne, Watts Dunton, Holman Hunt and the rest. But before they had become accustomed to his growing up he was already writing books which appeared one after the other in quick succession, novels and biographical, critical, impressionistic studies, books which were received, not unfavourably, for they were so well written, but not quite seriously, since what he wrote was so unlike what serious people say. During the first fourteen years of the century, when English literature was being dominated by Shaw, Wells, Bennett, Galsworthy, and a number of zestful writers preoccupied with social problems or by lighter essayists like Chesterton whose lightness could not conceal the same essential purposefulness, Ford pursued his apparently aimless, fanciful course, reading novels and a little history in a desultory way, playing the piano, looking at pictures, visiting music-halls for an hour's recreation— feeling there, as he would say, 'the great heart of the people'—talking about art much as the pre-Raphaelites had done. Pre-Raphaelitism was in his veins; perhaps it might be said that he was a sort of link between the votaries of pre-Raphaelitism in the nineteenth century and the neo-Georgians who fluttered into existence in the second and third decades of this century.

Highly serious critics like Edward Garnett were inclined to think of him as a dilettante—a fanciful, egotistic person who turned his back on 'real life,' moving irresponsibly from one unreality to another. And in a sense he did, in that his realities were often compositions of his active fancy, incompatible with hard fact, and not to be held down by any rules of severe common sense. None the less, the world in which he moved, smiling, egotistic, and seemingly irresponsible, was not wholly the invention of caprice. Within itself it was amazingly consistent; he clung tenaciously to certain governing ideas which were growing up in his mind. In the first place he wanted to be truthful to himself, to preserve 'those ideas which are a part of ourselves, which are our very selves'—ideas that deserve to be 'treated with some of the tenderness which is due to divine things.' 'It is not enough,' he said in *The Critical Attitude*, that 'the critic should say that we are nine parts gold to one part dross, for that one part will be to us dearest of all. And similarly for the novelist, it will be his function to present the world that he sees with tender regard for what it is, its gold and its dross, "crystallising modern life in its several aspects."' Hence the governing idea which he never abandoned, that the novelist should be intent 'merely to register—to constater.'

He was of course concerned, as so many conspicuous writers of his time were not, with the problem of style—but he would not have called it a problem—he disliked problems. He harped upon the expression *le mot juste*, as illustrated in Flaubert, though for him the search for it was no 'martyrdom.' Writing indeed was an art that had to be studied and even learnt—he audaciously affirmed that it was he who taught Conrad, with whom he twice collaborated, to write English—but once the faculty had been acquired it was as if for him style issued from inward grace and candour, through instinctive selection. He himself wrote fluently—perhaps too fluently—always giving as much heed to the sound and rhythm of sentences as to their meaning. A sentence that did not gratify his ear was to him intolerable.

In founding and editing the *English Review*, it has his avowed object to help to bring into being 'a sober, sincere, conscientious and scientific body of writers' who would 'crystallise modern life in its several aspects.' This was very ambitious, very high-sounding, but perhaps not wholly convincing, coming from one who in those years just before World War I still had something of the air of a trifler in the realms of gold, dealing so lightly if agreeably with eternal verities, weaving his fanciful tapestries of history with so much exactitude and so little authority, moving in a charmed and charming world but not a world of recognisable realities. Indeed, at the age of forty-one, in 1914, when that war started, it seemed as if Ford might have gone on to the end, an exquisite, fascinating trifler, with no clear bent, no central core, certainly with no definable character capable of leaving any deep impress on literature; he might have gone on just being 'Fordie,' that and no more. But then certain things happened, one consequence of which for him was the present series of novels, the Tietjens novels, which have been compared to Galsworthy's *Forsyte Saga*, but surely outstrip that work by virtue of a finer sensibility and a more elastic sympathy with human nature.

The events that produced a crisis for him were of two kinds. The first were in his private life, which I shall not discuss, for this is not the time to rake up memories painful to persons still living. Enough that Ford became involved in an intricate emotional situation from which his vanity and obstinacy made it difficult for him to escape. At the same time he had been introduced into a wider social world than he had hitherto known through his association with Violet Hunt on one side and the politician Charles Masterman on another. The second event was the war. He was over military age, but got a commission in the Army. He spent a few weeks on not very active 'active service' on the western front. But it gave him his picture of the war. A series of crises in his private life synchronising with a World War stirred Ford's emotional and perceptive life to the core. His writing acquired significance and poignancy. This combination of experiences produced the stimulus for his best books, *The Good Soldier*, and the four Tietjens novels, *Some Do Not*, *No More Parades*, *A Man Could Stand Up*, and *Last Post*.

Ford's avowed purpose in the Tietjens novels was to show 'what the late war (1914–18) was like.' 'If, for reasons of gain or, as is still more likely, out of dislike for collective types other than your own, you choose to permit your rulers to embark on another war, this—or something very accentuated along similar lines—is what you will have to put up with!'

'You see here the end of the war of attrition through the eyes of a fairly stolid, fairly well-instructed man.' From this it might seem that Ford, than whom none could have been less like a propagandist, had turned to the writing of propaganda. 'I hope,' he says, 'that this series of books, for what it is worth, may make war seem undesirable.' But the Prefaces in which these words occur are, after all, like most Prefaces, afterthoughts. All writing may become propaganda when it is poignant enough to stir the emotions, and thereby set up the train of thought which leads to opinions or convictions. It is only in this sense that these novels are propagandist. Ford's ostensible subject-matter is the war—the war as it is on the scene of action or the lines of communication, and the war as an atmosphere among the people at home, who remain their habitual pre-war selves, but modified by the unusual circumstances of war. His declared object is to make us look at this spectacle of war, and to show it without over-stating the horrors or the heroisms (thereby inducing in the reader indifference to both); and it occurred to him that he could not do better than view these struggles, mostly emotional struggles, through the eyes of a certain man he had once known, a Tory—'already dead, along with all English Tories.' He is the Christopher Tietjens of these novels—'the last English Tory, omniscient, slightly contemptuous—and sentimental in his human contacts.'

But the statement that the war is his subject must be qualified. The war was the governing factor in the life of that time, thirty years ago, just as the recent war with its sequel is the governing factor in the life of the present. War brings out the best and the worst in men and exaggerates the more primitive virtues and vices, but does not fundamentally alter human nature. It can afford the most amazing perspectives for the artist. Ford is concerned with the life, passionate and trivial, of certain people and groups of people, and the conflict arising from their loves, intrigues, vanity, ambition, obstinacy and weakness, honour and dishonour, a conflict which is heightened by the exceptional powers and disabilities conferred by the circumstances of war, and made more striking against the background of its more obvious tragedy.

It is for every reader to decide for himself whether he can quite believe in Tietjens as a real human being. 'The English Tory' as such is perhaps a figment of Ford's imagination. This obstinately chivalrous English gentleman (with 'the gentleman' somewhat over-emphasized) *sans peur et sans reproche*, masterful, arrogant, generous to the point of prodigality, reticent to the point of folly, honourable to the point of condoning dishonour, passionate yet steeled against passion, is a person hard to believe in, yet he does get across, striding powerfully through these pages, compelling some sympathy, some acceptance of his reality. We must, indeed, presuppose his reality, for all depends on him; and the fiction works. Whether such a person could ever have existed in real life we may question. But his existence is necessary for Ford's purpose. This Fordian ideal of an English gentleman is the peg on which this story had to be hung, and—fanciful or real—it acquires under his presentation reality at least within his system of thinking. Tietjens' personality is the foil against which the other characters are set in violent contrast.

The books present a series of conflicts. There is the conflict between him and his wife Sylvia, beautiful, arrogant, spoilt, and destitute of any sense of loyalty to country or husband, 'who considered that the World War was just an excuse for male agapemones,' of whose shamelessness Tietjens is in no doubt, though characteristically he refuses to divorce her, remaining in torture from love for another woman, Valentine, whom he neither accepts nor rejects. Sylvia is a brilliant piece of sardonic portraiture. In depicting Valentine, the clean, robust, courageous girl, in love with Tietjens as passionately as he with her, Ford reveals a capacity for probing genuine emotion such as one might never have suspected him capable of. There is no affectation here, no mere cleverness, but creative force of a high order in the long story of repressed passion between Tietjens and Valentine.

There is the conflict also between Tietjens and the whole order of established humbug which he discovers, first in the pre-war officialdom of the Government department he served before the war, and in many parts of the military machine which he is called upon to serve during the war. And there is the conflict between the private world of his domestic and social relations and his duty as an official or a soldier. Magnanimous to a fault, generous to the extreme of quixotry, we find him surrounded with careerists who borrow his money and exploit his talents and throw him over when they think he is down. Admirably drawn are the vain little coxcomb Macmaster, and the adroit Mrs. Duchemin (whom Macmaster marries) aspiring to salon fame and intellectual correspondences with budding celebrities. And there is Mark Tietjens, Christopher's elder brother, who is perhaps, like Christopher himself, a type rather than an individual—here the manner of portraiture is a little Galsworthian. But how Ford would have detested such a comparison!

The whole is a large-scale picture of English life in its public and its private aspects at moments when the world was approaching, enduring, or endeavouring to forget the war. The motive is the conflict between contrasted types of human beings living under the shadow of war or actually immersed in its ugly operations. The war scenes are done with a coolness, an insouciance, far more effective than any highcoloured rhetoric in conveying the cumulative horror of the thing. Ford may have had Tolstoy's *War and Peace* in his mind. These books are in no sense an imitation of that inimitable work, but Ford does, in his own way, seek to convey, as Tolstoy did, the pettiness and magnificence of individual human beings set against the terrific, ironic background of a fatuous war. I would not for a moment suggest that Ford can reach the splendour of Tolstoy. There are too many errors in tact, too many exhibitions of fancy or ingenuity, too many petulances incidentally revealed, for his work to stand up against so great a masterpiece. Nevertheless, I have little doubt that the Tietjens novels will come to rank far higher than the *Forsyte Saga*, and remain a significant expression of the time, a mature exhibition of passion, at a moment in literary history when so many of the more distinguished writers chose the insignificant and ran away from passion.

69. Morton Dauwen Zabel on *Trained for Genius (The Last Pre-Raphaelite)*

Nation, clxix, July 1949, 110–11

The American revival of interest in Ford's work was not to begin until 1950, with the first post-war reprinting of his fiction. Goldring's biography did not attract the attention it did in London, despite a front page review in the *New York Times Book Review*, but it undoubtedly helped set a reassessment in motion. The review printed below is probably the most thorough review the book—and Ford's reputation—received at this time.

The rough justice and grim irony that dogged Ford Madox Ford in life pursue him after his death in France ten years ago this summer. Today all his eighty books are, I suppose, out of print. He figures rarely, if at all, among the century's ranking novelists. Ignored or slighted in later life in his own country, he received there, on dying, the official obloquy and grudging sarcasm of obituarists of 'The Establishment.' (The only decent memorial notice I remember seeing was Graham Greene's in the *Spectator*.) France and America gave him such success as he finally came by, but after serving literature for fifty years in three countries, his only official honor was a degree from Olivet College, Michigan, of which he was gratefully proud. The irony persists even in the memoir by Douglas Goldring which was called *The Last Pre-Raphaelite* when it was published last year in London and now appears here as *Trained for Genius*.

Much as he exploited his Pre-Raphaelite ancestry, Ford knew the liability that glamorous inheritance laid on him. He was 'trained for genius' all too overpoweringly. It took him a large part of his life to find his real work as a writer. A sense of insecurity in his revered vocation never wholly left him. But it will be unfortunate if these titles mislead Mr. Goldring's readers. He was Ford's staunchest English friend; he writes with a mixture of amused realism and stubborn respect about the man he has always considered his literary guide and master; and he has never forgotten the debt he owed Ford for being taken on, at twenty-one in 1908, as sub-editor of the *English Review,* thus gaining privileged access to the highest conclaves of modern literature. This book is, in fact, the second of Mr. Goldring's tributes. In 1943 he published in London a memoir called *South Lodge.* Its pages are not incorporated in the present volume, which is a pity, for *South Lodge* is a better book than this one—a vivid evocation of the part of Ford's history Mr. Goldring knew at first hand, with a brilliant picture of literary and social London on the eve of 1914, a sound account of Ford's successes and miseries in that remote era, and a haunting portrait of Violet Hunt, that embattled 'woman who did,' from her disastrous entry into Ford's life until she died at eighty, alone, unforgetting, deranged, among her houseful of trophies, while the bombs of 1942 provided 'the orchestral thunder of a dying age.'

Mr. Goldring's will not be the last word on Ford. His biography is without exact scholarship, and his criticism, though roughly valid, yields to defensive polemic. Ford made a deathbed request against biographies. His American legatee honored this wish by refusing to cooperate. The Paris years are merely sketched, and the chapter on Ford's American career is completely inadequate, since none of Ford's important friends here were consulted. It is, moreover, a bold biographer who would venture on this task at all. Ford's own accounts of himself—*Thus to Revisit, Ancient Lights, Return to Yesterday, It Was the Nightingale*—were, for all their richness of content, always unreliable and often fantastic; 'impressions of truth' according to their author, congenital lying according to his enemies, incredible, embarrassing, wheezily garrulous even to his friends, with their quagmires of yarn-spinning and stories that never quite jibed twice. Had he really been dandled by Turgenev, had his chair stolen at a concert by Liszt, modeled for Densher in 'The Wings of the Dove,' gone to Eton, attended the Sorbonne? The reader could never be sure. And beyond these erratic records lies a muddle of gossip and legend and what a host of ladies had to say about their parts in it—Violet Hunt's *I Have This To Say: the Story of My Flurried Years*, Jean Rhys's *After Leaving Mr. McKenzie*, Stella Bowen's *Drawn from Life*, and a cloud of other documents in scandal, defense, and litigation. Ford had a genius for making messes. Even his strokes of fortune—friendship with James, collaboration with Conrad, contacts with Wells, Bennett, and other Edwardian talents, brilliant editorship of the *English Review* and the *Transatlantic*—were riddled by misunderstanding or mismanagement. His ventures in and out of marriage became an epic of error and tactlessness. Nor does the case become simpler when his file of eighty books and massive journalism are tackled. Novels, verse, essays, criticism, memoirs, biographies, travels, histories, sociology, they range from pot-boiling meretriciousness to distinction, the incessant outpourings of a polygraph who apparently wrote something every day of his life from fifteen to sixty-six. Criticism has hardly begun to make something of this vast bulk of print. (Mr. Robie Macauley's perceptive essay in the spring *Kenyon Review*, though it idealizes rather drastically at several points, may initiate a serious assessment and revival of Ford's achievements.)

The fact is that Ford's aesthetic origins and associations served him both well and badly. They made it impossible for him to live any other life than that of literature, and to live it whole-souledly and passionately. They also made it impossible for him ever quite to sell himself to journalism, propaganda, or profitably slick mass-production like such comparable polygraphs as Wells and Maugham. They kept him through five decades a lover of good writing, original talent, authentic invention. But his dedication to form, style, and the *mot juste*, coupled with his habit of pontificating, desire to *faire école* at all costs, and compulsive addiction to paper ('an old man mad about writing'), likewise kept him writing, prosing, repeating himself, when there was, very often, little actual substance to work on. Style, technique, manner, method were kept grinding away, half the time saying little and producing what can be, for long stretches, a garrulously tiresome parody of his intentions.

The better Ford was not a man spinning literature spiderwise out of his own entrails. For all his social, political, religious, and personal inconsistencies, he was a man who lived through and in his age. He never betrayed what Mr. Goldring rightly calls his highest merit, his unswerving loyalty to 'The Standard of Values' and to the art that supported that standard when, in a demoralized and violent time, every other support was likely to fail. He was also a man who, though often mistaken, pretentious, foolish, or deluded, was never essentially self-deceived. He knew in his own life the risks, ignominy, and treacheries of his period. Whenever he drew on his two soundest resources—his instinct of honor, his generous sense of justice—he wrote out of a saving reserve of character. He could locate and trace the problem of honor in history—the Katherine Howard trilogy or *Ladies Whose Bright Eyes*—and find an original means to define it there. He could define it even better in his own age—*The Good Soldier* and the Tietjens series—the first, as Greene says, 'a study of an averagely good man of a conventional class driven, divided, and destroyed by unconventional passion,' the second an 'appalling examination of how private malice goes on through public disaster,' both of them to be counted among 'the novels which stand as high as any fiction written since the death of James.' This estimate is high, perhaps, like Mr. Goldring's, finally too high, but if it errs it does so on the side of justice.

Traditionalist, *révolté*, Catholic, skeptic, 'small producer,' aesthete royalist, democrat, ritual-lover, iconoclast, fond father, erring husband, harassed lover, loyal to England, Germany, France, America—he was all of these by turns and never fully succeeded in localizing his civil or artistic loyalties. He came to reject half his work as 'worthless,' wrote day after day, found joy elusive and trouble constant, died at last in poverty (yet with two hundred manuscripts by young writers in his possession, recipients of his unflagging care and encouragement), was written off as 'dated' in England, soon forgotten in France, unread even in America. 'But,' said Graham Greene,

> I don't suppose failure disturbed him much: he had never really believed in human happiness, his middle life had been made miserable by passion, and he had come through, with his humor intact, his stock of unreliable anecdotes, the kind of enemies a man ought to have, and a half-belief in a posterity which would care for good writing.

Mr. Goldring presents Ford complete with all his errors and faults but with his honor intact too and with what D. H. Lawrence, who owed his debut to Ford and the *English Review* and who could understand Ford's kind of ordeal, called the 'dove-gray kindliness' by which he served literature. 'There was none too much of it left in the world, after Ford's departure,' adds Mr. Goldring, 'which is no doubt one of the reasons why some of us, who knew him, cherish his memory.'

For those who didn't know him, Ford left other, less elusive evidence. It remains their task to know the evidence and, now that a decade of posthumous probation has passed, to respect him for it.

70. William Carlos Williams on *Parade's End*, *Sewanee Review*

lxix, January–March 1951, 154–61

The republication in the United States of *The Good Soldier* and of the four Tietjens novels in one volume under the title of *Parade's End* elicited a good deal of critical comment, including reviews by readers who were encountering Ford for the first time. It also brought forth a number of essays and reviews by contemporaries and old friends, of which this review is perhaps the best example.

Williams (1883–1963) was the author of *Paterson* and one of the most influential American poets of this century.

Every time we approach a period of transition someone cries out: This is the last! the last of Christianity, of the publishing business, freedom for the author, the individual! Thus we have been assured that in this novel, *Parade's End*, we have a portrait of the last Tory. But what in God's name would Ford Madox Ford be doing writing the tale of the last Tory? He'd far rather have tied it into black knots.

In a perfectly appointed railway carriage, two young men of the British public official class, close friends, are talking quietly together. Back of their minds stands Great Groby House, the Tietjens' family seat, in Yorkshire, the north of England—its people, neighbors, and those associated with them just prior to the beginning of the First World War. It was a noteworthy transition period. It would be idle of me, an American, to try to recreate so highly flavored an atmosphere as that represented in this railway carriage. One of the speakers is Christopher Tietjens, a younger son to Groby's ancestral proprietor; he is a blond hulk of a man, a sharp contrast to his companion, MacMasters, dark-haired and with a black pointed beard, a smallish Scotsman for whom the Tietjens family has provided a little money to get him through Cambridge and establish him in town.

Sylvia, young Christopher's beautiful wife, has four months previously gone off to the Continent with a lover. She has sickened of him and wants to be taken back. The two men on the train, thoroughly well bred and completely British, are discussing the circumstances and its profitable outcome—Christopher, defending his wife, has consented to let her do as she pleases. There begins now to unravel (you might almost say it is Christopher's ungainly bulk itself that is unraveling) as intimate, full, and complex a tale as you will find under the official veneer of our day.

Four books, *Some Do Not*, *No More Parades*, *A Man Could Stand Up*, and *The Last Post*, have been for the first time offered in one volume as Ford had wished it. The title, *Parade's End*, is his own choosing. Together they constitute the English prose masterpiece of their time. But Ford's writings have never been popular, as popular, let's say, as the writings of Proust have been popular. Yet they are written in a style that must be the envy of every thinking man. The pleasure in them is infinite.

When I first read the books I began, by chance, with *No More Parades*: as the story ran the First World War was in full swing, the dirt, the deafening clatter, the killing. So it was a little hard for me to retreat to *Some Do Not*, which deals with the social approaches to that holocaust. At once, in the first scenes of this first book the conviction is overwhelming that we are dealing with a major talent. We are plunged into the high ritual of a breakfast in the Duchemin drawing room—all the fine manners of an established culture. There's very little in English to surpass that, leading as it does to the appearance of the mad cleric himself, who for the most part lies secretly closeted in his own home. Beside this we have the relationship of the man's tortured wife with Tietjens' friend MacMasters; the first full look at Valentine Wannop and of Tietjens himself before he appears in khaki —the whole rotten elegance of the business; Sylvia, at her best, and the old lady's 'You are so beautiful, my dear, you must be good.' Then it shifts to Christopher and the girl, Valentine, in the fog, linking the land, disappointment, the yearning for fulfillment and—

the ten-foot-deep fog itself covering everything but the stars of a brilliant sky overhead; we see Christopher in the carriage holding the reins, Valentine leaping down to find a road sign and disappearing from his view. Only the horse's head, as he tosses it, reappears to Christopher from time to time as the man sits there alone. Following that is the restraint and hatred in the scene between husband and wife, Christopher and Sylvia. He at table in uniform, she standing behind him, bored. Casually she flings the contents of her plate at the back of his neck, glad she hadn't actually hit him—but the oil from the dressing dribbled down on his insignia. He didn't even turn. It is their farewell as he is about to leave for the front.

This is the first of the four books. The war intervenes. *No More Parades*. The war ends. Tietjens is invalided home, his mind half gone. Valentine lives for him and he recovers. Mark, the present heir to Groby, the Correct Man, represents the family and England as a family. Living with his French mistress he suffers a cerebral hemorrhage and lies, during all of *The Last Post*, in a sort of summerhouse, where with his last breath, and as he holds the pregnant Valentine by the hand, the saga comes to an end.

Sylvia, through all the books, in her determination to destroy her husband, does everything a woman can, short of shooting him, to accomplish her wish. From start to finish she does not falter.

This is where an analysis should begin; for some, who have written critically of *Parade's End*, find Sylvia's extreme hatred of her husband, her inexorable, even doctrinaire hatred, unreal. I think they are wrong. All love between these two or the possibility for it was spent before the story began when Christopher lay with his wife-to-be, unknowing, in another railway carriage, immediately after her seduction by another man. It made an impossible situation. From that moment all that was left for them was love's autopsy, an autopsy and an awakening—an awakening to a new *form* of love, the first liberation from his accepted Toryism. Sylvia was done. Valentine up! A new love had already begun to shimmer above the fog before his intelligence, a new love with which the past was perhaps identical, or had been identical, but in other terms. Sylvia suffers also, while a leisurely torment drives her to desperation. It is the very slowness of her torment reflected in the minutiae, the passionate dedication, the last agonized twist of Ford's style, that makes the story move.

In his very perception and love for the well-observed detail lies Ford's narrative strength, the down-upon-it affection for the thing itself in which he is identical with Tietjens, his prototype. In spite of all changes, in that, at least, the Tory carries over: concern for the care of the fields, the horses, whatever it may be; the landed proprietor must be able to advise his subordinates who depend on him, he is responsible for them also. That at least was Tietjens, that too was Ford.

When you take those qualities of a man over into the new conditions, that Tietjens paradoxically loved, the whole picture must be altered—and a confusion, a tragic confusion, results, needing to be righted; it is an imperative that becomes a moral duty as well as a duty to letters.

Ford, like Tietjens, paid attention to these things. I'll not forget when he came to visit me in Rutherford, a town lying in the narrow sun-baked strip of good soil, land which the Dutch farmers cultivated so well in the old days, between the low Watchung Range and the swampy land of the Hackensack Meadows. It is one of the best tilled, you might almost say currycombed, bits of the Garden State, as New Jersey is still called. Old Ford, for he was old by that time, was interested. He asked me to take him out to see the truck farms. We spent the afternoon at it, a blistering July day when the sprinkler system was turned on in many of the fields, straight back into the country, about three or four miles, to the farm of Derrick Johnson, who personally showed us around. I was more interested in the sandpipers running through the tilled rows—birds which I hadn't seen up to then other than running on the wet sand of beaches as the water washed up and retreated, uncovering minute food. But on the farm they were nestling, here their eggs were laid and hatched in the heat between the beet rows on the bare ground. But Ford, who was looking around, questioned the farmer closely about the cultivation of the lettuce, carrots, dandelion, leeks, peppers, tomatoes and radishes which he was raising. It was all part of his understanding of the particular—and of what should properly occupy and compel a man's mind. He might have been Tietjens.

So far I have spoken in the main of Christopher and Sylvia, their relationship, their positions and their marriage. But there are other characters as important in the argument as they. Mark, Christopher's elder brother, the one man whom Sylvia has never been able to impress, should be put down as the first of these—as Ford, I think, recognizes, when he makes him the key figure of the entire last book, *The Last Post*. Mark, the perfectly cultured gentleman. Professor Wannop, old friend of the family, a studious recluse who has brought up his daughter, Valentine, in his own simple and profound ways, is gone. And there is, of course, Valentine herself, though she appears, generally speaking, little. She fills, however, a dominant place. *A Man Could Stand Up* is her book. General Campion, official England, is another to be named. He will carry off the girl, old as he is, at the close. At every turn he appears, often as Sylvia's instrument to thwart Christopher, triumphant officialdom.

But greater than he, Tietjens, are the men in the trenches, his special responsibilities, over whom he pains, a bumbling mother, exhausting himself to the point of mental and physical collapse.

Few could be in the position which Ford himself occupied in English society to know these people. His British are British in a way the American, Henry James, never grasped. They fairly smell of it. The true test is his affection for them, top to bottom, a moral, not a literary attribute, his love of them, his wanting to be their Moses, to lead them out of captivity to their rigid aristocratic ideals—to the ideals of a new aristocracy. Ford, like Tietjens, was married to them, and like Sylvia they were determined to destroy him for it. Even when he could help them, as Tietjens helped MacMaster, Ford got kicked for it and was thrown out of the paradise of their dying ideas— as much by D. H. Lawrence on one side, the coal miner's son, as by the others. He helped Lawrence but Lawrence soon backed out. And still no one grasps the significance of Tietjens' unending mildness, torn between the two forces—no one, really, but Valentine and Mark in the last words.

Sylvia's bitter and unrelenting hatred for Tietjens, her husband, is the dun mountain under the sunrise, the earth itself of the old diabolism. We sense, again and again, more than is stated, two opposing forces. Not who but *what* is Sylvia? (I wonder if Ford with his love of the Elizabethan lyric didn't have that in mind when he named her.)

At the start her husband has, just too late for him, found out her secret; and feeling a responsibility, almost a pity for her, has assumed a superior moral position which she cannot surmount or remove. She had been rudely seduced, and on the immediate rebound, you might almost say with the same gesture, married Tietjens in self-defense. She cannot even assure her husband that the child is his own. She cannot be humble without denying all her class prerogatives. Christopher's mere existence is an insult to her. But to have him pity her is hellish torment. She is forced by everything that is holy to make him a cuckold, again and again. For England itself in her has been attacked. But Valentine can pick up her young heels, as she did at the golf course, and leap a ditch, a thing impossible for Sylvia unless she change her clothes, retrain her muscles and unbend.

But there is a deeper reason than that—and a still more paradoxical —in that Tietjens forced her to do good; that as his wife she serves best when she most hates him. The more she lies the better she serves. This is truly comic. And here a further complexity enters. Let me put it this way: If there is one thing I cannot accede to in a commonality of aspiration, it is the loss of the personal and the magnificent . . . the mind that cannot contain itself short of that which makes for great shows. Not wealth alone but a wealth that enriches the imagination. Such a woman is Sylvia, representing the contemporary emblazonments of medieval and princely retinue. How can we take over our *Kultur*, a trait of aristocracy, without a Sylvia, in short as Tietjens desired her? What is our drabness beside the magnificence of a Sistine Chapel, a gold salt cellar by Cellini, a Taj, a great wall of China, a Chartres? The mind is the thing not the cut stone but the stone itself. The words of a Lear. The sentences of *Some Do Not* themselves are not likely for this to be banished from our thoughts.

Ford gave the woman, Sylvia, life: let her exercise her full range of feeling, vicious as it might be, her full armament of woman. Let her be what she *is*. Would Tietjens divorce her? When there is reason yes, but so long as she is truthfully what she is and is fulfilling what she is manifestly *made* to be, he has nothing but respect for her. Ford uses her to make a meaning. She will not wobble or fail. It is not his business. This is a way of looking at the word.

Ford's philosophy in these novels is all of a piece, character and writing. The word keeps the same form as the characters' deeds or the writer's concept of them. Sylvia is the dead past in all its affecting glamor. Tietjens is in love the while with a woman of a different order, of no landed distinction, really a displaced person seeking replacement. Valentine Wannop is the reattachment of the word to the object—it is obligatory that the protagonist (Tietjens) should fall in love with her, she is Persephone, the rebirth, the reassertion— from which we today are at a nadir, the lowest ebb.

Sylvia is the lie, bold-faced, the big crude lie, the denial . . . that is now having its moment. The opponent not of *le mot juste* against which the French have today been rebelling, but something of much broader implications; so it must be added that if our position in the world, the democratic position, is difficult, and we must acknowledge that it is difficult, the Russian position, the negative position, the lying position, that is, the Communist position is still more difficult. All that is implied in Ford's writing.

To use the enormous weapon of the written word, to speak accurately that is (in contradiction to the big crude lie) is what Ford is building here. For Ford's novels are written with a convinced idea of respect for the meaning of the words—and what a magnificent use they are put to in his hands! whereas the other position is not conceivable except as disrespect for the word's meaning. He speaks of this specifically in *No More Parades*—that no British officer can read and understand a simple statement unless it be stereotype . . . disrespect for the word and that, succinctly put, spells disaster.

Parenthetically, we shall have to go through some disastrous passages, make no mistake about that, but sooner or later we shall start uphill to our salvation. There is no other way. For in the end we must stand upon one thing and that only, respect for the word, and that is the one thing our enemies do not have. Therefore rejoice, says Ford, we have won our position and will hold it. But not yet—except in microcosm (a mere novel you might say). For we are sadly at a loss except in the reaches of our best minds to which Ford's mind is a prototype.

At the end Tietjens sees everything upon which his past has been built tossed aside. His brother has died, the inheritance is vanished, scattered, in one sense wasted. He sees all this with perfect equanimity—Great Groby Tree is down, the old curse achieved through his first wife's beneficent malevolence, a malevolence which he perfectly excuses. He is stripped to the rock of belief. But he is not really humiliated since he has kept his moral integrity through it all. In fact it is that which has brought him to destruction. All that by his upbringing and conviction he has believed is the best of England, save for Valentine, is done. But those who think that that is the end of him miss the whole point of the story, they forget the Phoenix symbol, the destruction by fire to immediate rebirth. Mark dead, Christopher, his younger brother, has got Valentine with child.

This is not the 'last Tory' but the first in the new enlightenment of the Englishman—at his best, or the most typical Englishman. The sort of English that fought for and won Magna Carta, having undergone successive mutations through the ages, has reappeared in another form. And this we may say, I think, is the story of these changes, this decline and the beginning of the next phase. Thus it is not the facile legend, 'the last Tory,' can describe that of which Ford is speaking, except in a secondary sense, but the tragic emergence of the first Tory of the new dispensation—as Christopher Tietjens and not without international implications. *Transition* was the biggest word of the quarter-century with which the story deals, though its roots, like those of Groby Great Tree, lie in a soil untouched by the modern era. *Parade's End* then is for me a tremendous and favorable study of the transition of England's most worthy type, in Ford's view and affections, to the new man and what happens to him. The sheer writing can take care of itself.

71. Caroline Gordon, *A Good Soldier*

From 'A Good Soldier', *Chapbook Number 1*, University of California Library, Davis, 1963

By the mid-fifties, Ford's literary reputation had slumped again. The Penguin edition was not reprinted, and stacks of *Parade's End* appeared in remainder bookshops. To many, it seemed that Ford's star was eclipsed for good. Yet accompanying this apparent decline was the gradual development of a much more solid appreciation and understanding of his work. Articles on Ford's fiction began to appear in the literary quarterlies, and by the early years of the 1960s, there were a number of books of criticism, generally devoted to Ford's fiction and written by American academic critics. In 1965, a second biography appeared which was widely reviewed and which supplied much new information not included in Douglas Goldring's book. At about the same time, Ford's own work began to come back into print, a collection of his criticism, the Henry VIII novels, some of the reminiscences and a new paper edition of the Tietjens novels. All of this activity indicates Ford's rise in literary reputation, and the increasing ease with which he has been accepted as one of the most important novelists of the century.

That Ford's new reputation is due to the enthusiasm of a new generation is only to be expected, but it has not prevented others who knew him from writing of him, not in the old, somewhat apologetic and explanatory way, but discussing him as a modern master. One such writer is Caroline Gordon (b. 1895) who more than any other single American novelist may be said to have been Ford's disciple. The comments printed below come from a longer critical essay.

In Ford's novels Christian archetypal patterns—in particular, Christianized rituals—appear, but these patterns of behaviour do not determine the form of Ford's novels in the way in which they determine the form of James' later novels.

Ford acknowledged James as his master, freely and frequently when he talked, as he loved to talk, with younger fiction writers about the mysteries of the art. It may be that his ready and generous praise of James inclined some of us to overlook these two masters' widely divergent approach to their art. I, for one, have come slowly, and by way of *Robin's Barn*, as it were, to a, or perhaps the, reading of Ford's novels which now seems to me the most rewarding. This key, it now seems to me, will serve to unlock all of the 'dramatic chambers' of his art. It was put into my hands, seemingly by chance, one day as three or four of us were lunching with Ford at his apartment on the *rue Vaugirard*.

On the day of which I speak Glenway Wescott was the last of Ford's guests to arrive. I remember that he walked straight across the room and put a book into Ford's hand, saying that he had had the luck to come across it in one of the book stalls on the *quais* that morning. Ford thanked him for the book, but made no comment on its contents. There is nothing, after all, that you can say about a book which you, yourself, have written. Or if you do feel that there are things that need to be said and try to say them you are likely to be haunted by a suspicion that the book wasn't written right. We went on talking about whatever we were talking about when Glenway came in and I, at least, didn't read *The Young Lovell* till years later. It begins:

In the darkness Young Lovell of the Castle rose from his knees, and so he broke his vow. Since he had knelt from midnight, and it was now the sixth hour of the day, he staggered . . .

The young nobleman, who expects to be made a knight in the morning, has been watching over his arms 'in the new French fashion' in the chapel on his father's lands in 'the north country' in the time of Henry the Seventh. Weakened by fasting, he has had visions of 'Behemoth riding crystal seas, Leviathan throwing up the smoke of volcanoes, Helen of Troy standing in the sunlight or, finally, of the Witch of Endor, an exceedingly fair woman, and a naked one, riding on a shell over the sea which has waves like dove's feathers.' The cock crows twice. He feels that it would have been a better omen if it had crowed three times, for he knows that between cockcrow and dawn, the old pagan gods who once ruled over this land 'have power over the lives of men.' He is overcome with a great curiosity to see them and at that moment a light 'of a rosy stealing nature fell through one of the windows' and he knows that eyes that can see in the dark are watching him and he is suddenly on his feet, 'reeling and stretching out his arms, with prayers that he had never prayed before upon his lips.'

Outside the chapel he comes upon an old witch who points to a hare digging in the loose dirt at the foot of a crag, and says, 'That man shall be your master.' He promises to drown her in his castle well, 'as soon as I get this business redded up,' rides over the top of a ridge, looks back and, seeing the flag being hoisted over his own castle, thinks of the sheep and oxen which are being roasted in the courtyard in celebration of his majority, then waves his hand and rides down from the real world, over a carpet which is composed of fluttering sparrows, 'with a pearly border of restless blue doves,' to a green hill 'where there stands a temple of pink marble and a woman sitting on a white horse holding a white falcon in her hand' smiles at him mockingly.

'But for you,' he thinks, 'I might have been the properest knight of all this Northland and the world' and hears her answering thought, 'But for that I had not called thee from the twilight.'

Ford's 'Belle Dame Sans Merci' is as beautiful and as without mercy as any White Goddess needs to be in order to convince us that a man turned his back on the real world and followed her over hill and dale. Like Thomas the Rhymer, like *Tannhäuser*, like all the heroes who have gone before him, the Young Lovell contemplates the lady's exceeding beauty for what seems to him a moment but which the reader realizes is many days. Indeed, a whole summer. When he rides back from Elfland, the trappings of his war horse and his parti-colored hose are faded, the way the colors of cloth fade if they have been exposed over a long period to all sorts of weather. Greater changes have come in his fortunes. His father is dead, and his false foster brother has put his mother in prison and has taken possession of his castle. The young knight recruits his followers, rescues his mother and wins his castle and other possessions back. He is aided in all endeavors by his *fiancée*, the Lady Margaret Glororem, who steadfastly maintained that he was alive when everybody else was convinced that he was dead. He is grateful to his *fiancée* and admires her beauty and her virtues but he does not take the relish in her society which he took before he rode over that carpet of doves and sparrows to a green hill to where a lady larger than life and twice as beautiful sits on her white horse and mocks him. Indeed, he feels a positive aversion from the Lady Margaret Glororem to whom he is affianced. The reader soon realizes that for all the fairy tale quality of the story here is a couple who will not live happily ever after and is not surprised when the Young Lovell, having set his worldly affairs in order, is off again, over the hill.

Here I think, Ford shows himself one of the first rank of imaginative writers. That is, he seems to me to belong among those writers who seek to plumb the depths of that chasm in the human imagination which men have agreed to call myth rather than engage in futile attempts to pervert or even transcend the archetypal pattern. In this romance everything happens in the poetic—that is to say—mythical order. It was the young knight's mother, 'a proud Dacre from the North,' who insisted on giving him the name of Paris at his christening. Paris, you will remember, was first called Alexander, and had the name of Paris bestowed on him as the result of a vision he had, as a boy, of three women, more than lifesized and fairer than any mortal women. The goddess on whom he bestowed the golden apple made him several fine promises on that occasion—and kept them. Paris fought bravely in the conflict between the Greeks and Trojans before the walls of Troy—not as bravely as his brother, Hector, but bravely enough. But we are not surprised, when in Homer's *Iliad*, Aphrodite, the goddess of Love, observing that he is weary, lifts him above the battle to rest for a while with her upon a rosy cloud. Homer, whom some of us regard as the first novelist of the western world, makes this pleasing incident subordinate in the action of his story. It is all of Ford's story and he tells it superbly in *The Young Lovell*.

The Young Lovell, after having regained his own castle, is fighting bravely on the battlements of 'The White Tower' which his father built long ago when twin water spouts which were discerned far out at sea early in the day suddenly loom over the battlements. There is a downpour of rain which hides every man from his neighbor, with thunder and lightning. And above the thunder a cry is heard, so loud and so fearful that the monk who is the Young Lovell's friend and spiritual adviser thinks that it did not come from mortal lips but from that false goddess who is 'the bane of all Christendom, who had cried out with the same voice' when in the form of a cloud or maybe of a rain spout she had hastened to the rescue of the hero Paris . . . 'at the siege of a strong Castle called Troy.'

This monk has among his other duties the care of a hermitage on the Young Lovell's land.

A holy man has dwelled for years there in a cave which is hardly more than a tunnel into the earth. Once a week a lay brother from the monastery thrusts a loaf of bread into the mouth of the cave and when a hollow voice murmurs '*Pax vobiscum*' returns the ritual answer. But when the monk next visits the hermitage, no hand takes the loaf of bread from him and instead of the benediction a foul stench rises from the hole. The hermitage is opened and the dead body of the holy man is taken out and given burial. The monk, Francis, as he supervises the burial, groans and beats his chest and looks fearfully around him, now out to sea, now towards Scotland. A great cloak is seen tossing over the churchyard wall and all hear a voice crying out in supplication.

An old monk whom the abbot sends to investigate reports that one who had been a good knight but had sinned so grievously that he did not dare set foot on consecrated ground until he was shriven, desired that the monk, Francis, might shrive him so that he might end his days in the dead hermit's kennel. The monk, Francis, cries out at that as if in deadly fear but afterwards goes outside the churchyard wall and remains standing there until the tossing form bends to the ground.

All this, we are told, passed in the black night. An old mason, so skilled at his trade that he can work in the dark, puts the stones of the hermitage back in their places, and the monks sing the canticle, *Ad te clamavi*, while the wind howls and the rain beats upon their upturned faces.

Meanwhile, in 'a very high valley' the mistress of the world, the goddess of pagan love, sits on her marble throne in her pink marble temple. At her feet sits 'a large woman, very fair,' and beside her lounges a dark shepherd, 'very limber in his bronze limbs.' He wears a tunic of goat skins and a Phrygian cap and holds in his hand a bow of ivory tipped with gold. They watch while a warrior, who sits upon what seems to be a steel horse, converses, apparently about feats of arms, with a hero who is naked except for his helmet which has a great nodding plume of horse-hair and his huge, round shield of triple-plated bronze. Then the hero and the warrior contend and it seems that the warrior might have won if the hero had not suddenly taken up a great marble rock and cast it upon both horse and rider 'so that they fell down among the asphodels.' But their wounds are anointed with oil and herbs and bound up and

Then all lay them down upon couches of rosemary, heather or asphodel, that were covered with the white fleece of rams, each person being with whom he would. And they fell to devising from couch to couch, some of times past, some of times to come, and others upon what would have been the issue of that late combat had it been fought upon the wearisome fields known to mortal man.

Meanwhile

... that knight thought never upon the weariness of Northumberland or upon how his mortal body lived in the little hermitage not much bigger than a hound's kennel that was builded against the wall of the church ...

I first read this novel when I was young enough to want to classify, to categorize, to assign its rank to any work of imaginative creation that came my way. It seemed to me then, as it seems now, something almost perfect of its kind. The same kind of book Ernest Hemingway wrote in *A Farewell To Arms*, only better. A true romance. One of the oldest stories in the world and one of the best, portrayed with consummate skill. I remember that I was much impressed on my first reading by the skillful way in which Ford adapted an incident from the *Iliad* to his own purposes: the moment when Aphrodite, seeing that Paris is tiring in the conflict, lifts him above the battle to rest with her upon a rosy cloud. Ford's handling of this archetypal situation seemed to me at that time only an adaptation. I hardly knew which to admire most: the skill he displayed in his adaptation or the boldness with which, it seemed to me, he contended with the greatest of all story tellers. It did not seem to me, however, that the kind of encounter which Ford was portraying in his novel could furnish material for a significant work of fiction, in our times. I have since come to feel that this novel, which is almost unobtainable and has been read by comparatively few people, is the key to Ford's life work.

72. Robert Lowell, Foreword to *Buckshee*

Cambridge, Massachusetts, 1966

By far the greatest emphasis of critics of Ford's work has been upon his fiction, although tribute has been paid to him as an editor and literary enthusiast. The republication of some of his last poems encouraged an assessment of his verse, and this essay by Robert Lowell (b. 1917), who had known Ford in the 1930s, when he was a student, is the most authoritative of the essays on his poetry. Like Pound, Cummings and Williams, Lowell also wrote a poem about Ford which was published in his volume *Life Studies*.

I first met Ford in 1937, a year or so after the publication of *Buckshee*, and two years before his death. Reading these poems is like stepping back in time to Ford in his right setting, France, to a moment when both he and Europe between the wars were, imperceptibly, miraculously, a little younger, hopeful, and almost at a pause in the onrush. When I knew Ford in America, he was out of cash, out of fashion, and half out of inspiration, a half-German, half-English exile in love with the French, and able to sell his books only in the United States. Propped by his young wife, he was plodding from writers' conference to writers' conference, finally ending up as writer in residence at Olivet College in Michigan. He seemed to travel with the leisure and full dress of the last hectic Edwardian giants—Hudson, James, and Hardy. He cried out, as if wounded, against the eminence, pomp, and private lives of Tennyson, Carlyle, and Ruskin, the false gods, so he thought, of his fathers. He was trailed by a legend of personal heroism and slump, times of great writing, times of space-filling, past triumph and past humiliation, Grub Street drudgery, and aristocratic indolence. He was the friend of all good writers, and seemed to carry a concealed pistol to protect them and himself against the shoving non-creative powers of editors, publishers, business men, politicians, college presidents, literary agents—his cronies, his vultures.

Always writers and writing! He was then at work on his last book,

The March of Literature, and rereading the classics in their original tongues. At each college stop he picked up armloads of Loeb classics, and reams of unpublished manuscript. Writers walked through his mind and his life—young ones to be discovered, instructed, and entertained, contemporaries to be assembled, telegraphed, and celebrated, the dead friend to be resurrected in anecdote, the long, long dead to be freshly assaulted or defended. Ford was large, unwieldy, wheezy, unwell, and looked somehow like a British version of the Republican elephant. His conversation, at least as finished and fluent as his written reminiscences, came out in ordered, subtly circuitous paragraphs. His marvelous, altering stories about the famous and colorful were often truer than fact. His voice, always *sotto voce*, and sometimes a muffled Yorkshire gasp, made him a man for small gatherings. Once I watched an audience of three thousand walk out on him, as he exquisitely, ludicrously, and inaudibly imitated the elaborate periphrastic style of Henry James. They could neither hear nor sympathize.

Largeness is the key word for Ford. He liked to say that genius is memory. His own was like an elephant's. No one admired more of his elders, or discovered more of his juniors, and so went on admiring and discovering till the end. He seemed to like nothing that was mediocre, and miss nothing that was good. His humility was edged with a mumbling insolence. His fanatical life-and-death dedication to the arts was messy, British, and amused. As if his heart were physically too large for his body, his stamina, imperfection, and generosity were extreme.

Ford's glory and mastery are in two or three of his novels. He also never stopped writing and speaking prose. He had a religious fascination in the possibilities of sentence structure and fictional techniques. About poetry, he was ambivalent. He had a flair for quoting beautiful unknown or forgotten lines, yet called poetry something like 'the less civilized medium,' one whose crudity and barbarism were decked out with stiff measures and coarse sonorities. Like Boris Pasternak, he preferred Shakespeare's prose to his blank verse, and thought no poetry could equal the novels of Flaubert.

He himself wrote poetry with his left hand—casually and even contemptuously. He gives sound and intense advice to a beginning poet: 'Forget about Piers Plowman, forget about Shakespeare, Keats, Yeats, Morris, the English Bible, and remember only that you live in our terrific, untidy, indifferent empirical age, where not a single problem is solved and not a single Accepted Idea from the poet has any more magic. . . .' Yet he himself as a poet was incurably of the nineteenth century he detested, and to the end had an incurable love for some of its most irritating and overpoetic conventions. His guides were always, 'Christabel', the Browning of 'My Last Duchess', the Rossettis, Morris, and their successors, the decadents. He is Pre-Raphaelite to the heart. Their pretty eloquence, their passionate simplicities, their quaint neo-Gothic, their vocabulary of love and romance, their keyed-up Christianity, their troubadour heresies, and their terribly over-effective rhythms are always peeping through Ford's railway stations and straggling free verse. For Ford and his ablest contemporaries, Hardy, Hopkins, Housman, Yeats, De la Mare, Kipling, and Pound, the influence and even the inspiration of the Pre-Raphaelites was unavoidable. Each, in his way, imitated, innovated, modified, and revolted. Ford's early imitations have a true Pre-Raphaelite brio, but he is too relaxed and perhaps too interested in life to have their finest delicacy, conviction, and intensity. His revolt is brave and resourceful, but the soul of the old dead style remains to hamper him. Even in prose, except for *The Good Soldier* and *Parade's End*, he had difficulty in striking the main artery; in poetry, he almost never struck it. His good phrases and rhythms grow limp or hopped up with impatient diffidence, and seldom reach their destination. The doggerel bounce and hackneyed prettiness of lines like—

> The poor saint on his fountain
> On top of his column
> Gazes up sad and solemn

(to choose a bad example) keeps breaking in on passages that are picturesque and lovely. His shorter poems are brisk, his longer diffuse.

Pound's FAMOUS COMMAND that *poetry be at least as well-written as prose* must have been inspired by Ford, though I doubt if Ford believed this a possibility or really had much fondness for a poetry that wasn't simple, poetic, and pastoral. I heard someone ask him about Pound's influence on Yeats's later style. 'Oh,' Ford said, 'I used to tell Ezra that he mustn't write illiterate poetic jargon. Then he'd go to Yeats and say the same thing.' This was tossed off with such flippant finality that I was sure it was nonsense. Years later, however, Pound told me the same story. He said too that Ford actually lived the heroic artistic life that Yeats talked about. There must be more to the story. Ford had no gift like Yeats for combining a conversational prose idiom with the grand style. I think he must often have felt the mortification of seeing the shining abundance of his novels dwindle away in his poetry to something tame, absent-minded, and cautious. He must have found it hard to get rid of his jingling, hard to charge his lines, hard to find true subjects, and harder still to stick to them when found. Even such an original and personal poem as 'On Heaven' is forever being beguiled from the road. Yet a magnificence and an Albigensian brightness hover over these rambling steps: Ford and Pound were companions on the great road from twelfth-century Toulouse to twentieth-century London.

Buckshee is Ford, the poet, at his best. It too is uneven and rambling —uneven, rambling, intimate, and wonderful. Gardening in Provence, or hearing a night bell strike two in Paris, Ford ruminates with weary devotion on his long labors, and celebrates his new young marriage —O minutes out of time, when time was short, and the air stiff with Nazi steel and propaganda! In his last years, Ford's political emotions were to the left, but his memory, pace, and tastes were conservative. He didn't like a place without history, a patina of dust, 'Richelieu's Villa Latina with its unvarying *statu quo ante*.' Above all he hated a world ruled by a 'maniacal monotone of execration.' I remember how he expressed his despair of the America he was part of, and humorously advised me to give up eating corn lest I inherit the narrow fierceness of the Red Indian. In 'Coda,' the last and supreme poem in this sequence, he is back in Paris, his great threatened love and symbol for civilization. In his dark apartment, he watches the lights of a taxi illuminate two objects, the 'pale square' of his wife's painting, 'Spring in Luxemburg,' and the galleys of his manuscript momentarily lit up like Michelangelo's scroll of the Fates. Then he says to his wife, the painter:

> I know you don't like Michelangelo
> But the universe is very large having room
> Within it for infinities of gods.

Buckshee coughs and blunders a bit in getting off, but in 'Champêtre,' 'Temps de Sécheresse,' and 'Coda,' Ford finds the unpredictable waver of his true inspiration. In these reveries, he has at last managed to work his speaking voice, and something more than his speaking voice, into poems—the inner voice of the tireless old man, the old master still in harness, confiding, tolerant, Bohemian, newly married, and in France.

Bibliography

EDWARD NAUMBURG, jr, 'A Catalogue of a Ford Madox Ford Collection', *Princeton University Library Chronicle*, ix, 3, April 1948, 134–67.

FRANK MACSHANE, 'Ford Madox Ford; Collections of his Letters, Collections of his Manuscripts, Periodical Publications by him, his Introductions, Prefaces and Miscellaneous Contributions to Books by Others', *English Fiction in Transition*, iv, 2, 1961, 11–18. See other issues of this journal, especially iv, 2, 1961, 19–29.

RICHARD A. CASSELL, *Ford Madox Ford: A Study of his Novels*, Johns Hopkins Press, 1961.

JOHN A. MEIXNER, *Ford Madox Ford's Novels: A Critical Study*, Oxford University Press, 1962.

DAVID DOW HARVEY, *Ford Madox Ford, 1873–1939, A Bibliography of Works and Criticism*, Princeton, 1962. This is the standard bibliography.

FRANK MACSHANE, *The Life and Work of Ford Madox Ford*, Routledge & Kegan Paul, 1965.

ARTHUR MIZENER, *The Saddest Story*, World Publishing, 1971.

Index

Addison, Joseph 181–2
Aiken, Conrad 70–4
Aldington, Richard 51, 148–51
Ancient Lights 9, 35–9, 117–21, 217
Anderson, Sherwood 219–21

Barrie, James 125
Benét, William Rose 79–83
Bennett, Arnold 33–5
Between St. Dennis and St. George 51–4
Bicknell, Percy 35–9
Bishop, John Peale 83–6, 169–71
Bromfield, Louis 93–4
Brooke, Rupert 76
Brown, Ford Madox 3, 4, 36, 117, 119–21
Buckshee 264–7

Call, A 33–5
Campbell, Roy 157–8
Cervantes, Miguel 182
'Chaucer, Daniel' 40–1
Chesterton, Mrs Cecil, *see* 'Prothero, J. K.'
Chesterton, G. K. 126–7
Collected Poems (1913) 7, 8, 55–8, 59–61, 62, 63–9
Collected Poems (1936) 79–83, 83–6
Colum, Mary 94–7
Conrad, Joseph 20–2, 23–4, 46, 98–100, 128–9, 131–47, 153, 155–7, 196, 206–7, 209, 213, 236–9
Conrad, Mrs Joseph 131–2, 143–4, 145–6
Crankshaw, Edward 231–9
Cummings, E. E. 95

Douglas, Norman 62
Dreiser, Theodore 47–51

English Girl, An 25–7
English Review 4, 6, 10, 35, 197, 205–212, 217–18

Face of the Night, The 5
Feather, The 5
Fifth Queen, The 24, 197
Fifth Queen Crowned, The 28–31, 31–33, 197
Flaubert, Gustave 84, 224
Flecker, James Elroy 208, 211
Fletcher, John Gould 222–4

Galsworthy, John 104, 242, 245, 246
Garnett, Edward 4, 5–6, 133–6, 140–2, 241
George V, King 9–10
Goldring, Douglas 14, 15, 55, 205–12, 232–3, 246–50
Good Soldier, The 6, 15, 44–6, 47–51, 198, 200–2, 236
Gordon, Caroline 258–63
Gorman, Herbert 186–93
Great Trade Route 159–61, 167
Greene, Graham 13, 14, 159–61, 162–163, 172–4, 177–9, 212–15, 236, 237

Hardy, Thomas 165, 206, 209
Hartley, L. P. 108–9, 113–15, 152–3
Harwood, H. C. 115–16
Haynes, E. S. P. 125–6
Henley, W. E. 2–3, 80
Henry James; A Critical Study 42–4
Hicks, Granville 194–204

269

INDEX

Hueffer, Francis 3, 4, 36–8
Hunt, Violet 123–7

Inheritors, The 20–2
It Was the Nightingale 157–9

James, Henry 42–4, 46, 165–6, 213–214, 236–9
Jepson, Edgar 6
Jones, Ada Elizabeth, *see* 'Prothero J. K.'
Joseph Conrad: A Personal Remembrance 8, 98–9, 131–47, 196
Joyce, James 100

Kipling, Rudyard 3
Krutch, Joseph Wood 90–2

Last Post 110–13, 113–15, 115–16; *see also Parade's End*
Last Pre-Raphaelite, The, see Trained for Genius
Lawrence, D. H. 249
Lewis, P. Wyndham 209–10
Little Less than Gods, A 152–3
Lowell, Robert 264–7

Man Could Stand Up, A 101–3, 103–7, 108–9; *see also Parade's End*
March of Literature, The 169–71, 175–177, 177–9, 180–5
Masterman, C. F. G. 25–7, 51
Mayne, Ethel Colburn 129–30
McFee, William 110–13, 145–7
Memories and Impressions, see Ancient Lights
Mencken, H. L. 98–9, 101, 142–5
Meredith, George 113, 117–18
Mightier than the Sword 164–6, 166–8
Millais, Sir John Everett 3
Mirror to France, A 189, 192
Monroe, Harriet 75–8
Morley, Christopher 137–40

Murry, J. Middleton 148–51

New Humpty-Dumpty, The 40–1
No More Parades 94–7, 98–101, 103–7; *see also Parade's End*

Olivet College 220–1, 225
On Heaven and Poems Written on Active Service 70–4, 75–8

Parade's End 11, 12, 13, 103–7, 190, 192, 201–3, 232–9, 240–6, 250–7; *see also Some Do Not, No More Parades, A Man Could Stand Up* and *Last Post*
Paterson, Isabel 103–7
Pinker, J. B. 6
Porter, Katherine Anne 11–12, 225–226
Pound, Ezra 7, 55–8, 63–9, 85, 215–218, 222–3
Pritchett, V. S. 13, 157–9, 164–5
'Prothero, J. K.' 122–7
Proust, Marcel 100
Provence 172–4
Pugh, Edwin 89

Randall, Sir Alec 51
Rascoe, Burton 98–101
Rash Act, The 13
Richardson, Samuel 87
Romains, Jules 85
Romance 23–4, 196
Rossetti, Christina 3, 36–7, 65, 80, 118–19
Rossetti, Dante Gabriel 117–21
Rossetti, William Michael 3, 9, 117–121

Scott-James, R. A. 28–31, 240–6
Shanks, E. Buxton 59–61
Shaw, George Bernard 52–3
Shifting of the Fire, The 19, 162

INDEX

Some Do Not 87-8, 89-90, 90-2, 93-4, 103-7, 172; *see also Parade's End*
Soul of London, The 5-6
Steele, Sir Richard 181-2
Stevenson, Robert Louis 2

Tate, Allen 227-30
Thus to Revisit 128-30, 148-51, 198
Trained for Genius 231-4, 246-50

Vanity Fair 93-4
Vive Le Roy 162-3

Walpole, Hugh 194
Wells, H. G. 128-9
Wescott, Glenway 225, 259

West, Edward Sackville- 175-7
West, Rebecca 40, 44-6, 51-4
When the Wicked Man 152
Whistler, J. A. McNeill 38
Wilde, Oscar 2
Williams, Charles 166-8
Williams, William Carlos 250-7
Women and Men 218
Wordsworth, William 71-2

Yeats, William Butler 7, 63, 68, 83
Young Lovell, The 258-63

Zabel, Morton Dauwen 154-7, 246-250
Zeppelin Nights 122-4

For Product Safety Concerns and Information please contact our EU representative GPSR@taylorandfrancis.com
Taylor & Francis Verlag GmbH, Kaufingerstraße 24, 80331 München, Germany

www.ingramcontent.com/pod-product-compliance
Lightning Source LLC
Chambersburg PA
CBHW052217300426
44115CB00011B/1723